An Extraordinary Ordinary Life

By Arthur Johnson

London Scientific Publishing

Published by London Scientific Publishing
Evidence House, Stokenchurch, HP14 3FE, England

© 2024 by Arthur Johnson

The moral right of the authors has been asserted.

A CIP catalogue record for this book is available from the British Library.

ISBN: 978-1-0686496-1-5

Printed by Dolman Scott Ltd.
www.dolmanscott.com

To the memory of my beloved wife, Sheila –
untiringly loving and supportive

Also, to all my children, grandchildren, and
great granddaughter, in the hope these small
insights into a slice of social history may
prove helpful in better understanding the
world today.

Contents

Chapter 1: June 1951 – To Egypt

Prelude

As a child, I remember my teacher showing the class a map of the world. Huge swathes were coloured red. Our teacher explained with some pride that the red parts were *our* empire, the largest empire in history. The British Empire! I'm not sure we knew what to make of it as not one of us had ever stepped a foot out of Britain – or thought we were ever likely to. When I was a young, the only way a working-class lad like me could travel the world was to defend that empire as a national serviceman. And that is precisely what took me to Egypt.

On the train

On the train at last! After two weeks' embarkation leave, I was on my way to Southampton to board His Majesty's Troopship Empire Ken, destined for Port Said, Egypt, before continuing to more British bases in the Middle East, Far East, then finally on to Korea.

War was raging in Korea between the West and North Korea, which was being aided, unofficially of course, by the Republic of China. I had heard rumours during our training that we were quite likely destined for Korea, which filled me with dread, not from the prospect of action so much as from the cold. Unfortunately, I am genetically a "nesh carrot" in my native Potteries parlance: I have always had an intense dislike of the cold. Paradoxically, in later years in the British Sub Aqua Club, I swam under the ice in a lake called Moreton Coppice, followed by a short naked swim to rinse off the French chalk that in those days was used to facilitate the smooth pulling on of the wet suit. But that is another episode in my life on which I shall touch on later.

I had received my national service call up papers in February 1951 ordering me to report to the RAOC training depot at Aldershot, Hampshire on the 15th of June. For two weeks, my fellow recruits and I were kitted out with boots, uniform, and all the basic equipment. We were taught how to stand at attention, to march and salute. We were then conveyed to Blackdown Barracks for six weeks basic training. We were declared fit after exhausting sessions on the assault course and taught to fire and maintain a rifle and Bren gun. This was followed by had lectures on the bewildering array of functions the Ordnance Corps provided.

I was then declared to be a technical clerk, ready for posting to the Armed Replacement Group in Egypt. We were then pumped full of a host of injections to prevent a dizzying number of horrible diseases. I still can't remember them all.

At this point, I hear you say, "Hang on, if this is an autobiography, why are you starting part way through your life?" OK. This is an autobiography *of sorts*. I am not starting with time and place of birth and so on, because, in my view, memories don't work like a diary. They are, instead, a collection of incidents, anecdotes and highlights triggered by personal, national and international events. In my case, there were two major watersheds in my life. The first was life before army service and after. The second was life before meeting Sheila, my wife, and afterwards.

Rather than stick to a strict timeline, I wrote this book according to the way memories and significant events came to me. For a long time, I found it too painful to think of my childhood. And even more so of Sheila after she died. So, I started with my army days.

The ship out to Egypt

To continue… back on the train to Southampton. When we arrived, we were "lorried" from the station to the dockside and found ourselves gawping up at what appeared to be an infeasibly huge ocean liner. Compared to the cruise liners that ply today's seas, it was not that big, but we felt we were boarding a monster.

We were given briefings about life aboard and each assigned a bed among the masses of three-tier bunks in the bowels of the ship.

Up the stairs – the gangway – and onto the deck we came. It was a glorious summer day with the sunlight glimmering on the flat, calm sea of the Solent. We looked out at the panorama of ships. Over on the right, only about three hundred yards away, we spotted a Sunderland flying boat, its four engines just starting, readying it for take-off. After several minutes warming up, the note of the engines increased. The propellers spun. The revs kept increasing until it seemed impossible the engines could turn any faster. Then, gloriously, it moved; the wake spreading from its bow. It ploughed on in full view for about half a mile before the bow rose even higher, and then, amid a cloud of spray, the Sunderland lifted into the air and gradually climbed until it was out of sight. That was the first and only time I ever saw a flying boat. It was mind blowing that such a big thing, with two stories of windows lining its sides, could free itself from the water's grip and lift itself into the sky.

In the morning, we feasted on a huge breakfast. In those days of austerity, when most foodstuffs were rationed, shipboard life seemed like luxury to us private soldiers. The next day continued pleasantly, until, on the third day, we hit the Bay of Biscay. I and my companions had never been on a ship before, and seasickness was dreadful. I staggered out of the toilets after another bout wishing that something would end it or me. I passed the entrance to the dining area, when a senior sailor grabbed hold of me and pushed a huge wet cloth in my hands and ordered me to clean up the massive array of sinks and stoves along one side of the saloon. I didn't even reach the sinks before another bout of nausea hit me, and I lurched out of the door on the other side in search of another toilet. Once there, I threw away the rag and staggered downstairs to my bunk. Lying flat on my back stopped the vomiting, so there I stayed. I don't remember for how long.

The only thing I remember of that episode was a kindly captain of the Service Corps coming over to me. "Dreadful thing is seasickness," he said. "Particularly on your first trip. You haven't eaten for a couple of days, but I know what might settle you down. A port and brandy." He re-appeared after several minutes with the drink, which I found warming and relaxing, and then I fell asleep. I never saw him again and never had the chance to thank him.

The next day, what a contrast! We had passed through the Straits of Gibraltar into the Mediterranean Sea. The weather was warm and continued to get warmer. The sea was like glass. The ship seemed to glide forward as though it were on ice.

3

The officers on board organised exercises from time to time which we found gentle and relaxing after the rigours of our basic training. We had a few lectures with film slides warning us of the horrors of venereal disease and on the basic geography of the Canal Zone. Most of the time like a holiday, relaxing in the wonderful sunshine with an occasional stroll around the deck before tucking in to the superb ship-board cuisine.

Before getting on the ship, my companion recruits and I had heard rumours that the American military ate all their meal off one plate – soup, main course and pudding. It had seemed almost too bizarre to believe. However, we discovered that the Empire Ken had its own version. As we queued for our dinner, we were handed large rectangular aluminium trays indented with shapes resembling a soup dish, dinner plate, pudding bowl and so on. Suddenly we understood why one plate: it made it easy to carry an entire meal to your table. It was a great idea. And a huge advantage when washing up.

After lunch one day, I went on deck and joined a small crowd of fellow recruits gathered around veteran army sergeant. Burnt a deep brown and wrinkled from years of service in the tropics, he had venerable appearance. He recounted his experiences in the Far East and spoke of the fascinations of India and the supernatural abilities of the sadhus (holy men) and others. We were captivated.

He then said he would demonstrate hypnotism. A young lad volunteered. "Close your eyes." The veteran instructed. "Hold out your arm. I am going to light this match and hold it under your forearm. You will feel no pain." He lit a match and waved the flame under the lad's forearm for several seconds, the flame visibly touching and spreading out over the skin. "Open your eyes," he commanded. The lad did so. His skin was white and unmarked with no reddening. He claimed he felt no pain during or after the experience.

The old sergeant then said, "Hold out your other arm and close your eyes. I will demonstrate a similar effect on your other arm." Again, the soldier closed his eyes and held out his other arm. The sergeant then held out an unlit match and touched the skin on the outstretched arm. As soon as it touched the skin, the soldier yelped in pain and jumped back in shock. "Sorry about that," said the sergeant. "It will form a small blister, but the pain will pass quickly. Thank you for taking part." The young soldier showed us his arm, no blister yet but the skin was clearly red and sore.

I don't know if it was trickery – perhaps the volunteer was an accomplice – but to me and the other onlookers it was extremely convincing.

The next morning, I was chatting to another regular soldier who had done a previous tour of duty in the Middle East. I was keen to know when we would be sighting Port Said.

"Two days' time," he said, "but tomorrow, you'll *smell* it."

Sure enough, the next day we saw faint tinge of sienna colour in the sky ahead, and then the stink hit us. I had never experienced anything like it: a fetid mixture of raw sewage and animals but also mixed with a curious, slightly sickly perfume. This stench was to accompany us everywhere we travelled in the Canal Zone except for the time we spent in the desert which more than sixty miles from the Canal.

A tortuous trip to our camp at Tel-el-Kebir

It wasn't long before the Empire Ken docked, and we prepared for disembarkation. My six comrades in the RAOC (Ordinance Corps) were the only troops destined for Egypt. We were shown the gangplank and descended to the dockside. I realised then how narrowly I'd escaped going to war. The toilet "griff" (rumour mill) was that the rest were bound for Korea. However, my relief was to turn out to be misplaced as, in the coming weeks, the whole world seemed to turn upside down.

I was the first person to leave the ship. Our instructions were that we had been assigned to the Armoured Replacement Group. "Just leave the dock and find the RTE desk." The instructions were so vague. We didn't know what the RTE was, or where to find it, or what to do when we did.

I learned that RTE was the Regional Transport Engineer, and I soon found it. Each railway station had one, as did bus stations or other points where troops were likely to find themselves. The docks led on to Port Said railway station where a small hut stood with a sign boldly announcing it to be the RTE.

Each of these huts was always staffed by a sergeant of engineers and sometimes one or two clerks. We had no papers, but the sergeant scanned his clip board and told us that we were a staff replacement for the Armoured Replacement Group stationed at Shandur. He scanned a map told us that Shandur was located at the far end of the Suez Canal. In fact, it was beyond the city of Suez and near a small port on the Red Sea called Port Tewfik. It was manned by Royal Engineers. We were in luck; it turned out that the train standing at this platform was destined for its terminus at Port Tewfik.

"The train will stop for up to an hour at Ismailia, a major city halfway down the canal," the sergeant explained. "Don't let anybody persuade you to transfer to another train. This train will take you right through."

Before he completed his paperwork and gave us our final instructions, he asked, "Who's in charge?"

"Nobody," I said. I explained that we had just finished our basic training as national servicemen, and this was our first posting.

"This is the army, lads," the sergeant emphasised. "There is *always* somebody in charge. So, who has the senior rank"?

"Nobody, we're all private soldiers," was our response.

"OK then, who's the oldest of you?" No reply.

"Who joined the army first?" he barked.

After a brief conflab, it turned out that I did as my intake group was 51.04. To explain: national servicemen were called up in fortnightly groups and given a group number that showed the year, 51, followed by the number of the fortnight in the year. My intake was on the 15th of February, which was the fourth fortnight. So, my intake group was 51.04. All my companions had group numbers ending in 05 or 06, which meant they joined slightly later than me. In the light of this, I was put in charge. I was reluctant but had no choice. I felt some trepidation, but, although I was I quite a naïve 18-year-old, the others were, by comparison, like lambs to the slaughter.

We boarded the train. The carriages were smaller than British carriages. However, it was a corridor carriage, with compartments on either side. Each compartment could accommodate five passengers. The windows had no glass, just wooden slats like a fixed Venetian blind.

6

The bench seats at each side were wooden slats with no upholstery. I closed the outer door and then the sliding door to the corridor. I turned to the group. Fortunately, there were very few passengers on the train, and we had this compartment to ourselves.

"OK," I said, "As I'm in charge. Have any of you travelled abroad?" Much shaking of heads. I, myself, had ever been out of England, but I had been brought up on travel books which my father borrowed from Burslem Library. These were to stand me in good stead for the whole of my stay in Egypt.

"None of us knows Egypt then, so we must follow a few ground rules," I said. "First, don't let any 'locals' into this compartment. [I'm ashamed to say we actually called them WOGS – these were brutal and unenlightened times.] Pile your kit bags against the door. Next, don't eat or drink anything provided by the natives except properly bottled mineral water. There is a toilet at the end of each carriage. If you need to go, don't go alone – always take least another one of us with you. Don't get out to stretch your legs at Ismailia."

They all nodded in agreement, so we settled down to a long trip on a slow train. As I said, the carriages were smaller than on British trains, but the way they travelled was also different – slower for one thing. But then there was the sound of the wheels on the track. British carriages have four wheel "bogies" at each end of the carriage. The length of the individual pieces of track in Britain are longer, and, as the wheels passed over the joints, they give out their characteristic, rhythmic "clickety clack, clickety clack". The Egyptian sections of track were shorter, and the rhythm had no pause between one bogie and the next. Consequently, the sound was a regular "clack, clack, clack". And, at each joint, the carriage bounced down and then up again. It felt like riding on a kangaroo bounding along the track.

After several miles, we were in an almost trance like state, when there came a scratching from the outside of the corridor door. Before I could stop him, the lad nearest to the door slid it open. We looked, our gazed centred on the space where you would expect to see a person's head. No-one there. A quick glance down and we saw a tiny figure. It was an adult Egyptian fellah with *no legs*. Just like the character "Shorty" years later in the film *The Good, The Bad and The Ugly*. This tiny figure held out a hand. "Baksheesh" he cried.

At this point, I stepped across and closed the door. "I know we all must feel enormous pity for the poor chap." He had, literally, no legs; they were cut off at the joint with the pelvis. "But if we start giving out any money, we will be besieged in this compartment by beggars of all kinds." My words must have had the desired effect on my companions as they all nodded silently.

There were no further incidents all the way to Ismailia. When we stopped there, we stayed in our compartment, wound down the outside window and spotted an Egyptian with a tray of iced Coca-Cola. We had each been given a small number of piastres (Egyptian pennies) by the Regional Transport Engineer, so we were able to buy one each. Fortunately, though the weather – it being mid-Summer – was hot, the design of the carriage, with its slatted unglazed windows and doors, maintained a steady cooling breeze while we were in motion. Standing still at the platform, the temperature gradually climbed until, after nearly an hour, it became a little uncomfortable. Just as I was thinking that we may have to leave the compartment to get a breath of fresh air on the very large platform, the engine gave a cough and gradually picked up its kangaroo motion continuing southwards. We passed the Great Bitter Lakes, a half-way point in the Canal and, I'd read, a helpful source of sea water to maintain the level of the Canal.

Later in the afternoon, the train stopped briefly at Suez, a smaller town, it seemed, than Port Said or Ismailia. It continued, as the RTE Sergeant had told us, to Port Tewfik, a tiny place with no visible habitation, just the single-story port building staffed by Royal Engineers and a simple wharf-side on the Red Sea. The stretch of water was miles wide, and the view continued to the Sinai desert and, beyond, the Sinai Mountain, where Moses is said to have been given the Ten Commandments. By this time in the afternoon, the sun was lowering behind us, giving a spectacular red light on the Sinai Mountains.

There was little time to contemplate the view. We found the engineers' office and they quickly consulted a map, bustled us onto the back of a three-tonner and drove off to Shandur. When we got to the spot on the map that was Shandur we found – nothing. No buildings, not even a tent or hard standing. Just a stretch of desert enclosed by a single-strand barbed wire fence enclosing a huge area. The only clue to previous habitation was the masses of litter blowing about in the wind which was growing stronger. The driver and his mate were worried that we were in for the "Khamsin". The word means "fifty" in Arabic: the wind was reputed to blow for fifty days and fifty nights.

There was no alternative but to drive back to Port Tewfik. The RTE Sergeant, who appeared to be in charge of the small port detachment, spent some time on the field telephone with British Army Headquarters in Fayid, near Ismailia. Apparently, he learned that the Armoured Replacement Group had moved, *months* ago, to Tel-el-Kebir. To get there would involve driving north, halfway up the Canal, to Ismailia and then taking the Cairo Road, heading west for another sixty and more miles to Tel-el-Kebir.

This was an impossible prospect at this time of day; the sun was beginning to sink over to the west. With admirable speed and efficiency, the engineers erected seven new beds and bedding from their stores, gave us an excellent, late hot dinner, and we settled in for our first night in Egypt.

After their decision to put us up for the night, we had time, before the evening meal, to stroll around the dockside. The Red Sea water was as clear as crystal, so inviting to hot, dusty travellers. I said to the rest of my small group, "I fancy a swim; anybody like to join me?"

"But we have no swimming trunks," one lad replied.

"Who the hell is watching us here?" I replied, stripping off my khaki drill, boots, puttees and so forth.

I dived in. The water was perfect. Just like a swimming pool. The high salt content made us more buoyant, and swimming was effortless. After our initial splashes entering the water, we were surrounded by little fish, the biggest about four inches long. They were attracted to our skin and started nibbling particles of dead skin. Not painful, just a slight tickling.

After about half an hour, we climbed out. There was no need to towel off; the air was still very warm, and we dried as we dressed. It was one of the most enjoyable swims I've ever had. (It was in stark contrast to swimming in the River Derwent one year on Boxing Day. I only did it because it was a charity event, otherwise I wouldn't have braved the cold. I ended up dodging the occasional ice clump and getting swept down a couple of weirs.) But I'm digressing from the warm Egyptian climate.

An early breakfast next morning, then on to the lorry again, heading north to Ismailia. Once there the driver and his mate quickly found the main road to Cairo, and we headed west towards the capital city of Egypt.

At this point a little description of the geography. The Canal Zone lined the west bank of the Canal, from north to south. However, a finger of the zone stuck out, lining the north side of the Ismailia-to-Cairo road, heading due west to the capital and the great river, the Nile. The surrounding land was complete desert, except that a canal, only about 20 yards wide, carried water from the River Nile eastward to Ismailia where it terminated. This canal was called the "Sweet Water Canal". Its purpose was to carry water for irrigation of the desert alongside the Cairo Road. The irrigated area created a strip, about a mile wide, on the southern side of the road. The ground, mainly sand dug out of the Canal channel, had been dumped all along our side of the road, forming a long, continuous embankment. This would be burned into our memory in a couple of months' time.

It was pleasant, driving along an extended oasis on our left. Date palms, cornfields, sugar cane and a variety of vegetables made a pleasant change from the stark desert we had been travelling through on our way to Ismailia. The only buildings on this strip were the occasional single-story houses, windowless and roughly built of sun-baked bricks and roofed by a crude thatch of dried palm fronds. There lived the "fellahin", the Egyptian term for peasants, who tended the crops, irrigating them using a primitive contraption called a shaduf, a simple, hand-operated device, which had been in use in Middle Eastern countries and India for thousands of years. It was a flimsy see-saw on a pole with a short rope hanging from each end. On the water's side hung a bucket and, on the other side, a counterweight made from a ball of dried mud. This was an ancient but simple and ingenious method of raising water and emptying it into channels that ran through the fields. To our untravelled eyes, it was like being transported back to a scene from the bible. The only distraction was the lorries and overloaded buses racing back and forth on the road. There was no habitation on our right, except for very occasional British bases and a military aerodrome called Kasfareet.

Eventually, we reached the only road junction we had come across. The road from it led north for only half a mile before it stopped at the mighty British military base of Tel-el-Kebir. Armed guards emerged from the low guardhouse. They inspected our driver's documents, and they raised the red and white banded barrier pole to allow us to continue a further hundred yards to the main gates. We then crossed a bridge over an anti-tank ditch, then a minefield, then a fence consisting of layers of rolls of Dannart barbed wire, then the main, high barbed-wire fence with wooden machine gun towers at hundred-yard intervals. These formidable layers of defences surrounded the huge depot for a distance of well over twenty miles. The base dated from the Second World War or earlier. It was the main base for supplying our forces in the Western Desert. Pretty well everything an army could need was supplied from here. They had everything from darning needles to guns, and from ammunition to vehicles. There were B vehicles (soft skinned), A vehicles (armoured tanks, armoured cars, and armoured scout cars), E vehicles which covered bulldozers, excavators, graders and road-laying vehicles, and so on.

The area contained well-spaced hangars and store buildings and accommodation for the thousands of troops manning it. They were housed in proper brick-built barracks, not huts or even tents, which some other units had to rely on elsewhere in the Canal Zone. There was even a cinema, a huge out-door swimming pool, shops, restaurants, and cafés, owned and staffed by Greek or Egyptian entrepreneurs.

We were still recovering from our shock at army communications – or lack of them – from finding that the Armoured Replacement Group (ARG) had been transferred here to Tel-el-Kebir. We were now in for another shock. The ARG was indeed based here, in a huge building called 21 Shed. It contained stores, workshops, and offices, *but no living quarters*.

This was six years after the end of World War II, but there was still a great deal of military preparedness needed in the Middle East, for which

TEK (Tel-el-Kebir) was responsible. As a result, the base was nearly full when the ARG was transferred here. (It was transferred, by the way, because military intelligence had foreseen the coming revolution in Egypt. Shandur, where the ARG had been based, was not considered secure.) Because the base was nearly full, there was room for the ARG operations, but not accommodation.

However, the British Military Hospital which lay outside TEK, a further fifteen miles along the Cairo Road, had been transferred to Fayid, and all its female nurses (QARANCs), who by the way were all commissioned Lieutenants, shipped back to the UK. This had provided accommodation for ARG troops in the abandoned single-story wards. However, this meant that they had to travel in the backs of lorries, to and from work, along fifteen miles of the Cairo Road each day. This was to have consequences in the coming weeks. More of this later.

Getting to know "Fort Zindenouf"

The hospital was just off the Cairo Road, and we turned off at an unmarked junction, leading off to the north, to get to it. We drove in through a simple, open, unguarded break in a single strand barbed wire fence. It was astonishingly less secure than the TEK base.

A short drive forward, and a group of bungalow type buildings appeared. One of these had a small sign: "HQ ARG". Everywhere seemed deserted. As we drove up from the main road, Pip Orchard, one of my group, had exclaimed, "God, Fort Zindenouf." Anybody reading this who is old enough to have seen the 1930s black and white film *Beau Geste*, starring Gary Cooper and Robert Preston, would appreciate the comparison with the scene from that film set in the French Foreign Legion outpost of that name. Stuck out in the desert. No breaks in the scenery. Just sun-baked dusty desert. My heart sank at the prospect of spending the rest of my national service in this desolate spot. (We did, in fact, adapt to the place, and camaraderie developed in the months to follow.)

A corporal, stripped to the waist, only a simple wristband denoting his rank, stepped out of the building. We jumped down from the lorry and followed the corporal to another bungalow, which housed the stores. We were each supplied with a mattress, pillow, blankets and pillowcase. Then, we were led to the nearest unmarked bungalow.

"There are spare beds and footlockers in here," instructed the corporal. "Settle yourselves in, and then report to the office, and make sure you read part-two orders for tomorrow. Don't forget to read them each evening. Then you'll have no excuse for not knowing mealtimes, parade times, dress requirements, plus any further instructions."

The hut was occupied by a dozen other soldiers, who were also stripped to the waist, lounging on their beds for the afternoon siesta.

The main meal of the day came after the day's work and was referred to, on the daily printed orders posted outside the main office on the veranda wall, as tiffin. It was a hearty meal. Before our tiffin, we would shower and get changed out of the denim overalls that we, the non-officer "other ranks", wore. (I was the sole army clerk under the officer in charge and his sergeant. Though there were also a couple of educated Egyptian male clerks as well.)

After tea, we strolled across to the veranda to consult the part-two orders. Part-one orders were also displayed, and these described the standing orders, fire drill etc and the ranks and appointments of the officers and WOs in charge. WO stands for warrant officer, the senior non-commissioned rank. Warrant officers were not saluted, like the commissioned officers were, and, although they were ranked below the most junior commissioned officer (second lieutenant), in practice they were highly respected. For example, an RSM (Regimental Sergeant Major) was outranked by a lieutenant. However, despite his higher rank, I have seen a lieutenant standing before the RSM on the parade ground visibly trembling with trepidation.

Reading the orders, our first shock was the early rise. At 0500 hours "gunfire". We looked at one another for some enlightenment, but no-one had a clue. The explanation was that the sergeant major in charge of discipline in the ARG was a Scotsman from the Scots Greys. Apparently, the term gunfire was used in Glasgow to refer to the early morning cup of tea – hot, strong, sweet and milky. It lived up to its name. It was welcoming and made sure we were well awake in the wee early morning hours. Like the rest of the food and drink served before the imminent uprising, it was truly excellent. In fact, it was the finest tea I have ever drunk before and after my national service.

Next item on the orders, PT at 0530 hours, followed by breakfast at 0630 hours. Then parade at 0730 hours, and finally, embussing at 0800 hours, when we climbed on the back of four or five three-ton lorries.

The working day was 0830 hours to 1400 hours with no breaks, although we could grab the occasional Coke or glass of water. After work, the return to our quarters at the abandoned hospital was an informal arrangement. We just climbed on one of the three tonners waiting outside 21 Shed and got driven back to the old hospital.

Once "home" after our first day at work, we really felt the heat. Egypt in June was quite hot, at times approaching ninety degrees Fahrenheit, so it was off with the denims, under the cold shower, then change into shorts (and vest if you wanted it). The water tower was fully exposed to the sun which meant that its contents were lukewarm, all the better for a thorough wash to remove the desert dust. We were covered in it, like the wartime General Rommel, who in the news films, was continually slapping his uniform to remove the dust.

Like most people, I had assumed the desert was all sand. In fact, a lot of it is just hard, sun-baked clay covered with fine dust and littered with stones of various sizes. Also, it wasn't uniformly flat. It was criss-crossed by ravines (wadis). And there any large sand dunes where we were stationed. There were areas of picturesque golden sand dunes, but these were not uniformly spread over the country. They were to be seen in the desert that the Suez Canal had cut through – I'd seen it for myself. They could also be found in other areas, like the "Great Egyptian Sand Sea" to the south of El Alamein. General Montgomery, a great logistician, had used it to his advantage in 1942, luring Rommel into meticulously planned minefields in the relatively narrow area between the Mediterranean Sea in the North and the almost impassable Sand Sea in the South.

Decent and refreshed, we followed the crowd to the cookhouse for our first tiffin. There was a short queue outside the cook house, and it took only minutes before I was standing under the veranda facing a group of cooks. They were proper cooks from the Royal Army Catering Corps, with a sergeant of that regiment watching proceedings with an eagle eye. The first surprise was how relaxed and jolly the cooks were, after the sullen, off-hand crews at the training camps. It was a hint that the morale at this unit was high. The next surprise, another pleasant one, was the quality and quantity of food. Steak and chips, with a side salad of some Egyptian greens that looked like the pak choi that, in later years, became popular in the UK. Also, there were spring onions and a gleaming, deep red tomato. I was given my pudding at the same time, a sugar-glazed yeast bun, stuffed with fruit and still warm from the oven. I learned that these buns were not a daily pleasure but were very much looked forward to by the troops as a special treat.

The dining room was a separate building, only about twenty yards away, but the experienced troops had forewarned us that we had to run the gauntlet as we crossed the short distance to the dining room. "Look out for the bloody shite hawks," they cautioned. "They'll have the meat off your plate like lightening if you don't keep your eyes peeled."

I was lucky. I got to the dining room (called the mess) without incident. We newcomers really enjoyed our first dinner – sorry, "tiffin". After the tip-off, I kept a wary eye out for the shite hawks, which constantly circled in the sky. Almost inevitably I grew over-confident, and then one day, a couple of paces after leaving the veranda with my loaded tray, I was momentarily stunned by a blow behind my right ear as a hawk swooped past me, the knuckle of its left wing giving my head a mighty crack. In milliseconds it had seized the sliced beef off my plate and disappeared. Up in the sky they looked small, like pigeons, but that day, I realised they were much larger and heavier than I'd assumed. As you can guess, my attention never wandered after that.

As part of our kitting out with mattress, sheets, blankets, and pillows, we had all been given a pottery mug and eating irons – knife, fork and spoon. The procedure after every meal was the same everywhere I was posted. After leaving the mess, we passed a cleaning station. This again, never varied. It consisted of three large oil drums lying on their sides, cut in half horizontally and filled with (if we were lucky) hot water. Each container carried a label: "Wash", "Rinse" and "Sterilise". One could tell the quality of the officers in charge by the way this apparatus was maintained. If you were lucky, as we were at ARG, the drums were filled with hot, relatively clean water, with the final one lightly dosed with chlorine.

I shudder when I remember what it was like at the Napoleonic era Salamanca barracks we stayed in briefly on our way to Deepcut training barracks. The water in their tubs wasn't hot and looked like soup which got thinner as you progressed from "Wash" to "Rinse" then "Sterilise". After the last one, I always took my mug and irons to the wash house for an extra quick rinse. This wasn't necessary at ARG. Even during the difficult times after the uprising.

Life continued in quite a relaxed routine, although we were busy at the 21 Shed at TEK receiving and scrutinising requests for vehicles from various army units in the Canal Zone, then filling out the paperwork, then organising the despatch of the tanks, spare kits etc.

I mentioned before that Military Intelligence was on the ball, anticipating the coming troubles, and as a result, demand for stuff increased. Also, we were busy receiving new vehicles from the docks at Port Said and ferrying them to the ARG at Tel-el-Kebir.

Any new tanks or heavy armoured cars couldn't be driven from the port. Regular lorries carried spare parts and equipment from the port, but when it came to the tanks and armoured cars, there were large "low-loaders" pulled by heavy tractors. The drivers were incredibly skilled. It was fascinating when we could briefly watch them in action, loading things like a sixty-ton Centurion tank up on to the low trailer, chaining and fastening it down.

On a couple of occasions, we didn't have enough staff amongst our crew of tank or cavalry troops to fetch the entire load, so I was pressed into service as the armed guard on a three-tonner fetching a load of spares, referred to as "kits". The guard wasn't there because of the risk of terrorism at that time. Rather, drivers had to be accompanied by an armed guard to ward off any "cliffty wallahs". This was what the common thieves were called.

Their ingenuity was legendary. For example, at Tel-el-Kebir at an isolated section of the perimeter, under the noses of the guards and their searchlights and Bren guns in the watch towers, a gang had driven a bunch of dogs ahead of them across the minefield to explode a path through. In the confusion, some of the cliffty wallahs cut their way through the barbed wire entanglements (Dannart wire) and main fence to hide until the following night. They then sneaked out with the goods they had stolen.

I was told, and everybody I asked swore it was true, that they carried a hose pipe that they then inserted into a petrol storage tank and pumped a sizeable volume of petrol through to their gang members on the outside. Whether that was true or not, I don't know. I never saw any actual evidence myself of that scale of theft.

A favourite trick of the cliffty wallahs was to secrete themselves behind a rock formation which caused the road across the desert to bend to get round them. An approaching lorry would slow down for the bend. This gave a thief the chance to jump on to the back of the lorry. If the lorry was not transporting troops in the back, it was a prime target. Once on board, the thief would surreptitiously, using his spanner, loosen and then remove the nuts securing the spare wheel, which was fastened to the outside of the back of the cab. He would then wait for the truck to slow down for the next bend, push the wheel off onto the sandy roadside, and then jump off and hide himself in the rock formations surrounding the bend. If he was not spotted – and invariably he wasn't – the rest of the gang would pick him up with the stolen wheel.

Terrorism to come

Jumping forward in time. One incident with cliffty wallahs I actually experienced was in the later months of the emergency. I, with half a dozen fellow ARG troops, was in the back of a three tonner. I know I'm getting ahead of myself, digressing forward to the uprising which was declared on 2nd October of that year – 1951.

Actually, the terrorist activity started before then. The Egyptian staff disappeared, clerks, storemen, and the complete laundry staff. Losing the laundry staff was a particular problem as they provided a vital service in that climate. Our sweat-soaked clothing had to be washed daily, our khaki drill uniforms beautifully pressed, and the lapels/collars smartly starched.

Another big problem with the disappearance of the Egyptian workers was that there were no flushing toilets at the old British military hospital where we lived. A huge, many handled, iron bucket stood underneath each wooden garde-robe ("toilet hut"). Huts, stood in a row, way off in a corner of the camp. Not having any labouring/cleaning staff to empty and clean them was a challenge. I'll describe the consequences of this later when I cover the terrorist events.

However, I am digressing, because telling you how the cliffty wallahs would rob goods lorries, reminds me of when we troops were the cargo in one of the lorries. One day, a dozen of us were travelling from TEK to Port Said. All were sitting on the floor of the truck, except a full corporal and me who were standing near the back, holding on to one of the vertical struts that held the canvas cover. As we slowed for a bend, a cliffty wallah tried to board us. He must have thought the lorry was empty, because the canvas covering prevented a proper view. We were all armed with our personal weapons. I had a .303 rifle with a bandolier of 100 rounds. The others had Sten guns.

The corporal was a cavalry NCO from the 16/5th Lancers. Like a number of the cavalry men, he had taken advantage of the emergency to help himself to various items from the kits that were issued with every new tank. Each kit equipped the tank for a particular theatre of war in which it might operate – Arctic, European, desert or jungle. But the tanks only carried the kit for the environment they were operating in – the desert in our case.

The remaining kits were held in the RAOC kit stores, which our troops had access to during the emergency, particularly because general discipline had been relaxed, and we few RAOC staff who actually ran the group were so busy receiving, readying and issuing vehicles. The corporal in our truck, like a few of his mates, had got hold of one of the great machetes, in a beautifully tooled scabbard. This was part of the jungle kit for slashing a way through thickets. He wore it attached it to his army belt, like a medieval knight.

At any rate, the first thing we were aware of was two sets of fingers holding on to the tail board. This was over seven feet from the road, so the thief's head was below, out of sight. The corporal was a big chap, tall, dark-haired with a Clark Gable moustache, a regular soldier, not a national serviceman like the rest of the crew. The eight fingers appeared, and in an instant, the corporal, with lightening re-action, drew his machete and smacked it down on the fingers of the thief's left hand. There was a howl from the thief, who disappeared behind us, as the driver, completely unaware of this fracas, accelerated from the bend. Three finger ends, from the second joint, lay on the truck floor, and we carried on without any fuss. It made me admire the skill and speed of the corporal, but also to question the general callous attitude that some of us Brits had towards the Egyptians.

Calm before the storm and a slip at the pool

That was one of the incidents during the terrorist campaign, but in the peaceful days beforehand, we were busy at work but relaxed in our off-duty hours. One Saturday, we were transported to Tel-el-Kebir for a spot of relaxation. We were able to sample the most popular item on the menu in one of the Egyptian cafés, namely "eggs a sheeps" as the waiter called it. Although the food at the hospital was good and plentiful, we, like teenagers everywhere, had insatiable appetites.

In fact, being filled by good regular food and getting regular exercise caused a general improvement in the health and appearance of many of us. I guessed from the short stature of the Glaswegians in our unit, army service was the first time they had experienced good and plentiful food and exercise. I recall that at eighteen, when I was first called up, I was five feet and six inches tall and weighed nine stone. When I was demobbed two years later, I was five feet nine and a half inches tall and weighed just over ten stone.

Back to our Saturdays at TEK. The swimming pool was a great treat for me, as I had always loved swimming. It was great in the hot summer, but I imagined, after experiencing the Egyptian winter, which was surprisingly cold, that it wouldn't be a popular attraction once summer had passed. At the time I'm describing, it was really hot. Walking on the stone clad poolside was almost impossible. The builders had relieved that problem to a large extent by creating a channel running all the way round the pool along which was a constant stream of cool water. Unfortunately, despite the running water, it harboured a slight growth of algae or some other sort of slime. This made the channel a bit slippery, a problem I became acutely aware of during a later visit.

I was walking along the channel when I slipped and fell backwards over the edge of the pool, only half a metre away. As I fell, the centre of my back caught the edge. It felt a little sore, but it didn't seem serious.

It ached the next day so reported sick. I was taken to the Royal Army Medical Corps Medical Centre for an X-ray. The RAMC medics couldn't see anything, so I was put on four days' light duties.

Terrorism starts

A curious thing is coincidence! During my light duties the terrorists started their mischief.

Our officer commanding at the ARG, Major (Paddy) Bruen, ordered that every soldier be issued with a personal weapon. No choice, you were given either a rifle or a Sten gun plus the appropriate ammunition. We were instructed, because we were in an isolated camp (the abandoned British military hospital, with no fortification and fifteen miles away from Tel-el-Kebir itself), to carry our weapon *everywhere*, to work, to meals, to the toilet, to the showers. We even had to take it to bed. Because of the reputation of the terrorists, who would probably include many of the skilled cliffty wallahs, we were ordered not to leave our guns by the bed but to go to bed with our weapon beside us.

In addition to carrying weapons everywhere, the workload increased, and if that was not enough, we had to carry out additional guard duties. Guard duty involved a squad of a dozen or more troops, with a junior NCO as guard commander, occupying the main office annexe for 24 hours.

The commander organised the various duties. We each served two hours "on" and four hours "off", when you could rest on the beds in the annexe, but not expected to sleep. Doing the two-hour periods was called "being on stag". Different soldiers would have different duties. For example, two were assigned to stand on each side of the main gate to 21 Shed; two were assigned to patrol the shed and its immediate surroundings; other pairs were sent to patrol sections of the tank park, where the "unfit" vehicles were stored. I was excused guard duties while sick, but at the end of my four days, being a lance corporal, I was to be the guard commander the following period of twenty-four hours.

I forgot to tell you, before my first guard duty, I acted as one of the first orderly officers. Normally this duty was carried out by a junior commissioned officer, but because we were a small unit, away from immediate reinforcements, they used a sergeant, corporal or even a lance corporal like me. One of the duties of the orderly officer was to organise and supervise troops on punishment duties. These were the chaps who had committed some misdemeanours and were on "jankers", the term for being on "fatigue" duties.

I've already mentioned one of the unpleasant duties normally carried out by the Egyptian labourers, which was to remove the iron buckets from a hatch at the rear of each toilet compartment. These was emptied into a large pit that had been excavated during World War Two and was still being used for that purpose. What you often find in situations like that was that the NCO in charge would pick on some inoffensive private, not a troublemaker, to do the dirty jobs. In our unit there was a group of Glasgow lads, the same age and length of service as me. They were an aggressive lot and stuck together causing the senior ranks some nervousness. This reverse favouritism really annoyed me, and as it happened, the nearest private unoccupied soldier was a Glaswegian chap named O'Hara.

He was short, like all the Glasgow lads, but powerfully built. He had flaming red hair, freckled skin, and was a real neanderthal knuckle-dragger, with an intellect to match.

"O'Hara," I ordered. "Toilet duties. You can join this pair and empty and clean the toilets."

"You can go and f*** yourself," was his reply.

I didn't waste any time. "You're on a charge," I said. "Report to the guardhouse now."

He strolled away in the opposite direction, so I went to the main office, reported to the lieutenant in charge, and the papers were immediately drawn up. You can imagine that during an emergency we were classed as being on active service. Any lapse of discipline was viewed extremely seriously. The performance of the whole unit rested on complete unity and discipline.

The next morning, I reported to the main office at 21 Shed, the HQ of the ARG, dressed in khaki drill, properly turned out. With much deafening shouting and stamping of feet, the accused and I were marched in very quick time into the OC's office. "Mark time – Halt."

We stood in front of the officer commanding our unit. For some reason it wasn't Major Bruen, it was a strange major from the No. 5, Royal Ordnance Base in Tel-el-Kebir. The charge was read out: "Charged under Section 40 of the Army Act, with conduct prejudicial to good order and discipline, whilst on active service."

The major asked for my evidence. I explained that the toilets needed emptying and cleaning and, from the group of soldiers on fatigues, I had ordered O'Hara to do the job.

"What was the defendants reply?" the Major asked.

"He told me to f*** myself, then walked off with a gesture of contempt," I replied.

At this, I thought the major was going to have a fit. He went scarlet in the face, then exclaimed, his voice shaking with indignation, "A gesture of contempt!"

He didn't even question O'Hara. "Remanded for Commanding Officer's orders. Dismissed."

We were frantically marched out in quick time, just as we had been marched in. Outside, O'Hara was sent off to his normal job on the tank park, and I made my way to our kit stores office. The squadron major, Urquhart, accompanied me. "By God he's in for it now. Remanded for the commanding officer." he muttered.

A few days later, we were marched in again, with the same intimidating, aggressive, ceremony. This time, facing us was the commanding officer of Combined Ordinance Services, a lieutenant colonel. A repeat performance, and the sentence was announced: fifty-six days at detention barracks. O'Hara was marched away. Anybody who has seen the film *The Hill*, starring Sean Connery with Harry Andrews as the sadistic RSM, will appreciate what he was in for! I never saw him again.

One remaining recollection of O'Hara was a few days after he joined the unit, fresh from basic training. He was assigned to a labouring job at the tank park with a group of workmates who had been in the ARG for some months. It was mid-summer, and the other lads wore just denim trousers and boots plus their army beret. O'Hara obviously wanted to fit in with the others, so he went to work similarly attired.

After working in the blazing sun all morning, he was badly sunburned. The next day, once at the 21 Shed, he discarded his denim jacket and went off to work again. I was horrified at the sight of his bare back. It was a mess, almost one, huge swollen yellow blister. I don't know if he didn't feel pain or had declined to report sick. Perhaps someone had told him that sunburn was considered by the army to be a self-inflicted injury and subject to punishment.

A tease backfires and an ambulance for me

Back to my stint as guard commander. I settled down in the guard room at 21 Shed, deputed the first "stag" to their various posts, then lay down for a spell on one of the beds. No sooner had I relaxed than came the loud sound of a .303 being fired.

The chap doing duty as guard at the entrance gate had been approached by one of the very few Egyptians who had not deserted us. It appeared he was cheekily hard-faced individual. He'd been teasing our guard, saying he was going to enter the compound. The guard, as it happened, was another unfortunate Glaswegian who promptly levelled his rifle at the Egyptian, holding at waist height. The Egyptian laughed and brushed it away, so our soldier promptly pulled the trigger, blowing off the Egyptian's middle finger.

The Egyptian started screaming uncontrollably, so a couple of our resting guards rushed out and dragged him to stand in front of me, his finger stump pouring with blood. He wouldn't stop screaming, so in desperation, I punched him hard under the chin. He was stunned but quietened while I organised the first aid box.

Just at that moment, there came the repeated clanging of a bell, and with its engine roaring, an ambulance drew up outside the open door.

"Good God!" I said, "Who sent for an ambulance, and how've they got here so quickly?"

As I said this, the ambulance driver and his mate quickly opened the ambulance doors, pulled out a stretcher and ran with it into the guard room. They dropped the stretcher by the blood soaked Egyptian and said to me, "Are you Corporal Johnson?" (The full-term lance corporal was not used in daily conversation. In the same way the lieutenant colonel was always referred to as "the colonel") As soon as the ambulance men knew who I was, they picked me up, despite my protests, laid me down on the stretcher, picked it up, and carried me to the waiting ambulance.

The ambulance crew drove me to the hospital in TEK, where I was given another X-ray and then put to bed. An RAMC doctor came to see me and explained that the junior doctor who had taken the original X-ray had not spotted that I had a wedge compression fracture of the first and second lumbar vertebrae. This had been picked up when all X-rays were routinely examined by a senior doctor.

I was transferred to the main hospital for the Canal Zone, at Fayid, near Ismailia. There I was taken, without delay, to the plaster room, where I was sat with my back upright and bent backwards like a banana. Then I was plastered from my groin to below my Adam's apple, a most uncomfortable position, which brought on a low-level pain. This, unfortunately, got worse. I was annoyed to learn later that a junior doctor had entered on my notes that I was neurotic for demanding pain killers when the banana position caused a dreadful aching.

After a few more days, the consultant orthopaedic surgeon, a large bluff lieutenant colonel, came to see me. He recognised immediately how "sore" it must be to be fixed in that position.

"This climate is not the best environment for fractures, and limbs in plaster take longer to heal," he said. "Your injury is not so serious in the scheme of things, so I'm going to prescribe a few days bed rest in a recommended position, and then an on-going course of physiotherapy to build up the muscles along your spine. If you follow this regime, you'll heal better than being in plaster, plus it will avoid a long period of post-plaster weakness."

Later that day, the sergeant physiotherapist came to me and gave me some gentle exercises to do while I was confined to bed. After that, in each of the following four weeks, I did two or even three long sessions in the gym, until my back was so strong that it would support me on two chairs, one under the back of my head and the other under my heels.

The next four weeks were boring. Again, the QARANC nurses had been repatriated to the UK, and the native auxiliary staff, just as at Tel-el-Kebir, had fled for fear of terrorist reprisals. There were no newspapers, no books to read. The male nurses recognised this. They couldn't access their small library for some reason. The only books they could lend me were textbooks: *Anatomy for Nurses* and *Physiology for Nurses*.

The other patients on the ward were soldiers recovering from malaria, gyppy tummy and other illnesses They were not well enough to be good company and seemed too unwell for much conversation. There was one patient, however, in the corner bed. His name was Harry. He was a corporal from the Royal Corps of Signals. He had been transferred to Fayid from Khartoum in the Sudan, one and a half thousand miles to the south. He had been bayoneted in the leg. His femur – the big bone between the hip and the knee – was fractured.

Again, presumably because of the climate, he was not in plaster. Instead, he was being kept in traction, with the leg being pulled lengthways to keep the two halves of his femur in line. This, to avoid shortening his leg when it healed.

His bed was raised more than two feet from the floor, so that the doctors and nurses could help him without having to stay bent over the injury. He lay on his back with the upper part of his body raised into a partial sitting position. His injured leg was uncovered. A hole had been drilled through the head of the tibia bone just below the knee-cap. A rod was threaded through the hole, protruding a couple of inches either side. A hoop was fastened to its two ends, and a non-stretchable cord ran from the head of the hoop to a pulley that was beyond the foot of the bed and about three feet above the level of the mattress. From there, it descended to a frame holding heavy iron weights, that could be added to or taken away as necessary, to provide the required "pull" on his upper leg.

Each end of the rod was passed through a cotton wool pad, and this was regularly moistened with Friars' Balsam, described in the dictionary as a "protectorant", although it is no longer used. The nurse would moisten the pads as he rotated the rod a few times to stop the hole closing (which would prevent the rod being removed after the thigh was healed).

Harry, who had been in this position for more than six weeks, didn't know how much longer he would have to endure it. He was not in great pain and was surprisingly cheerful and glad of my company.

"You think it's hot here," he said. "It can reach one hundred and ten and higher in the shade!" (In those days, we talked about temperatures in Fahrenheit. Today he would have said forty-five Celsius.) His khaki drill jacket was hung up behind his bed, and it was bleached almost white by the sun.

One day, without being able to say goodbye to Harry, I was collected in a hurry, along with my few belongings, loaded onto a pedestrian ambulance with some other patients, and whisked off to a convalescent depot at Deversoir. As was typical of the army, there was little communication. I had never heard of Deversoir.

It was rather disappointing to see that there were no accommodation buildings – it was all tented. A score of tents were stood in military-style rows on the desert sand, along the Suez Canal. It was at the end of the first section of the canal, where it entered the first of the Bitter Lakes. With a little exploration, I found a bungalow office/medical centre and the cookhouse/dining mess. Fortunately, it was, like the hospital at Fayid, in a malaria-free Zone, which after Tel-el-Kebir, was a great relief.

At Tel-el-Kebir, we had to wear long khaki drill trousers after sundown, and our khaki shirts were rolled down to the wrists. We were each given a small applicator containing DDT, an oily liquid to be applied to exposed skin. It was altogether an uncomfortable precaution during hot, sticky summer evenings. At Tel-el-Kebir, we also had to sleep under individual mosquito nets, which were stifling as they restricted any flow of air.

At Fayid I had a bed outdoors on the veranda, with no extra clothing or nets. This was a welcome luxury, which continued throughout my stay at Deversoir.

Because of the army's emergency arrangements, there were few if any Egyptian staff to help, and the food gradually became more basic in the absence of fresh meat and vegetables.

It wasn't too bad when I'd settled in. I had a proper steel bed with proper mattress and bedding, with a little bedside cabinet. Also, a footlocker to keep my boots and uniform in.

Each tent was the same: square with a centre pole and low canvas walls, which were rolled up during the heat of the day. The floor was laid with good, concrete square blocks. This was a help, as we could easily sweep away any loose sand which blew in from outside.

Bed bug aside

Another relief after Tel-el-Kebir, was the absence of bed bugs.

I forgot, earlier in this narrative, to mention the problem they caused at Tel-el-Kebir. You will remember I described the "wards" we used for living in. They were lightly built, with rush and plaster walls and a palm thatch roof. Presumably because they were designed and built as hospital wards, the floors were made of a whole concrete raft. The concrete was good quality and carefully finished with a smooth final coat, which was almost like marble. Our beds were typical army beds made of angle iron.

The senior corporal in our room explained a drill we carried out every day after tiffin, before we settled down for a relaxing afternoon. Our standard uniform contained a pair of gym shoes, described as pumps or daps or sneakers, depending on your home dialect. The drill was to select one bed out of the twenty, strip it bare of bedding, and draw it into the centre of the room, which fortunately was quite spacious. We gathered round with raised gym-shoes in hand, while the corporal and another chap at each end of the bed lifted it up about a foot off the floor, then smacked it down as hard as they could.

The bed bugs spent daylight hours gathered in bunches like tiny red grapes in the inside corners of the angle iron. Banging the bed onto the floor dislodged, hopefully, all the bugs which then scattered, quite quickly, in all directions. They were surrounded however, by the gym-shoe army. Each of us used our pumps with their smooth flat soles to flatten the bugs as they scattered. This didn't take long. After a few minutes, the floor was red from the blood-filled bugs, which had fed on us during the night. A small mop-up party soon washed it away, as the smooth, even, floor was so easy to clean.

This daily carnival of the bugs was, happily, brought to an end just before I went on that fateful guard duty. As I mentioned earlier, it was the year 1951, only five years after the end of World War II, and DDT was being used more widely. During out time, it was introduced into the Canal Zone.

One morning as we paraded before work, a party of white-overall-clad medics entered each hut with what looked like hand grenades – a heavy steel container, sealed at the top with a break-away nozzle. I watched, before leaving, as this medic broke the seal, held the bomb aloft in his hand, and marched the length of the hut and back. It must have been a heavily concentrated version of DDT, hence the white suits and respirators. Miraculously, we never saw a bed bug again, before or after my hospital stay. This Ghost Buster squad also treated any areas where wastewater might gather such as rain gutters or any open containers. Mercifully, the number of mosquitoes was greatly reduced.

Back to the convalescence centre

So, back to Deversoir. I was surprised at first by the tented quarters. However, I got used to it quite quickly. We had electric lighting, and after rolling down the canvas walls, it was all rather neat, tidy and cosy, with only four occupants. The food was somewhat Spartan because of the emergency. By this time, it was August, and although the history books tell you the troubles began with the abdication of King Farouk on 2nd October 1951, the problems started well before that date. Despite that, it was quiet and peaceful here at Deversoir. We had no visible armed guards, unlike at Tel-el-Kebir. They were necessary there because of the massive problems posed by the many cliffty wallahs.

Life proceeded in a peaceful, relaxed way, as you would hope for at a convalescent centre. The weather was hot but calm, with no sandstorms or traffic noise to disturb the quiet. We spent time sunbathing, however, for chaps with a fair, sensitive, skin like me, you had to watch the clock and limit the exposure.

The camp was located on the west (right) bank of the canal, just at the very point where, at the northeast corner, it opened up into the lake. My tent was at that very point, only thirty yards from the water's edge. The canal itself was lined with huge concrete blocks, to prevent the bottom and sides being eroded by the wash from passing ships. The blocks descended into the bottom of this huge canal in great steps sloping down to the bottom. It was amazing to sit at the top of these steps watching a massive tanker or liner passing by, only ten or twenty yards from each side of the canal. Their speed was limited to about ten or so, miles an hour. They appeared absolutely colossal, towering above me.

The next amazing sight was the bow wave. Although the ships weren't moving fast, at that closeness they seemed to speed past. Immediately after the bow of the ship passed, the water level was sucked down to a depth of about fifteen or even twenty feet, then after a distance of twenty to thirty yards, the bow wave followed, racing over the concrete stairs to pass right by our feet. As the water receded and this hollow was revealed, we could see short seaweed clinging to the concrete, and amongst the weed, as the water drained, we could spot the occasional seahorse.

A game developed amongst the fitter blokes amongst us. The trick was, as the bow passed, we would clamber down these massive blocks – a depth of up to twenty feet in some cases – pluck a seahorse from the sides, then scamper back up again, ahead of the bow-wave racing towards us. The seahorses seemed to expire very quickly. We then laid them on the sand under the fierce sun for the rest of the day. We then polished the desiccated creature with boot polish and kept it as a souvenir. I only took part once in this escapade. I gave it up after reflecting upon the sight of the massive bow wave racing towards me. Also, I thought it was senseless cruelty inflicted on the little creatures.

It was peaceful and quiet at Deversoir. The nearest village, or any sort of building, was miles away. There was no main road either to disturb the atmosphere of the place. The food was adequate, but lacking variety and fresh vegetables. (We were reduced to eating hard tack, the thick, brick-hard biscuits, as fresh bread couldn't reach us from the British Army Bakery). As I've said, these privations were caused by the Egyptian staff deserting because, we assumed, of threats from the Egyptian Liberation Army who, we were told by the few NCOs, had an avowed aim to sweep the British occupiers from their country.

Because of the lack of media in those days, we couldn't see the big picture of the political situation. We, those of us who had remembered their schooldays history lessons, knew that the British were not actually an occupying force. We were there because of the treaty between the British, French and Egyptian governments. The British forces were stationed there to guard the canal and the surrounding area. Also, it was recognised that the Middle East in general, and the canal in particular, were so important to us from the point of view of our island's reliance on maritime trade and sources of oil from neighbouring Arab countries.

The way a minority of our forces behaved could have led the political activists to see us as occupiers. Also, it was known that there was a great deal of communist sympathy in the Egyptian Liberation Army. It wasn't clear if they operated with the approval of the Egyptian government or were an unofficial terrorist organisation. It was early days yet, before the troubles really broke out. Meantime, we convalesced in peace. Boredom wasn't a major problem. Most of us were glad to have a break from hospital treatment, and before that, the hard work and loss of uninterrupted sleep when on frequent guard duty.

Pioneers aside

At this point I want to mention the role of the Royal Pioneer Corps. Most us conscripts had no proper concept of the structure of the army. The general attitude we had towards the Pioneers was to regard them as general labourers. This was because they did most of the dirty and unpleasant duties. During the previous world wars, they cleared up behind the front line, gathering up the dead bodies, labelling them, recording what personal information they could, and then burying them. This was unpleasant and dangerous work so near the front line. They also helped the Royal Engineers and infantry regiments in clearing mines, then moving on to help lay new minefields. When they were not used in these unpleasant roles, they did almost continuous guard duties.

Before the troubles began, the whole Canal Garrison was guarded by these Pioneers. They were mercenaries from abroad, like the Ghurkhas from Nepal. The Ghurkhas were, and still are, proud and fiercely effective infantry. They, like the rest of the infantry, carried out only their own domestic guarding.

However, in the Canal Zone, the Pioneers were recruited from Mauritius, a beautiful island in the Indian Ocean. Climate and scenery don't provide a lot of employment, so there was a large population of young men who were drawn, like the Ghurkhas from Nepal, to a three-year tour of duty. Nearly all their time was spent on guard duties. Two hours on and four hours off. I thought it must have been soul destroying. I never found out what happened at weekends, whether they had time off or carried on relentlessly with their two on and four off.

The Mauritians were small, brown skinned, men whose ancestors had settled Mauritius, mainly from India, for generations. I don't know where their barracks were. We never had the opportunity to mix with them because of the emergency or troubles, call it what you will. (Years afterwards, the BBC called it "The Suez Emergency: The Forgotten War of the Conscript Soldier.")

At Tel-el-Kebir, as I described earlier, the main base was surrounded by massive defences, including watch towers which were, from memory, about thirty feet from their base to the roof of the hut on top of it. Two Mauritians manned each tower, one scanning the area with a search-light and his mate at the ready with his Bren gun. After two hours, they would be relieved, spend four hours in the guard room, after which, they would be back for another two hour "stag", either on the tower, guarding the gate, or patrolling inside the perimeter.

Although, as I said, we didn't get to mix with them during our regular posting, we did get the chance to get to know the ones who were convalescing with us at Deversoir. They were a decent bunch of fellows, always clean and smartly turned out, with smooth pale brown skin and gleaming, healthy looking black hair.

Crocodile Lake

One day, quite out of the blue, a young doctor officer from the Royal Army Medical Corps at Fayid came and introduced us to a very kind looking lady from the Church Army. I had no idea what the Church Army was and neither did my fellow national servicemen. It turned out they were similar to the Salvation Army and had no connection with the military. They have a history of social work and rehabilitation. The lady was friendly and helpful, and throughout the short time we saw her, there was no overt attempts to evangelise to our mostly heathen community. But there was an open invitation, for anyone that was interested, to attend the occasional church service, held by a visiting Church Army officer.

The main reason for her visit was to ask if anybody was interested in a trip to Lake Timsah and a picnic on the beach. There was no shortage of volunteers – we had been held in benign prison conditions for weeks, and as I said earlier, convalescing and relaxing didn't solve the boredom.

So, the next day, two, or perhaps three, lorry loads of us set off for the lake. Lake Timsah was also known, I later learned, as Crocodile Lake. How it got that name puzzled me – the water in it was salty as the Canal passed through it. The Canal took shipping from the Red Sea into the Mediterranean, all sea water. I guess the Sweetwater Canal may have emptied into the lake with its water from the Nile, but I never found out how that affected the salinity of the lake. Nowadays, there is a bit of greenery in spots around the lake, but in 1951 it was sand everywhere.

The picnic was a great success. In those days, portable refrigerators had not been invented, so the crates of Coca Cola and other mineral waters were placed in the shallows near the edge of the beach. There was no beer, because the Church Army rather frowned on alcohol, and in my view, it would have been a bad idea to drink it in the heat of the day.

The food was a real treat, proper white bread sandwiches, pastries, savoury and sweet, plus cakes. Egyptian food was delicious, as fifty years later, Sheila and I found on a Nile Cruise. The picnic was a foretaste of that experience. The cakes and sweetmeats were absolutely delicious. I guess the Church Army, being based at Fayid, had developed friendships with the local populace so weren't dependent on British Army supplies.

After the food came the drinks, cooled enough by the lake water to an acceptable level. But, shock and horror, the organisers, having done such a great job, hadn't brought a bottle opener! However, rescue was at hand. As I mentioned earlier, we were a mixed bunch of British soldiers and the Pioneers from Mauritius. A few of the Pioneers, however, had been recruited from the Seychelle Islands. These islands were in the Indian Ocean near to Madagascar. The inhabitants of the Seychelles were African rather than Asian. We had just one of these Seychellois soldiers amongst us. He was a magnificent giant of a man, with coal-black shiny skin, close cropped hair, and the most brilliant strong white teeth. Like all the Seychellois he was full of good humour. He sat in the shallows by the drinks crates. When any of us wanted a bottle, he'd grab one from a crate, and putting the edge of the bottle-cap between his teeth, he would effortlessly flip it off.

I have always been fond of swimming. The lake water was at the perfect temperature for a dip. So, I asked if any of the others would care to accompany me in a swim across the lake. I'm not sure of the distance. I know the lake is five miles long, so I guess it was less than three miles wide. What added interest to the idea was the sight of the monument to Ferdinand de Lesseps on the other side. De Lesseps was the French engineer who constructed the Suez Canal, starting the digging in 1860. The monument stood on a tall sand dune and was basically an obelisk standing on a stone platform.

My idea was based on a naïve understanding of distances and underestimation of the power of the sun. To keep off the worst of the sun, we wore our khaki drill shirts over our swimming trunks, leaving our legs bare. The water was lovely, and to swim in water with a high salt content was easy. On the other side, we started our way walking up the dune. With no other features around us, we hadn't got a grasp of the scale of the height. The farther we walked, the steeper it got, until we were on all fours, at times, and the obelisk didn't seem much closer.

Eventually, we reached the top of the dune. The views weren't in any way spectacular, just desert with the blue Suez Canal heading up to the north and Port Said. So, we turned to examine the monument, a massive stone obelisk. It had an inscription on a metal plate on the side of the large concrete (or was it stone?) block. I'm writing this exactly seventy years later, so I can't recall what it said. The inscription was in French, of which I knew only a few words. It seemed to commemorate the creation of the Canal under de Lesseps' guidance, with a date (1850, I think).

We now faced the return journey. Getting down was so much easier, half walking and half sliding down the steep, deep, sand. A problem now appeared – sunburn. The top half of my body was protected by my shirt, but in swimming trunks, my bare legs and feet were not. It wouldn't have been so bad if the sun shone from the same direction during our trip. We were walking roughly north, so as we went up the dune it shone from the east on my right. It was way past midday coming down. The sun was now in the west, so the same leg, the right, was exposed to the sun.

The swim back to Deversoir helped a lot. As I swam, I remembered, as a child during the war years, reading accounts of the work of Sir Archibald MacIndoe, a talented burns specialist in the south of England, who was treating RAF and other aircrews who had crashed in burning planes. He noticed that the burnt aircrews who had ditched into the English Channel had a much better survival rate than the chaps who had come down on land. He developed a technique of treating burns with saline solutions and had much success with it. Success in terms of patients' surviving, but unfortunately, he couldn't do much about the scarring and terrible disfigurements. Survivors afterwards formed a club called the Guinea Pigs Club.

I remembered reading about them so vividly. My two brothers and I became horribly fascinated by the war, which started when I was seven years old. I was still fascinated when, years later, I read accounts, which were not published during the war, of the problems faced by air forces on all sides. Particular among these was the problem of fighter plane design. Finding space for fuel tanks was difficult.

I recall that the Hurricane had a tank immediately in front of the unfortunate pilot. The extremely flammable liquid caught fire easily and burned intensely, fanned by the powerful slipstream blowing it directly onto the unfortunate pilot. Some headway was made, eventually, to lessen this danger. But I must avoid getting bogged down in war history. That is a subject for writers more experienced and skilled than me.

So, getting back into the highly saline waters of Timsah, we reached shore and returned with the Church Army to the convalescent depot. The sunburn was rather extensive down my right leg, and it was rather sore. However, it didn't blister (which could have been due to the involuntary saline treatment), and after a few days of lazing in our neat little tent, it was healed. I never reported sick, because it had been dinned into us that sunburn was regarded by the army as a self-inflicted injury, and you would be liable to be put on a charge. I didn't really think, even though we were classed as being on active service, they would punish a convalescing patient but knowing the queer ways the Army thinks at times, I kept a low profile.

It was high summer now, and time was spent after lunch having a siesta or just relaxing on one's bed. Time passed at a leisurely pace, so there was time to indulge in afternoon reveries. My thoughts would wander back to the hectic days of induction and basic training, and then further back to call up, school days, and early work.

Chapter 2: Getting a Job

Prelude

As I sit here about to write this chapter, I reflect on the fact that every one of my highly educated grandchildren has enjoyed a wonderful university education. They have bachelor's, master's and doctorates coming out their ears. How different it is to two generations ago, when university was an alien concept to me and my pals in the Potteries.

Leaving school

I left school a few days before my fourteenth birthday. Middleport School, in Burslem, one of Arnold Bennett's "Five Towns", from the book series of the same name. The five towns are, from north to south: Tunstall, Burslem (the mother town of the Potteries), Hanley, Longton and Stoke.

Since Bennett's day, the towns have been federated into the city of Stoke-on-Trent. OK, why was the whole city called Stoke-on-Trent, when the town of that name already existed? And, to deepen the mystery, Stoke is the smallest of the towns that make up the city. My education hadn't stretched to such puzzles. Also, there were six towns, not five. Bennett ignored Fenton. Personally, I guess that the title *Anne of the Five Towns* had a better ring it than *Anne of the Six Towns*. To this day, some of the residents of Fenton remain miffed by their exclusion.

As I said, it was at the time of my fourteenth birthday in December 1946. I hadn't been to grammar school. As a child I was somewhat a sickly lad. I caught scarlet fever when I was ten, so I didn't sit my "eleven-plus" exam. I was in Bucknall Isolation Hospital. Bucknall was a suburb of Tunstall and was somewhat rural, which is why it was chosen for the site of this hospital for infectious diseases. In those days, eighty years ago, there were no antibiotics. Alexander Fleming had discovered penicillin, but it was some years before it was in mass production and available to the general public.

"Nowadays," a nurse told me, "we regard scarlet fever as tonsillitis with a rash." No matter the name, it still killed a lot of children of my era and was talked about in hushed tones by our neighbourhood housewives.

I remember my father telling me about the team from the local public hygiene department coming to our house, which was to be "stoved" because of the scarlet fever. The bedding plus all soft furniture, the little that there was, were moved out into the back garden. Every door and window was covered by sheets of a special paper and sealed around the edges with adhesive tape. Special fumigating candles were lit before sealing up a room. The sealing tape wouldn't come off around architraves and window frames, which meant my father had to strip and re-decorate the house.

I can't remember how long I stayed in hospital, only three weeks or so, but it meant I missed the eleven-plus exams at school. I was blissfully unaware of the significance of this. Mother and Father never discussed anything of importance with us children. They had very much a working-class outlook on life and regarded such matters as being beyond their type.

My mother also had some strange ideas, not based on information and facts, but on rumours and gossip. Although, in her way, I suppose she cared for us and did wonders with the rations during the war, ensuring we never went hungry. She actually believed that education was not a good idea! I remember, years later when my wife, Sheila, and I visited them and talked about our children. Gary, the eldest, was studying hard for his O-levels.

My mother turned to Sheila and said, "It's not good for them, all that studying. He'll get brain fever." By then, we had become used to her strange ideas – she would have been considered very old fashioned, I'm sure, even in her grandparents' age.

Although I missed the eleven-plus exams, a couple of years later, I sat the thirteen-plus exams, getting good results to the surprise of my headmaster. I suppose it was something of an achievement, because I did no revising, and homework was actively discouraged by my mother.

My mother's main concern was that I was nearing an age where I could bring an extra wage into the household.

Job interview

After the thirteen-plus results, I was offered a place at either Burslem College of Technology or Burslem School of Art. I didn't get to take up either, discouraged, again by my mother, who was continually hinting about shortage of money.

A few days before the beginning of the Christmas school holidays, a director of Burgess and Leigh – a local pottery firm – had approached the school. He had vacancies for two school leavers in the company office. The headmaster called another pupil, Beryl Bailey, and me to his office to meet the man from Middleport Pottery, as it was known. Arrangements were made for me to go to the office to be interviewed by Mr George Lloyd, the office manager. He talked with me in the main office, standing by his desk. After a few questions about arithmetic and basic English, he was keen to get a sample of my handwriting. He handed me a pen and pointed to a pad on the centre of his desk.

The office was so old, dating back to the founding of the company in the late nineteenth century, that, even in the nineteen forties it drew gasps of astonishment from first-time visitors. The desks lined one wall and Mr Lloyd's desk projected from a wall on the opposite side. Talk about Dickensian! They were designed for clerks to stand up to work at them, although each had a tall stool to sit on if they fancied a change of posture. They were not individual desks; each was joined to the next in a fixture lining one wall of the office.

Then, a further surprise, the desktops were not flat, they were sloping upwards at an angle of about thirty degrees and edged at the bottom, nearest to the clerk, by a heavy brass lip. The whole set up was designed around the huge brass bound ledgers. These were placed above the brass lip, which stopped the ledger from sliding down and onto the floor. At the top of the slope was a horizontal ledge in which were inserted two porcelain ink wells, one for black ink and the other for red. The ledgers were kept safely in the directors' office, so every time a clerk needed one, in order to "post" (meaning to enter) invoices or money received, he would have to knock quietly at the directors' door, ask permission and come out with one or more, if he had the strength to carry them. I'm not joking, those ledgers weighed a ton.

Fortunately, I never rose high enough in rank – or in height – to use them.

So, returning to my interview; Mr. Lloyd looked round and found a stool upon which I could stand and from there clamber onto his stool. The pen was a "dip" pen. (Ball pens hadn't been invented yet). It was much bigger than the pens at school, and the nib was a great silver steel spear. I found it rather scratchy, but I was able to write my name, address and the numerals from 0 to 10. He didn't tell me what to write but he seemed pleased by my initiative in deciding for myself.

The final step was a brief chat in the directors' office with Mr Denis Leigh, who, with his brother Kingsley, was joint managing director. Mr. Denis, as all the staff in this Dickensian world addressed him, asked me what I had done at school, and if I had any plans for the future. I told him that I intended to enrol at the Wedgwood Institute in Burslem for a commercial course. The course covered Pitman shorthand, typing, education into various commercial and legal documents, commercial mathematics (whatever that was), commercial geography etc. This involved attending the institute for two hours in the evening, three times a week.

Denis Leigh seemed a kind, avuncular figure, but was not very approachable and kept to his office. The only times I saw him was when his fountain pen was dry. He would emerge, holding it at arm's length and call, "Lesley, fill my pen, would you." Mr Stubbs, whom we all knew as Frank, would jump off his stool and rather obsequiously, in my view, hurry to take the pen. He would then later scratch on the director's door to return the pen.

Many years later, I learned that, when I was away doing my military national service, Mr Leigh had an envelope delivered to our house with a Christmas gift of cash, which in today's money would amount to nearly a hundred pounds. Mother never told me of this and pocketed the lot as a contribution to housekeeping, as was her perceived right. Similarly, while in Egypt, I entered into a voluntary savings scheme to deduct a sum from my pay, leaving me one shilling and sixpence of my own. When I was demobbed, I looked in the savings book, which Mother had kept. It was empty. Again, she believed that anything I earned was for her household.

Starting work

Getting back to my first job, I started to work at thirty shillings per week. Mother took twenty-five shillings, leaving me five of my own. On the other hand, I had bed and board and basic clothing. Things like a new suit or overcoat, I paid for myself.

I arrived at Burgess and Leigh Ltd. (Middleport Pottery) at 9.00 a.m. on Monday 6th January 1947, just over twenty months after the end of World War II. The posh part of the factory was a two-storey building, lining the beginning of Port Street, about 200 yards walk down Albion Street, where I lived. The top-storey contained the "glost" warehouse and some of the decorating shops. Like all industrial premises from the industrial revolution, the term "shop" described a working place – a room or shed like a "machine shop". The ground floor was pierced by a short tunnel with a weighbridge built into the ground and, alongside it, the doorway into the "lodge" and the offices.

I've already given a part-description of the office, a thirty-foot square with windows (frosted glass for privacy) on the north side, behind which was the main row of Dickensian desks. The left hand of the row, however, dropped down to a horizontal ledge at table height. This was the "post desk". (Nowadays it would be the equivalent of the mail room). This was fortunate for short arse me. (In those days I would be under five feet tall) There was one chair for the sole occupant, me. The tabletop had room for a set of scales to weigh parcels, and a shelf above it for the large book of postage stamps, the Post Office Guide and the despatch books, one for home market despatches and the other the export version.

I was told that my job title was "Forwarding Clerk and General Office-Boy". Looking back, it was an extremely responsible position even for an experienced clerk, let alone a green school leaver. I was trained by a man, I don't remember his name, who happened to be the uncle of Beryl Bailey, my co-starter. He was a big chap, recently de-mobbed from the Royal Air Force, impatient to work his notice. He was leaving for a better job. This was good for me – I had always been a quick learner with a penchant for doing things my way.

First duty for me was to make an early start and collect the mail from the main post office in Burslem. This was mile walk up a steep hill to Burslem and back. If the weather was at all inclement, I used the frequent bus service, a penny per trip. As I said, I was expected to walk and no question of "bus money", so I quickly developed a way of reimbursing myself for this – and no more – from the cash box I was responsible for. I used the cash box when I needed to buy high value stamps for parcels. Regular mail envelopes used the standard stamps kept in the stamp book.

Once back in the office, my next job was to take my despatch books down the driveway from the lodge to the packing house at the bottom of the drive, standing on the canal-side. Why it was called the packing house instead of packing shop was, I guess, because no manufacturing process was done there. In the packing house, threading my way through piles of straw, I searched for newly packed crates each with a copy of the order form standing on it. I entered the details in the appropriate despatch book.

Home crates needed a proper label with the customer's name and address, which I wrote out in my neat handwriting. (Well spotted, Mr Lloyd). The export crates didn't have labels but a marking board, about a foot square, made of plywood or hardboard on which the glost warehouse manager had stencilled the mark of the importer. It seemed curious that the home crates bore the detailed address, but the export crates, which had to travel so much farther, carried a board with the importer's initials surrounded by a triangle, a Staffordshire knot, or other symbol. It was explained to me that stevedore or dock labourers in some of the countries couldn't read, and each importer at the port of destination had a warehouse or "go down" associated with one of the marks. OK, it worked; in the four years I did the job. Only one crate had ever gone missing, involving a lot of palaver with marine insurance.

Once that task was done, I needed to arrange transport. In those days, after the privations of the war, there was little or no road transport. Everything from Middleport Pottery was despatched, either by rail for "home" traffic, or by canal for all the exports. Home crates were loaded onto a flat-bed trailer with pneumatic tyres, and horse drawn to our local station at Longport, a mile away in the opposite direction to Burslem. My involvement ended once they had been loaded onto the trailer.

It was a different matter with the exports. When I had judged we had a boat load, or enough to justify using a boat, I would order a barge from the Anderton Canal Company. The barge would carry the cargo to the Anderton's depot at Runcorn. This was a short journey of about thirty miles towards Liverpool Docks. Back in the office, I would notify the London office or agent of the appropriate importer. Then I would wait for the agent to select the ocean steamer. This was relayed to me, and I would give Anderton's the instructions to "lighter" the crate or crates to the steamer to be loaded on board. The loading of railway trailers or Anderton's barge didn't happen every day, probably three or four times a week. I'll never forget the first load I supervised.

My first load – a dray and shire horse

The winter of 1946/7 was a harsh one throughout Europe. Britain suffered from storm damage and from the snow and heavy frosts, making conditions, already difficult from the war years, really hard. Rationing was still in force. Bread was rationed from 21st of July '46 to 24th of July '48. Average body weight fell, and potato consumption increased. Certain foodstuffs that the 1940's British citizen would find unusual, for example whale meat and canned snoek fish from South Africa, were not rationed, but the taste, even after the canners had cut away the poisonous parts, were not popular.

It was early morning in January, past snowfall everywhere, but the air was dry. My little despatch books in hand, I scurried from the office, where I had just delivered the morning post (mail). The worst of the snow had been cleared from the drive by a gang of our pot bank labourers. "Bank" was the Potteries word for "factory" but, for some unknown reason, seemed to be reserved for pottery factories. Down at the packing house at the foot of the drive, the British Railways' drayman was waiting to be loaded underneath the hand wound crane. The dray was the usual flat-bed trailer with four pneumatic tyred wheels. These tyres made a considerable difference to the horse pulling it along poorly maintained Potteries roads.

Harry, the drayman, had already manoeuvred the dray so the horse was facing uphill towards the factory exit. Harry was a wizened little man. He was a brown, almost gypsy-like chap, and he and his horse, a magnificent huge shire horse, were devoted to each other. In fact, I learned later the shire, named Tom, had recently been suffering from an infection called "grease" in one of his massive hooves. All the time that Tom had been confined to his stable while the infection healed, Harry had stayed with his devoted companion, sleeping in the straw in his stall. Now they were back to normal duties, so it was the first time I'd seen the pair.

The next job was for me to point out which crates should make up the load. Then, the head packer, Mr Moss, discussed briefly the contents of each crate which, because of the dense straw packing protecting the contents, were not visible. If a crate was a consignment of "flat ware", meaning plates and dishes they were loaded at the back of the dray with other "flat" crates alongside. This left the lighter "hollow ware" (jugs, bowls, mugs and cups etc), for the front end, which made the steering easier. A couple of apprentice packers manned the crane. The crates were pretty much the same size, about five feet long, four feet wide and deep – so, you can imagine they could be quite heavy. The crane stood on a pivot right on the edge of the canal, so it was used to load canal boats or trailers.

The loaded dray, containing up to 15 crates and weighing somewhere around one ton, was then ready for the off. Already facing up the slope to the lodge and exit, it wasn't an easy job for Tom. The slope was about ten percent, which wasn't too bad, but it was paved with really ancient cobblestones. Not the usual stones, they varied in size from as small as a teacup to as large as a dinner plate, and they were a variety of shapes. They were not flat either; they all had a smooth surface, but were always slightly domed. This, and the slope, made it a challenge for Tom.

He stood waiting, wisps of steam rising from his glossy broad back and from his nostrils. "Come on Tom," called Harry. Tom leaned into his harness, well-practised in what was wanted from him. His colossal feet slipped slightly as he sought to get purchase on the uneven ground. As he strained, his huge hooves shot sparks from the stones as his feet stamped and scrabbled to get moving. All the packers got round the back and side to lend a hand, including me contributing my tiny pennyworth. The dray gathered pace, and after about fifty feet, it had sufficient momentum to carry on up the bank to loud cheers from us, the helpers.

We all loved Tom and looked forward to his visits. Always groomed and combed, his glossy deep brown coat and white feet were a sight to see. With that his harness, well rubbed and with gleaming horse brasses, he was a credit to Harry.

Unfortunately, or fortunately, depending on your views on progress, the railway company discontinued horse transport after about two years of me starting work. The same rubber-tired drays remained, but they were hauled by a peculiar motor vehicle. It had a cab like a lorry, but much shorter and it had only one wheel at the front. These mechanical work horses did the job a bit quicker than the old horse. I never knew what happened to Harry and Tom. I just hoped they were found decent alternative employment.

Loading barges for the export trade

Now, turning to the export trade. Just as I ordered a dray when there were enough railway bound goods to fill one, I ordered a barge when we had accumulated a sufficient load or, to be truthful, when Mr. Moss's nagging at me to make room in his packing house became too much. The packers were on piece work: they were paid by the number of crates they packed, so it was understandable that they couldn't put up with standing idle for want of space.

You know, as I reflect on all this, I think it was a hell of a responsibility for a fourteen-year-old lad when you take into account the further complications of arranging the onward shipping from Runcorn, through Liverpool or London. Also, in those days, before tannoy had become established, I had to act as the "searcher/finder" of managers in various parts of the pot bank, so that they could answer an incoming telephone call.

I was kept busy, but rarely was it hectic. The "Ansaphone" duties were, for me, pleasant interludes. A particular recipient of these phone calls was Mr. Lowe, the "clay manager". He had enormous responsibilities covering all the aspects of potting, from testing samples to ordering the correct ingredients - clays of different types, stone, flint. Also, he was responsible for the processes of mixing and producing the clay body for making plates, cups and saucers, and similar ware. Then he dealt with the liquid clay, called "slip", used for casting larger and more intricate shapes like teapots, ewers, basins, jugs and vases, plus the Toby jugs. Burgess and Leigh were quite renowned for these Toby jugs, second in reputation only to the famous Doulton figures.

The "clay end" of the factory (pot bank) was like a warren. Like most of the pot banks, it was built alongside the Trent and Mersey Canal. This allowed clays, stone etc to be brought up from mainly Devon and Cornwall by barge and unloaded at our own wharf, a few hundred yards along the canal from the packing house, from where all finished goods were despatched Over the years, the factory had grown. Shops had been extended and additional shops had been built, either alongside, or over existing shops. It must have been a nightmare in later years when health and safety laws revealed some dubious constructions and practices. It was easy to get lost in the maze, but luckily my memory served me well and I never failed to track down the wanted manager, unless he'd neglected to sign off at the lodge if he left the factory for some reason.

It was always a "he". Women didn't fill managerial roles until you came to the finished goods departments, such as the decorating shops – underglaze and on-glaze, separate departments. Mr. Lowe was a distinguished, grey-haired figure, nearly always deep in thought or discussion with a leading worker. Underneath, he proved to be a particularly nice man. At first, he was quite distant with me, perhaps somewhat flummoxed by this eager youngster with his constant questions and observations. Then he began to relax and teach me a few things.

I remember once telling him about an experiment I'd been carrying out at home making a firework out of two bolts screwed onto a nut, one at each end with the shavings from match heads in the space between. When tightened then dropped from a window they made quite a crack as they hit the brick-flagged floor.

He told me about his early experiences in the First World War with explosives. We went into his laboratory where we made a larger version of my bomb using, I think, sulphur and some nitrogenous ingredient. We took this out onto the outside balcony of his lab and dropped it onto an empty area beside the coal heap for the Lancashire Boiler. It made a hell of a bang. We laughed triumphantly, then he sort of shook himself out of this unaccustomed playful attitude and resumed his serious, slightly worried, demeanour. He often gave me little tips about potting, but neither of us had much play time.

Chapter 3: Around the Pot Bank

Prelude

Today, we are so used today to seeing footage of shiny modern factories, full of electronics and robotics. It is hard to believe – even for me who lived through it – how different factories were when I started work. I thought you might like to join me in a tour around our pot bank so you can see how much things have changed.

The great steam engine

One of the many fascinations, for me, of this factory was the Lancashire Boiler. This mighty steam engine drove the network of belts and pulleys used to carry its power to the various pot making machines. The boiler was a huge cylinder, more than twenty feet long and about six feet wide. It was built into a shallow pit. The end that coal was shovelled into faced the end of the pit where a large pile of coal stood, its contents pouring onto the concrete floor of the pit as a cartload was added to the pile. The boiler man was a tiny red-haired chap. He had an enormous shovel, which he used from time to time to throw the fuel (was it small-sized anthracite?) into the fire hole. He didn't have any assistant or back-up. I often wondered what would happen if, for example, he caught 'flu!

Next to the boiler stood the engine house. I spent many a spare quarter of an hour standing by the engine, watching with absolute fascination this behemoth of a machine with its large crankshaft and mighty flywheel. The cylinder lay horizontally with the steel trough along which the sliding block ran. This extended the reach of the con-rod to drive the flywheel. A raised walkway ran alongside it, with a handrail separating me from the cylinder, about two feet away. The steel flywheel was so big that, at first, I couldn't believe a wheel that size could be manufactured.

A strong steel shaft ran the length of the engine shop. Pulley wheels of different sizes were threaded on one end. A stout belt, about four inches wide, went round the end of the flywheel shaft then ran up to shaft on the ceiling. Another belt wrapped round one of the pulleys on this ceiling shaft and from there disappeared through a hole in the ceiling. This, I was told, turned another shaft running just below the shop above.

A system of belts powered machinery where potters were smacking lumps of clay onto horizontal potter's wheels. As the clay spun round, it was fashioned by the potters' wet hands into a plate and finished off with the aid of a "profile tool", which shaped the rims and curves on the back of the plate. This belt system was obviously modelled on Richard Arkwright's first mill at Cromford in Derbyshire. He is credited as being one of the fathers of mass production.

As I passed through these various shops, on returning to the office when my errand had been completed, I watched with my youthful curiosity all the various processes. There was the slip house where the clays and ingredients were mixed in a huge "blunger" – a deep, tile lined pit with a big shaft ascending from its centre. Large blades extended from this shaft giving it the appearance of a giant form of a modern food processor. When I think back at the various machines in that factory, I thank God for the modern health and safety laws and rules. I'll try not to digress too much, but I remember, years later just before the Health and Safety Act was introduced, an accident that happened involving that blunger.

It was during the summer holiday fortnight. All the pottery factories closed, so that during that "downtime", deep cleaning and machine maintenance could be done. On one occasion, an engineer was working on that shaft. He was inside the pit, handling the shaft. All power had been turned off; only the electric lights remained. Somehow the power came on and the shaft began to spin. I'm not sure how it happened, but there was nobody in the vicinity to switch it off. I had nightmares about the worker coming onto the area and seeing the pureed engineer. It is widely believed that this particular accident gave rise to the modern "permit to work" system which ensures that a worker has to be both accompanied when doing this sort of task and given permission, in writing, to do it.

Two very different designers

Another wonderful man I loved chatting with was the designer, Ernest (Jones, I think), a brilliant man of striking intelligence with a flair for the work he did. He was a much younger man, recently de-mobbed from the Royal Navy. We had some lovely chats in his studio, where he worked alone, except for consultations with the head mould-maker about any problems with the plaster of Paris moulds for casting his new creations. So, he welcomed my intrusions bearing messages or alerting him to come to the office so he could take a telephone call. Amazing isn't it, to think how old-fashioned Middleport Pottery was in those days. In fact, most of the pot banks had no switchboard or telephone extensions – apart from Wedgwood's, who were shortly to build their New Model Factory out in the country at Barlaston – neighbouring the Trentham Estate, a well-known visitor attraction.

Ernest was an extremely talented and interesting man. He was also an athlete. This became clear during a tragic incident one day in Autumn. I've described how pot banks lined the north side of the Trent and Mersey Canal. On the south side were open fields stretching up to the Wolstanton escarpment with its great clay quarry. It was rough land, not fit for agriculture, so was a great play area for us children. After school we would call to Mother, "We're going down to the fields." We played football and cricket or just larked about, jumping the Fowlea Brook, as boys did.

One day, a gang of boys, about eight years old, were playing on the other side of the canal. One fell in. As I and others heard the screams from the paintresses passing the scene, I dashed to our side of the canal to see what I could do to help. I had, not many months previously, done a life-saving and artificial respiration course with a small group of the more talented swimmers from Middleport School. The canal water was the colour of orange chocolate. It was impossible to see a sign of whomever it was that had fallen in.

I started ripping off my clothes only to see the large figure of Ernest, stripped to his vest and long johns racing down the bank. He dived in and began to surface dive into the murky depths, until after a few minutes, before I had finished undressing, he stood up, waist deep in the water, holding the little boy's body in his arms. I and others helped Ernest with his tragic load onto the canal side. I will always remember the way the boy's lifeless body slumped onto the cobblestones. As his head fell the last few inches it made a hollow knocking sound. Strange, how little details like that stay in one's mind.

Later, I had cause to go to Ernest's studio with a message. This was actually a few days later, but Ernest and I were somewhat subdued. I delivered my message and then caught sight of Ernest's latest work: a small Toby jug of Mr. Micawber. It was one of the first of this figure which had been cast, fettled dried and fired in the biscuit oven. He and his fellow jugs were ready for the next stage in their production: underglaze painting before dipping in a transparent glaze and firing in the glost oven. Ernest allowed me to pick it up and examine it.

"It's beautiful," I said admiringly. "But you know, although they look so smart in their finished state, in all their glorious colours, I personally prefer them in this unadorned biscuit state."

Ernest gave me a look, was silent for a moment, and then said. "You have got good taste, lad, use it."

Ernest's fellow creator was the "Head Artist", Mr Archibald Bennett. He was older than Ernest. And as different as chalk and cheese. Ernest was a down-to-earth character, well-educated and practical, as well as a gifted designer. He had no affectations – what you saw is what you got.

Mr. Bennett was completely different in many ways. He wanted the world to see that he was an "artist" by his dress, his manner of speaking, and in his general demeanour. He was tall, slim, angular, with long hair (most unfashionable in those days of "short back and sides"). He always wore a tweed suit, colourful but not "loud", often with a primrose shirt, and always with a heavily patterned bow tie. Outdoors, he almost always wore his "deer stalker" hat in a tweed to match his suit. He cut a sort of "Sherlock Holmes" figure.

He claimed that he was dyslexic. A new word in those days that didn't exist in common parlance. People who couldn't spell or read properly had "word blindness". I have since learned that people with dyslexia are more likely to see three dimensional images in their minds than non-dyslexic people. This could have accounted for his choice of profession. I saw a few examples of his work, mainly floral decorations on the tableware, which was popular with customers in the USA particularly.

The pottery industry was always a labour-intensive business. Fortuitously, many jobs called for manual dexterity and a careful touch, so it suited womenfolk, which kept overall costs lower in those days, before feminism and equal pay. However, wages for women gradually increased thanks to the efforts of CATU, the Ceramic and Allied Trades Union.

Partly to offset labour costs and the demand from overseas for more artistic and elaborate decorations, there began a continuing shift to lithograph patterns. These were designed by extremely talented artists. The real specialist in this area was the firm Johnson Mathey. They were, and still are, a large company in the USA dealing with precious metals, bullion and various sophisticated products. They had a factory in the nearby town of Kidsgrove, where metal-based colours were produced. They also held most of the market for lithographs. These were beautiful, elaborate patterns in sophisticated colours, shades and backgrounds that were printed in reverse on special, strong glossy paper.

When the ware (cups, saucers, teapots etc) had been glazed and fired in the glost kiln, they passed to the decorating shop, where experienced ladies with nimble fingers would cut out a section of the pattern sheet that would fit the size of the piece of ware. This section of pattern was placed on the cup etc, then skilfully pressed firmly and in the correct position, using special brushes like a pestle in shape with firm but soft bristles.

The cup was placed on a potter's board to dry out the oils in the pattern. After a period, the cup had the paper backing peeled away and placed onto another board which, when full, would be carried to the "hardening on" kiln to be fired again but at a lower temperature and for a shorter spell.

So, returning to Mr. Bennett, many of his "on-glaze" patterns, as they were called, were still popular, but these were not put onto the glazed ware with lithographs. The firm employed a lot of "free hand paintresses" who would recreate his patterns. Mr. Bennett didn't oversee these processes, but fired samples would be sent to him, so that he could satisfy himself that they were "up to snuff".

I didn't spend much time in conversation with Mr. Bennett, but I once remarked that I had joined, only for a short period, the Boy Scouts. Mr. Bennett, with one of his characteristic flourishes, waved his hands in front of himself. "No, no, no!" he exploded. "A dreadful militaristic organisation which is encouraging the martial attitude of our populace. Look at Germany with its Hitler Youth. We'll be going down the same path." I quite agreed in principle, but he didn't seem to want to discuss it, merely dismiss it as a dangerous idea.

Back around the pot bank

Before leaving his office, in a walled off corner of the decorating shop, I noticed one of the placers picking up a loaded board and carrying it off for placing into the hardening-on kiln. It never failed to impress me the way pottery workers used these boards. The load was often precarious, with dozens of pieces of delicate coffee cups and saucers, or extremely heavy flat ware, like plates. For example, a large dinner plate can weigh nearly a kilogram (over two pounds), so a board loaded with four dozen plates would weigh ninety-six pounds – the weight of a teenage girl.

Imagine carrying that on your head and threading your way through cluttered workshops, up and down flights of stairs. I remembered my father at one time worked as a glost placer. He had a home-made device consisting of four or more ladies' stockings rolled up into a ringed sausage shape. This was worn on the top of the head, underneath his cap. It helped to keep the load level and even, and it also reduced wear and tear on his unfortunate scalp.

I could go on, describing the various processes and workshops in Middleport Pottery. I became almost expert at describing them to people. Starting at the clay end with its "slip house" where liquidised clay from the blungers was filtered and magnetised to remove any iron particles. Then it was pumped through large hoses up-stairs to the casting shop, where the liquid slip was hand poured from giant ewers into moulds made of plaster of Paris. The filled mould was left for a specified time, depending on the thickness required of the piece of pottery.

Then the mould was tipped onto a large row of draining racks, after which the mould was taken to the drying shop, carefully removed from its mould and placed onto racks, which were fastened onto a device call "the mangle". The mangle was a chain driven apparatus holding horizontal boards full of ware. The whole thing was contained in a brick-built tower, lined with pipes carrying steam, that was carefully controlled to reduce the temperature at the correct rate to ensure proper drying and to avoid cracking from overheating.

All the loaded boards were lifted in the mangle up towards the top of the tower, where it became progressively hotter, then descended on the other side, where the ware was taken off to be fettled (mould markings cut off with a sharp little knife), brushed and polished with a damp cloth. After further drying, it was off to the "biscuit" oven, where the ware underwent its first firing.

I will briefly describe the other processes. I didn't want to end up writing a treatise on pottery manufacturing; it's just that, occasionally, I grew enthusiastic about all its complexities.

There was the "sagger house". Why it was called a house not a shop, I never discovered. I'll save this for later for when I describe my father's early employment as a "sagger maker's bottom knocker".

Then there was the "mould making shop", an overwhelmingly complex and skilled collection of activities, where Mr. Maddox, the head mould-maker, was another kind gentleman who seemed to appreciate my curiosity and spent time explaining, even demonstrating, the mould maker's art.

Starting from Ernest Jones's new model, he would create the "case". This is in the shape of the finished article but larger to allow shrinkage during firing. This was surrounded by a container made of metal or plastic. The case was coated with a film of liquid soap, to prevent the liquid mixture of plaster of Paris sticking to it.

Plaster was poured into the container and, when the plaster had dried, it was removed from the case. This removed plaster became the mould. The case was carefully wrapped and placed in special storage, to be used again when a mould had become worn, and a new one was needed. Moulds were used to produce "flat", or basic "hollow ware". The plaster mould placed on a horizontal potter's wheel, which I described earlier when I talked about the engine house. I've also described the casting shop where the hollow ware underwent its initial production.

Before the next stage in production, "dipping" with glaze before glost firing, I should mention "underglaze" decoration. Ware was carefully selected in the biscuit warehouse after it had gone through the first firing to convert the clay ware into hard biscuit ware.

At this point, I should mention that dust and any other contaminants were vicious and costly enemies of the potter. A tiny speck on the dipped ware would leave a visible raised, discoloured mark on the fired piece, either ruining it or condemning it as a "second" – second quality. Standards were extremely high; there were no thirds. Failing the seconds test meant going to the "shard-ruck". This is where sub-standard smashed ware was tipped, giving rise to the characteristic white speckled hillocks among the Potteries. I was amazed at such perfectionist standards with a product which, through each of its many stages of manufacture, ran the risk of destruction.

After its first firing at a very high temperature, the clay ware was transformed from its delicate dried state into a hard ceramic state, strong against pressure but, like all pottery, breakable if dropped or hit by a hard object. From its protective saggars, it was taken into the biscuit warehouse, where rows of ladies sat on low stools behind low benches on each of which stood the mouth of a powerful extractor fan.

Each lady had a pile of newly fired products on her left. She would pick up a bowl, for example, and a stiff brush, again in the form of a pestle. Placing it on her lap, or on the bench, she would vigorously brush the piece of biscuit ware all over and inside, holding it so that the fan could suck away any dust or sand (which was used in the saggars to keep the unfired ware in place).

Most of the cleaned ware was passed to the dipping house for glazing, as I said earlier. It would then either be plain ware, or overglaze decorations could be added. (And you will recall that the overglaze decoration could be added with lithographs or by paintresses.)

But, although most of the cleaned ware would go to the dipping house, not all of it would be. A selection was held over for the underglaze decorators. You will recall that one of the things that these decorators did was to paint the Toby jugs before they were glazed.

The saggar maker and his bottom knocker

I'm trying not to get ahead of myself when describing the various jobs, so I'll take a step sideways to talk about the saggar, a (mainly) square shaped box with rounded corners. The word's origins are a bit of a mystery, but an old book I once found in Burslem Library claimed it was a corruption for an old French expression to "safeguard" ceramics. If you don't mind, I'd like to dwell on it briefly because of my father's experiences.

The saggar was made out of "fireclay", an unrefined local clay used to build the interior of kilns (hence the name). To give strength to the saggars, a quantity of "grog" was mixed in the clay during its preparation. Grog was pieces of old saggars, broken and crushed into crumbs. This was added to the clay while it was being mixed and extruded from a giant toothpaste-like tube. Each saggar-maker would cut himself a length of grog-enriched clay and carry it to his low steel covered workbench.

He would select a frame whose width was the desired height of the saggar's sides. He would then firmly plonk the lump of clay onto the bench inside the boundary of the frame. The frame consisted of a mild steel square section, about three quarters of an inch (20 millimetres) thick and it would define the height and perimeter length of the saggar. Then he would raise his "maul" (pronounced "mow") a short distance and start to hammer the clay to make it spread out. The head of this maul was more than fifteen inches in diameter and about five inches thick, with a steel band around its circumference to protect its shape. The maul was held in both hands below waist height, with the dominant hand holding the handle an inch below the maul's head – again, a medieval French word, this time for hammer or mallet.

By the saggars maker's side stood a horizontal wheel, like a potter's wheel but not powered. On that, he would wrap his already-moulded clay strip around a wooden interior mould, that was in the shape of the saggar's walls. He would then cut clay to length with a short, sharp wooden paddle and join the two ends with the aid of a little water, into the finished shape – minus a bottom.

A "bottom" had already been made by his "bottom knocker", actually his apprentice. The saggar bottom was placed on the wheel, and the clay walls, wrapped around their wooden mould was placed on top. The bottom was two or three inches wider and longer than the saggar itself. So, the saggar maker slowly turned the wheel with his fingers, using his sharp little wooden tool to spread and form the protruding bottom upwards to seal it firmly into the sides. The completed saggar was carried away to racks, standing over a network of hot steam pipes, to dry sufficiently for the saggar not to collapse when the wooden mould was removed.

The saggar house was actually a cellar, poorly lit and hot because of the steam pipes – not the most pleasant of working environments. My father never spoke of his experiences in the "saggar hole", as he called it. I do remember seeing the apprentice saggar maker doing his job of fashioning the saggar bottom. Essentially, he used the same procedure as the saggar maker but confined himself to just making the bottoms of the various saggar types. The same sort of outline iron ring placed on the bench. The clay then hammered to spread it to fit inside the ring.

Willow ware

I am still resisting the temptation to say too much about pottery production, but I can't pass on to other things from the biscuit warehouse without saying some more about underglaze decoration. Middleport Pottery was famed for its "Willow ware". The decoration showed a traditional Chinese picture based on one of their old legends.

I remember Miss Adams, our English teacher at Middleport School, telling us the story of a rich man's daughter who fell in love with his secretary, who was promptly dismissed. The rich man built a long fence around his estate to keep his daughter from meeting her lover. However, the young man manged to get over the obstacle. He was spotted by the rich man as he and the girl fled using a small bridge to cross a small river. The river was partly hidden by a large willow tree, but the father kept them in sight and chased them onto the bridge. He was rapidly gaining on the couple; I guessed his daughter was hampered by the "lily walk" that was caused by bound feet.

The couple were saved though: the gods took pity on them and turned them into doves. You can see a sample of "Willow ware" by Googling it. You'll see the picture of the three people on the bridge and a pair of doves above them. The pattern was printed in cobalt blue on a pure white background. This pattern was a favourite in the American market, and we produced it in some quantity.

To create the pattern, the image was first printed on the reverse of strong tissue-like paper using a thick oil and wax colour. The tissues were printed off a metal sheet engraved with the picture. I loved chatting to the engraver in his tiny studio, just off the biscuit warehouse. The door was firmly locked, because he needed a quiet place to work. He would allow me inside only for important messages.

Mr. Wilson was a tiny old man, as quiet in his speech and manner as his job suggested. He sat at a workbench with a high-quality lamp shining onto his work and a strong magnifying glass mounted on an elaborate stand. Before him was a large copper plate and alongside and in front of him were the master drawings he used to create a pattern on the copper sheet. After using a steel pen to outline the main features, he set to work using an extremely sharp tool nesting in the palm of his hand. He would gouge out a stronger set of lines and shades to form the Willow picture.

Apparently, it took several days to etch out a pattern, and he would carefully and gently polish any pieces of "swart" (copper shavings) from its surface. The finished piece would be sent away to a specialist firm for electro plating with steel. The steel was hard enough to prevent the surface from being quickly worn away when the copper sheet was used to print the patterns onto the paper. The plate was stored, with others for different shapes and sizes of ware, in a rack by the printer.

To produce the paper transfer, the steel-plated sheet was placed on his bench, which was heated to quite a warm temperature. His printers' ink stood in a large blob on a corner of the heated surface. Using a fine steel pallet knife, the printer would carve out a quantity of the heated ink and place it onto the centre of the pattern. The knife, a fine steel one for the combination of strength and delicacy required, was used to spread the thick, heavy ink over the surface of the pattern, spreading and scraping to ensure all the grooves in the pattern were properly filled.

When he was satisfied that the pattern was properly "inked", the printer used his knife to scrape the pattern's surface clean and return the surplus ink, with a consistency something like oily tar, back onto the ink pile in the bench corner. Next, he would pick up his "polisher", a hand-made pad of corduroy, cloth filled with cotton rags. The corduroy provided the proper surface he needed to properly polish the pattern plate to remove the tiniest dots of ink from it. This hot plate, now properly inked, was placed on a side bench beside a large hand-roller. A pile of tissue paper stood on his other side. He would dip a brush into a weak solution of soft soap and tepid water to liberally soak the pile of tissue. Then this wet paper was carefully placed on the hot steel pattern sheet. The sheet was then fed into a large roller. The drum was wrapped with a thick felt covering. The whole thing was, again, heated. He hauled on a long steel handle to pass the pattern through the rollers. When it emerged, the pattern plate was placed on the bench, then the paper was peeled off and placed on a rack to partly dry. The printer was producing these patterns in quantity to feed one or more underglaze patterns.

A decorator would place one or more pieces of pattern on the particular ware she was decorating, then gently smooth and press them into place, just like the overglaze lithographers. However, you may recall that with the overglaze lithographs, the paper was simply peeled off. Underglaze patterning was different. After brushing the transfer sheet onto the piece of biscuit ware, it was placed into a deep tank of clean water to soften the tissue enough for it to be peeled off, leaving the pattern in place on the jug etc...

The next phase was dipping the ware into a mixture of "frit" (finely ground glass) and the required metal-based colour or, in the case of plain white or Willow ware, a white glaze. When finished and having undergone its glost firing, the Willow ware had a beautiful effect, bright, colourful, with the colour looking like an integral part of the object, not just a pattern painted on to it afterwards.

Off around the pot bank again

The glost warehouse was where the fully finished ware was examined, sorted into best and seconds, then finally assembled into the customer's order The orders were packed large wicker baskets., ready for "carrying down" to the packing house. The glost warehouse was upstairs (second storey), so it wasn't easy to transport the ware from there.

The carrier down, effectively a labourer, would, unaided, lift a basket weighing up to a hundred-weight (112 lbs or 50 kg) onto one shoulder. He adopted a special gait for this with his left hand on his hip to take the weight of the loaded basket on to his shoulder and upper arm. His right hand reached up to hold on to the forward edge of the basket. Then he would walk through the warehouse, down two short flights of rickety stairs, then cross the uneven cobbles to the packing house on the other side of the driveway.

The usual carrier down was Thomas (not Tom) Findlay. He was actually, the sister of Mrs. Findlay and lived with her at her newsagent's shop. Poor Thomas was a small, frail looking man with bad feet. He was a little "slow", as retarded people were called it in those days, and he was put upon by various under-managers for all sorts of extra jobs. Poor Thomas, he was a gentle, harmless soul. I felt sorry for him, but I never was able to witness any actual physical abuse, so couldn't help him. To this day, I feel guilty about my inaction.

I've skipped a number of jobs on this brief outline, but anyway, the best of the glost ware was selected for the "on glaze" decoration. This consisted of lithograph transferring which I touched on earlier, and a type of decoration called "free hand" painting. Rows of (mainly young) women sat at a long bench. They had in front of them a selection of brushes. A lot of these brushes, especially the ones used for delicate work, were made of Russian sable and were extremely costly. (Years later, when I took up water-colour painting as a hobby, I discovered this when fitting myself out with a selection of these brushes – made by the same firm that supplied to the old pottery industry.) These ladies painted standard patterns of decoration, mainly floral themes, entirely by hand, some of them without a stipulated picture, sometimes entirely based on their own ideas. They always seemed to be a happy lot, sometimes singing together.

In one corner, separated from the singers, was the "band and liners". I used to watch them working in fascination. Beside them and a little forward, each had a horizontal wheel, like a mini potter's wheel, with a thick spindle descending from the middle. The paintress would place a plate, bowl or other circular pot on the wheel then gently nudge it with her finger so that it was spinning absolutely dead centre on the wheel. She would then take her brush with a sawn-off handle, dip it into a quite thick pot of oily paint, then stroke the brush on the side of the paint pot to get it fully loaded but not dripping.

The pure sable hairs of the brush were long, but she would place it on the edge of the plate while turning the wheel with the fingers of her other hand. This would paint a broad band of colour completely round the pot. Not a hint of where the band started and finished. This was called "banding".

Another skill used the same technique, but using a thin brush with extremely long bristles to paint one or more concentric thin lines, either instead of or in addition to the band. This part of the job was called "lining". If was often done by the same lady that did the banding, or it was the job of specialist "liner".

All the decorators were smartly dressed, usually with a bright wrap-round apron. This alerted me to class distinction, which I've met in all walks of life. Top of the hierarchy were these paintresses, descending through underglaze decorators to clay workers – "throwers" or "turners", to the "mould runners". These lads and girls would fetch the plaster of Paris moulds from their store and carry them to the potter that they were serving.

Many of the potters were on piece wor", so the mould runners were under pressure to keep up with the potters' demands. They and the potters wore white overalls, but on their feet, which would get absolutely covered with clay, they wore an old, worn-out pair of shoes called "trashers". These girls were often poorly educated, and some of them were considered quite "common" at least that was the term. They had a reputation for de-trousering any young lad who was strange to their world and rub clay onto the unfortunate individual's nether regions. I never suffered, or witnessed, these legendary pranks, but I remember having to run the gauntlet at Christmas to avoid the clutches of these girls (and older women).

Taking on the factory visits

By this time, I had reached the advanced age of sixteen. An innovation introduced by Barry Leigh, a younger director, was to encourage factory visits. It had publicity benefits and foresaw the gradually increasing interest of the public for historical sites. Middleport Pottery was an old pot bank, dating from before 1888. (There is an interesting article about it on Wikipedia, where it was described as being a more modern design than previous factories.)

At first, the visits consisted of older schoolchildren. It was some years after I left that it became the visitor attraction it is today. These factory tours fell to the lot of poor Mr. Lowe, who had enough on his plate without this added burden. It was my job, when the party had arrived, to find Mr. Lowe and, without being asked or required, to go along with the tour. Doing the tours added more structure and knowhow to my pottery knowledge.

One day, a pre-arranged tour party arrived when Mr. Lowe had suddenly been taken ill. I stepped into the breach, conducted the tour to the evident satisfaction of the schoolteachers who were escorting the party. So, it just became an accepted job for me.

I remember Mr. Lowe describing to the girls and boys the high temperatures in the firing process. "Eleven hundred degrees Celsius", caused raised puzzled glances from the kids, so I suggested, in a quiet moment to Mr. Lowe, that explaining it in terms of how much hotter it was than a boiling kettle, would be helpful. He agreed, and I gradually introduced more "lay" English expressions, which made an obvious improvement in the interest the youngsters showed.

Jolted out of these early memories

Back to Egypt, where my afternoon reverie was broken by the sounds of boots on the floor of the tent and the clatter of mugs and eating irons as we made ready to stroll across to the mess for our evening tea.

The next day, I learned that I, and a few more convalescents, were fit to be returned to our units at Tel-el-Kebir. Climbing on to the ubiquitous three-tonner, we were driven to Tel. Five of my group were dropped off at the main guardroom, then the truck left with me to be delivered up the road to the ex-hospital camp and the ARG. I settled back into the daily routine of travelling to Tel-el-Kebir itself for our work then back to the hospital to shower, get changed, take tiffin and undertake our off-duty chores, which had previously been carried out by Egyptian labour.

One of these was laundry duty. Previously, dirty washing had been taken out of camp and returned washed, dried, ironed and, in the case of our KD's (Khaki Drill uniform), beautifully starched. In those deprived days, we sought out scrap five-gallon drums, washed the insides, and mounted them on a ring of stones with a fire underneath. For fuel we raided the deserted part of the old hospital for old chairs, cabinets, racks and anything that was combustible. We had access to the abandoned stores with lots of hospital soap, which we used to hand-wash our laundry.

Drying was no problem; it was late summer, and the sun was fierce enough to dry stuff in less than an hour. We didn't have to worry about smartness as most of us wore underpants and vests with our denim trousers and jackets on top. The officers and NCOs wore KDs, laundered by troops unfortunate to be on punishment "fatigues" duty.

The "troubles" hadn't really started yet. On the eighth of October 1951, the Egyptian Government abrogated the treaties binding various parties and Great Britain, France and the USA. It was the start of the terrorist campaign. Before that date the British Forces intelligence knew where things were heading and had started taking precautions. Major Bruen ordered that every man jack of us was armed with a personal weapon. We didn't have a choice; some were given a .303 Lee Enfield rifle with a stout cotton bandolier containing fifty rounds in ten clips of five. Others were given a Sten submachine gun with a magazine containing 30 rounds, plus a spare mag to stick on his belt.

We were instructed to carry this armament with us wherever we went: dining mess, to work and into our bed at night. Some griped that this was a little over-the-top, but nobody disobeyed the order. Our OC (Officer Commanding) ARG, Major Bruen, also, in view of our hardships, had dispensed with the usual "bull" of "barracking" our bed each morning and polishing boots. He had also discontinued the formal parade that we did each morning before climbing onto our three tonners to go to work.

Chapter 4: Once to Every Man

Prelude

Looking back over my long and fortunate life, there are many forks in the road. I sometimes wonder what would have happened had I meandered left rather than right down one of these. Often the fork is so gentle you don't even realise you are changing direction. But there can be moments when the juncture is so sharp that you know your life could go one way or another – or even end.

The young men who were sent out on military service to defend the British Empire often experienced moments like this.

This one is mine.

The ambush

The title of this chapter comes from the title of a thrilling chapter in one of the "Jungle Books" my father used to borrow from Burslem Library. The author, a famous big-game hunter, wanted to bag an African buffalo. He had shot a bull but failed to kill it and was following a trail of blood spots through the tall grass by a river. He was already aware of the legendary aggressiveness of the buffalo, but his African Guide had also warned him of their vindictive habit of escaping when wounded and then circling back to surprise its hunter from the rear. Despite these warnings, the hunter failed to see or hear the wounded bull until it charged from behind.

His African guides fled. I can't do justice here to the words the hunter wrote to describe his experience, but this is what happened. The bull's first charge caught him in the back and flung him to the ground. Next a wicked curved horn pierced his side and tossed him several feet into the air. As he landed, he was caught again on sharp horns and repeatedly hurled into the air. Between the tosses, the bull trampled him: his one-ton weight crushing the hunter's rib cage.

The bull paused sucking in air and snorting angrily making ready for his next charge. The hunter lay paralysed, wheezing, barely able to breath. Seconds ticked by as he waited. Suddenly, a quotation from his classical education flashed into his mind, "Once to every man…" For him, in that moment, it meant that in every man's lifetime, he undergoes a life-threatening episode. And this was his.

The bull renewed its attack, goring the hunter again and again. Suddenly shots rang out. The bearers and the guide had returned! The bull turned tail and thundered away through the grass. The crew tended to his wounds as best they could and carefully strapped him onto a stretcher improvised from nearby undergrowth. Once to every man…

The day after we'd been issued with our weapons, we climbed aboard four lorries. One of the main tasks of ARG was to retrieve abandoned armoured vehicles left in the Western Desert after the many battles that had raged there. These were then triaged. The vehicles that were only fit for scrap were loaded onto flat beds at the TEK railhead to be conveyed out and onwards to Port Said where they would be shipped back to Selby in Yorkshire. The small number of vehicles that could be overhauled were fixed in our workshops in Tel-el-Kebir and re-issued to cavalry or infantry units as required.

Our little convoy of lorries was headed by a "Dingo" (Daimler Armoured Scout Car). This had a driver peering over the top with his mate at his side armed with a Bren gun – famed as being one of the war's most useful light machine guns. Bringing up the rear, after the lorries, was a giant "Staghound" armoured car, complete with its two-pounder gun. Theoretically, this massive, armoured car was obsolete having been superseded by a modern Daimler armoured car. However, we had a Staghound complete with Bren gun. The Staghound had been recovered from the desert and restored into working order – but we had no ammunition for its mighty two-pounder gun.

We bowled steadily on towards Tel-el-Kebir with the Sweetwater Canal running along to our right with its embankment of excavated sand between the canal and the road. On our left was another smaller sandy embankment with a shallow ditch between it and the road. The road was unusually quiet. There were none of the colourful buses loaded with fellaheen and their goats and chickens. None of us noticed the absence of traffic which might have served as a warning.

The dozen or so of us in our truck were sitting on the floor with our backs against the sideboards of the lorry. The lorries all had a series of metal hoops straddling the lorry made to hold a heavy canvas tarpaulin to shelter cargo or occupants from the weather. The canopy it formed was almost high enough for the troops to stand under. I generally sat on the left side of the lorry dosing or, if the canvas was off, lazily watching the canal. However, on this occasion, I happened to be gazing over the heads of the chaps on the other side of the lorry. Suddenly there was a noise above the sound of the engine. A strange roaring sound. At the same time, a tightly spaced row of holes appeared in the canopy about a foot or so over the heads of my mates. Then came a crashing of metal and breaking glass from the cab. Immediately the truck veered across the road and crashed cab first into the ditch with its back end sticking up into the air. There was a split second of frozen silence. None of us said a thing but we leaped over the tailgate into the shallow ditch.

Strangely, I didn't feel scared. There wasn't the time. I ran, bent double, back down the road to where I had spotted the remnants of a dried brick wall. It had only one course of bricks left – about five inches high – but I flung myself down beside it, placed my rifle on top and aimed at the embankment. I don't remember feeling terrified as I lay in the dirt, but I do remember my stomach clenching tightly as I waited to be hit by a bullet. I remembered the force of .303 bullets from training. The bullets smacking and thudding into the bank over my head when I was in the hole at the end of the practise range winding targets up into place. I remembered the instructor bellowing, "303 bullets have a two-ton striking force so keep your heads down, lads."

That was my "Once to Every Man" moment.

Then things went quiet. Heads popped up from our side of the road and our men opened fire with their personal weapons. The crash of .303 rifles, the sputtering of Sten guns with their nine-millimetre rounds, and the sustained chattering from the Brens from the head and tail of the convoy.

I raised myself slightly but couldn't see anybody. There came a shout from the Bren gunner in the scout car. He was higher up than the rest of us who lying in the ditches and he could see across the other side of the canal. "They've run back across the cornfield towards those buildings," he yelled pointing towards a couple of low mud huts. We cautiously raised our heads. At this our firing immediately started again.

A few of us climbed back over the raised back of our lorry to get a better view. Nothing. No-one. I never saw a soul although lots of silly buggers were emptying their magazines firing across an empty field. I surprised myself at how cool I felt throughout the incident. I hadn't fired a shot. Despite looking quickly and keenly as our truck crashed, I never saw anything to shoot at. It didn't make sense to me to shoot at nothing. The others, however, kept firing until they exhausted their ammunition.

Our truck was left in the ditch, to be recovered later. Bullets had smashed the windscreen and ripped up the roof of the cab. An older, experienced soldier said later, "That was a German Spandau machine gun firing at us. No doubt recovered by Bedouin from drifting sand in the desert battle fields and sold to the terrorists." Miraculously, the driver and his mate were unharmed. In fact, none of us suffered a scratch.

I don't know who was supposed to be in charge of our convoy and I never did find out. I remembered the Royal Engineer's sergeant picking me out at Port Said with the words, "This is the Army, lads, there is always somebody in charge." But, on the day, I never saw or heard an officer. However, we did hear on the grapevine later that poor Major Bruen had faced a court of inquiry because of the waste of over a thousand rounds of ammunition. And in such a short space of time too.

You need to remember we were not trained infantry. For the most part, we were national servicemen doing their two years' compulsory service. Many, like me, had undergone only six weeks basic training mainly devoted to inculcating discipline: lots of marching, drilling and physical training. I had been taught how to hold, strip, clean and re-assemble a Sten gun but not to fire it. I had fired only ten rounds on the rifle range. Apparently, there was insufficient ammunition! I was a mere lance corporal, outranked by full corporals and sergeants. None of us had the authority, wits or time to establish order over a bunch of trigger-happy teenagers.

Back at the hospital base, a squad of armourers had set up cook-house boilers. Those who had fired their weapons had them cleaned by boiling water poured through a funnel down the barrel. The remainder of the day was a day of rest. This was the last proper rest for some months before the troubles began in earnest.

The army (our non-infantry troops) never ceased to amaze me with its amateurish approach. Outside the single barbed wire fence, just beyond the bath house, was a large dump full of empty beer cans – we no longer had luxuries like beer, but the old cans were still there. The Egyptians would take the empty cans and made Molotov cocktails of them. Not many, it's true, as they didn't have access to much petrol. However, these were a nuisance when they were flung over the wire into our base during the night. It wasn't like being in battle, but terrorist incidents like this kept us constantly "on the qui-vive". This army vernacular comes from French guards who used to ask visitors to a castle: "Qui voulez-vous qui vive?" meaning "Who do you want to live?", in other words, whose side are you on?

Things were less exciting for a spell, and we had a quiet Christmas. Despite the shortage of fresh food, the men of Royal Army Catering Corps in our little camp did their best to make Christmas a little better for us. We had resumed our daily convoy to Tel-el-Kebir and back, but we no longer used the Cairo Road – the senior officers must have considered it too risky. Instead, they reconnoitred a route across the desert from the hospital to the depot at Tel-el-Kebir. Because of the rocky outcrops and many deep wadis that criss-crossed the desert, it was a slow winding route and increased the distance from roughly ten to fifteen miles. It was bumpy and very dusty.

But we took it on the chin and work carried on. In fact we were very busy because of the heavy reinforcements being brought into the Canal-Zone. It was rumoured there was going to be more than one division, and we needed to keep them supplied with armoured vehicles. These were mainly armoured cars, scout cars and Bren carriers, plus E Group vehicles which included bulldozers of various sizes and road-building equipment. It also meant an increase of shipments coming in through Port Said. Reinforcements from the infantry helped. I had one trip as armed escort to and from Port Said – it was my first and my last.

Military driving

I was, along with two officers and a senior sergeant clerk, busy with all the paperwork involved in supplying the vehicles. I was, however, occasionally dragged into duty as a driver to help "de-mothball" new vehicles and then give them a brief running-in stretch around the tank-proving course. As part of mothballing, the engines of new vehicles had upper cylinder lubricant poured underneath each spark plug. When the tank or whatever was started, white clouds of lubricant poured from the exhaust. We would them drive each vehicle round and round the course until smoke no longer appeared. We then passed it on to the brilliant Royal Electrical and Mechanical Engineers to run a battery of checks before passing the tank as fit for issue.

I rather enjoyed it when I was pressed into driving vehicles round the course. I remembered reading that after the Second World War, the Germans appreciated the quality of the kit left behind by the British Expeditionary Force at Dunkirk. They, apparently, admired our seventeen-pound anti-tank gun which was a match for their 88mm but had the advantage that it was easier to manoeuvre into place and presented a lower target to the opposing force. They eagerly commandeered any Bren Carriers for their own use.

These tiny, wholly tracked little armoured vehicles could reach speeds of over fifty miles per hour on roads and even forty on rough ground. I loved them. One slight drawback was that the driver's compartment was very short with just enough space for a man to squeeze in between the vertical steering wheel and the bulkhead behind which was the engine radiator. In very hot conditions radiator could boil over and splash small amounts of hot water on to the back of the driver's neck. Fortunately, it only happened to me once when I was running-in vehicles.

We didn't issue many main-battle tanks as we were dealing with a terrorist insurrection rather than major battles. However, I did have an opportunity to drive one of the newly designed Centurion tanks. An experienced driver from the Sixth Tank Corps drove it round the roughest part of the course, but I was given the chance to drive this magnificent beast on the flat. I felt so privileged to drive it. The controls though huge were so well designed and smooth in operation. On those early models they had conventional controls. A huge clutch pedal under your left foot and an equally large accelerator under your right. The gear lever was between the legs, with large billets sliding out from its foot as a gear was selected. Like all tanks there was no steering wheel, just two brake levers on the outside of your left and right thigh. The trick was to pull the left brake to turn left and right on the other side. It sounds crude but the Centurion was a delight to drive and steer.

A quiet Christmas, then things heat up in 1952

1951 Christmas passed without incident. After Christmas there was the occasional bomb, but these were flung or placed so haphazardly that there were no injuries. One incident at the hospital camp involved the old lavatory left over from the war years. It was several hundred yards away from the side of the hospital that we occupied. The lavatory was a very large, deep pit in the sand, partly surrounded by an array of wooden compartments joined together in a semi-circle. The doors opened to the outside of the circle. Inside was a wooden bench seat with a hole at the rear, placed so that any "soil" slid down into the pit behind. In the days when it was in use, labourers would shovel a layer or sand over the contents to bury it.

The terrorists, presumably unschooled in western ways, assumed that this isolated structure was important and placed a bomb there. It was rumoured to be the equivalent of a few pounds of TNT. Anyway, we were awakened at about 3 am by a loud crump and thud. It was dark, too far away, and at the far side of the camp, so we left it to the guard duty to deal with and went back to sleep. When we got up in the morning there was a dreadful smell. The buildings on the other side of the camp were covered in a sandy gloop which was dripping off the edges of their canvas lateen roofs. Fortunately, I wasn't involved with the work party of defaulters who spent a good few days clearing up the mess.

In 1952, things on the terrorist front hotted up! We were still travelling to work across the desert as the powers-that-be still thought it too risky to travel by road. I agreed. The Cairo Road could have been tailor-made for ambushes with its almost unbroken sandbank between the road and the Sweetwater Canal and the crop-fields behind it.

In addition to the heavy workload, we were also required to do regular guard duties. At that time, we were at the extreme western edge of the Canal Zone which was even further west than Tel-el-Kebir. I learned years later that sixty thousand troops were despatched to the Canal Zone after King Farouk's deposition. (But it may have been before then – I'm no history buff.) The extra troops were mainly infantry and some armoured forces. The powers-that-be wanted the infantry "up front".

The whole of the Canal Zone was cramped for accommodation, so they made tented accommodation for many of the new troops at Tel-el-Kebir. The idea was to give each infantry battalion some experience at the sharp end, so they posted one battalion at a time to spend a fortnight in our abandoned hospital. There were still plenty of unused wards at the opposite side of the hospital from where we were billeted. I've mentioned before the appalling lack of communication in some areas of the army's operations. This was no exception. The first we knew of any of this was the arrival of the Grenadier Guards. However, they didn't bother us at all as they were based on the other side of the hospital and did their own catering and supplies.

Since we started work, we were allowed a siesta each day which gave us the opportunity to watch our neighbours hard at work digging trenches just inside the single barbed wire fence. They were digging, what I believe in my limited military vocabulary, were called "sangars" – short trenches surrounded by sandbags which were big enough to house a Bren gunner and a rifleman. The sangars would be made bigger according to need. The Guardsmen were a magnificent sight. Stripped to the waist, well-built and tall – not one under six feet. They were overseen by a lieutenant. These were all Etonian, Harrovian public school types affecting an effete manner and speaking to their subordinates, in what seemed to me, some disdain.

Even when they were working the Guardsmen were extremely disciplined. If wearing a cap, they saluted every time an office came into view. If their hands were occupied, for example if wheeling a barrow full of sand, they would execute a smart "eyes left" as they passed. I kid you not, I observed one guardsman execute his eyes-left salute which resulted in him and his wheelbarrow falling into a freshly dug trench. In between our "wards" and the infantry "wards" on the opposite side of the hospital, lay a big open space of levelled-off dusty ground which served as a parade ground. I watched with some admiration as the Guardsmen carried out their morning parade. Such precision and synchronisation of movement and timing. They occupied their sangars day and night which gave us a sense of added security.

You may remember I described the short stretch of road which left the Cairo Road at a right angle and travelled about half a mile or so to the hospital gates. Halfway up this road, the Guards built a sangar and trained their weapons on the Cairo Road. A small detachment of Guards stopped an Egyptian bus at random. The passengers were urged, at gunpoint, to get off the bus and line up on the roadside behind the bus. The guns in the sangar were trained on this line of passengers in case any of them turned out to be terrorists. It was a hazardous operation because any suspicious movement could cause a tensed-up Bren gunner to let fly a burst of .303s. In the now notorious absence of briefings or communications, we were surrounded by rumours, known in troops' parlance as "shithouse griff". This is how we learned of a Bren gunner allegedly shooting a member of the searching detachment.

After their fortnight's stint in the front line, the Guards left. No communication. No noise. No rubbish left behind. Impeccable Guards discipline.

Instead, I was awakened that Monday morning by a loud, ungodly screeching. Half-dazed by sleep, I was scared. My bed was near a window, so I leaned across and in the half light of the early morning I could make out a Scots Piper marching up and down the lines of the wards on our side of the hospital.

It wasn't long before the rest of my ward's crew woke and we hurried out to see what the hell was going on. The dawn light was increasing by now and we could now clearly see this chap with kilt, sporran and plaid sort of shawl, marching briskly up and down. The show lasted a few minutes more and then he disappeared. Squadron Sergeant Major Urquhart, our Sergeant Major, explained later, "It is the Highland Light Infantry." In later years, they gained for themselves a name and reputation when stationed in Germany as the "poison dwarfs" after on a drunken spree in the town of Minden where they had trashed it.

As I explained earlier, a lot of our "bull" including the morning parade was suspended because we were hard stretched working as well as having to carry out regular guard duties. We had the opportunity, later, to see the Highlanders on one of their regular parades on the open stretch of parade ground. They were all unbelievably short. I couldn't see a single man taller than five feet four inches. I could be wrong, but they seemed very similar to the Glaswegians in our own unit: small, active and aggressive. Colin, one of my mates, had been to a minor public school and was quite well educated. He reckoned that the Highland Light Infantry were drawn from the Gorbals tenements in Glasgow. These were notorious for the poverty of the residents' insecure employment, and for generations of malnutrition. The other Scots people in our unit came from the Highlands or Eastern Scotland, cities like Edinburgh, Dundee and Aberdeen. In contrast to the Glaswegians, and indeed the rest of us, they were big, raw-boned fellows and much more civilised in their speech and behaviour.

The infantry stints continued, each regiment being given a fortnight on the front line to keep them occupied and add some realism to their training and experience. After the Highland Light Infantry, it was the turn of the Coldstream Guards. I was impressed by the precision of the Grenadier Guards, but the Coldstreams took it to another level. I never worked out the purpose of all this drilling. But it was great to watch.

After the Coldstreams came the Royal Inniskilling Fusiliers. Like all fusiliers they wore a large, coloured feather bloom on their berets. And coming from Ulster, they wore a uniform of shawls and kilts similar to the Highland Light Infantry: I was surprised when I first saw them on parade. Instead of tartan, their kilts and shawls were plain, bright orangey brown with no patterning at all.

Their band of pipes, drums and fifes practised daily on our parade ground. Being a music lover, I loved it, but it drew groans and rolled eyes from most of my mates. I'll never forget them marching and playing the song from "The White Horse Inn". Josef Locke made it popular: "Out on the plains the weary soldiers are asleeping. From across the fields, the scent of new mown hay. And they see in their slumber a great army passing by. See them pass by, those dragoons those guardsmen." And so on. I can't remember all the words, but I can hear the music sometimes when I'm falling asleep. When we hosted the Sussex Regiment for their fortnight, they marched with their fifes and drums, but no other instruments, endlessly playing "Sussex, Sussex, by The Sea". Other regiments followed, like the Lancashire Fusiliers, and others whose names I can no longer recall.

Mr Churchill and the fitness drive

It was at about that time (working from memory more than seventy years later) we were told by one of our sergeants that Mr. Churchill had become Prime Minister in Westminster and had been looking at the state of things. Allegedly, he was dissatisfied with the state of the Army's physical fitness. He had issued an edict that the army should institute and implement an on-going fitness programme. God knows, I thought, whoever briefed him about that. Could he not appreciate that we were over-worked, relatively poorly fed, and in the midst of these troubles? Surely, we shouldn't be bothered with such nonsense. However, it was taken seriously by our senior officers. Major Bruen issued an order that on Saturday, when we wouldn't be doing our regular jobs, we should undertake a route march. No, we were not at work, but we were cleaning the camp to maintain hygiene, doing our own laundry, cleaning our weapons etc.

Saturday arrived. We formed up on the parade ground where we used to have a morning parade at 8.00 a.m. It was about September time, I think. So long ago. Some details like the Spandau ambush are so clear that it might have happened yesterday. But that march across the desert doesn't stand out. Probably because there wasn't any serious incident. At that time of the year, the weather is cool in the morning but as the day goes on it becomes as hot as it is at the height of summer. Our engineers had cut through and fashioned an extra gateway at the back of the camp facing in the direction of Tel-el-Kebir so we could avoid the roads completely.

We were dressed in battle order which meant we didn't carry the full field service order of large backpack, side pack, and greatcoat. We wore our army belt with its attachments. Two magazine packs at the front, small pack at the back and, on our hip, our felt covered water bottle. On the other side we had our bayonet "frog" with its sheathed bayonet. We also carried our personal weapon. Unfortunately for me, mine was a Lee Enfield rifle with four clips of .303 carried in my ammunition pouches at the front. It was no joke carrying a .303 for any distance. With a full magazine of ten rounds, it weighed over 9 pounds, and for me, not the biggest of chaps, I felt every pound after a few miles.

We were ordered to completely fill our water bottles, but our major made it clear we were not to drink from them. This was presumably to give us an idea of the reality of enduring the desert on foot and to learn how to conserve our drinking water.

Off we went tramping over the dusty desert. We soon discovered the realities of the terrain. You couldn't go straight from A to B. There were rocky outcrops which we had to skirt around and wadis which crisscrossed the landscape. On foot the wadis were difficult to spot until we were suddenly upon one. Most were narrow gorges, about twenty feet across but with steep sides down to the bottom which could be anything from five to twenty feet deep. Major Bruen kept scanning the landscape for routes to skirt the wadis. If none could be found, we would have to scramble down into the wadi then up the other side. With all our kit, it was extremely tiring.

Fortunately for us, the Major was a big chap: at well over six feet tall so he could see farther than most. Unfortunately for him, he was big with it. He must have weighed 18 stone. As the morning wore on, the sun became fiercer, and we began to sweat heavily. And Major Bruen sweated more than most. He was wearing his officer's peaked cap which was warm in itself. Sweat was forming on his head, running down the underside of the peak in rivulets, and then pouring down in front of his nose. He must have been suffering terribly, but he kept doggedly marching on with us following. None of us had taken a sip of water.

Alongside of him at the front of the Company was Captain Nightingale and Lieutenant Robertson. Eventually, after what seemed hours, Bruen stopped. Unbidden we slumped to the floor. The three officers were consulting a map and discussing earnestly which gave me a suspicion that we were lost. One of our lads, thinking he was out of sight, surreptitiously uncorked his water bottle. It was brand new – we had never used them in our usual daily procedures – so it made a loud pop. The major spotted the culprit straightaway. "Put that man on a charge!" he barked to his lieutenant.

He turned to the rest of us, "You will not open your water bottles until I give the order." It was obvious to me we were lost. Perhaps fearing the worst, he wanted us to conserve our water. As if to confirm my suspicions, he announced that the unexpected obstacles were causing slower progress than expected reaching Tel-el-Kebir. He then turned us round and led us off back in the direction of the hospital. I knew from my innate sense of direction which has served me well over the years, that the hospital lay in a westerly direction. By this time the sun had passed its zenith, so I knew that if we kept the sun to our left and the shadows to our right, we would get back OK.

After a few more hours of slogging through the barren moonscape, we finally caught sight of the hospital water tower ahead and a little to our left. We finished up on our parade ground where Major Bruen said, "I hope you found that experience useful in knowing how to cope with the bad terrain hereabouts. Also, it has proven a useful test to you of endurance and self-discipline in resisting the temptations of your water bottle. Dismissed."

Strangely enough, there was no repeat of the exercise. Nor were there any further efforts made to improve our physical endurance. I guess the major thought, like me, "Bugger this for a game of soldiers, Mr. Churchill. Come out here and share the conditions for yourself before making any more crackpot edicts."

Christmas is coming

So, the weeks wore on to Christmas. We had a couple of quiet months apart from work where we were still busy issuing vehicles and repatriating wrecks to the UK for scrap. But before I go any further…

The Armoured Replacement Group was the result of experience and ideas gained during the Second World War. The idea was to have a forward base as close to the front line as could be safely managed. From there, if a tank or armoured vehicle was knocked out, it could be replaced and sent into the front line complete with a crew. As well as importing new vehicles into the theatre of war, they would recover knocked-out or damaged vehicles, wherever practical. These vehicles were either sent for scrap or repaired, overhauled and got ready to go back into action. Any survivors of the damaged vehicles were hospitalised and then, when fit, they too were brought into Armoured Replacement Group. There they would be formed into complete crews – driver, gunner, machine gunner, tank commander etc. – ready to go back into action.

The unit was under the command of the Royal Ordnance Corps. The staff consisted of the officers, kit storemen and drivers. There were also small detachments from other groups. The Royal Electrical Mechanical Engineers who examined, repaired and serviced vehicles. The Royal Signals, who installed and serviced the radio communications in each vehicle. Then there were the Royal Engineers who were unbelievably skilled and resourceful at overhauling bulldozers and had a huge lorry and flatbed trailer equipped with sophisticated winches for extracting damaged tanks from sand. Finally, the Royal Artillery, who were experts with mobile guns like the Sexton, a twenty-five-pound artillery piece mounted, instead of a turret, in a Sherman tank.

The rest of the ARG was made up of odd survivors of tank regiments and cavalry regiments who rode armoured cars instead of horses. Ours was a motley crew of members of, for example, the 16/5th Lancers, the 17/21st Lancers (with their skull and cross bones cap badge as a memento of their part in the Charge of the Light Brigade), Scots Greys, Household Cavalry, Dragoon Guards, Royal Hussars and others. They used their experience with the various types of vehicles to assist REME, Royal Engineers and so on to recover, repair, service and drive to the waiting receiving units.

No doubt you will be wondering where these tankers and cavalrymen came from if the war had ended six years ago. In practice, if a soldier didn't fit in with his parent regiment, it was convenient sometimes to transfer him to ARG. This happened with soldiers who had been ill and left behind in hospital when their regiment was posted to the Far East or Germany etc. Also, any malcontent or troublesome offender would find himself got rid of to ARG. We got quite a few of these. But, interestingly, these scoundrels all seemed to fit fine in with the relatively free and easy, but hard-working environment at ARG.

Christmas came and went. It was surprisingly cool after the torrid summer. And all was quiet on the Egyptian Liberation Army front – at least as far as our sector of the Canal Zone was concerned. There were no luxuries, but our cooks were able to get flour and bake a limited supply of our own bread. They got their hands on fresh eggs and vegetables from time to time.

A new year and a new regime

As the new year started, January 1952, the emergency in Egypt calmed down. It was obvious that the higher authorities had been giving some thought to the future of the Armoured Replacement Group. It had been formed during the war and it had served its purpose. It was decided to re-title it as the "A" Company of the Royal Army Ordinance Corps (RAOC), Vehicle Regiment, Tel-el-Kebir.

However, the accommodation difficulties were not solved. "B" company (soft skinned vehicles) were still based in the actual garrison at Tel-el-Kebir, but we remained in our abandoned wards in the old military hospital up the Cairo Road. Although titled the "A" company, we would still have responsibility for "E" vehicles (engineering, bulldozers, road-building machines, etc.) Major Bruen, being a Royal Ordnance officer, remained as officer commanding of the company.

The company sergeant major, a squadron major of the Scots Greys Cavalry, was, I believe, posted back to Germany. I hoped he would be O.K. because it was obvious that he had a drink problem. At the last morning parade, before the ritual was abandoned in the time of emergency, he stood swaying at the head of the company (or squadron, as he insisted on calling it). I could smell the whisky fumes standing yards away.

In his place, a new company sergeant major was brought in from the Royal Ordnance Corps. It was obvious, we didn't need to be told, he'd been brought in, now the emergency was ending, to get a grip on the company. He changed us from a rag-tag bunch (but skilled and hard-working crew) that looked and behaved like "Popski's Private Army" into the orthodox ROAC Vehicle Company.

After quickly making the administrative and senior NCO arrangements, he turned his attention to us, the "other ranks." He was the man for the job. Company Sergeant Major Straight who, when in the infantry, had won his Military Medal. He was a Londoner and a veteran from the Second World War. He looked the part too. Six feet four inches tall, lean, tough looking, ramrod straight military bearing with an eagle eye and a voice which could blast the paint from the trucks waiting for us on the parade ground. He didn't carry a pace stick, the usual instrument of office for a sergeant major. Instead, he carried an ebony staff, about five feet long with a silver head.

He re-introduced the morning parade, before we embussed to Tel-el-Kebir. The usual procedure on these parades was for everyone to make our own way on foot to the end of the parade ground. The sergeant major would stand at the head of the parade ground and shout to the loosely assembled crowd. "Company 'shun." Then, "Stand at ease." Then, "Stand easy." Next, he would shout, "Right markers. To your stations. Quick march."

This triggered the junior NCOs in charge of each platoon of twenty or so men to march forward, four of them in line astern. When the last of the four NCOs had marched 60 paces, he would, quietly, call to the one in front of him, "Up" and this last NCOs would immediately halt. The rest would continue until the last of the three had marched 30 paces, then he would call "Up" and thus the system would continue until the markers were properly spaced.

The Sergeant Major would then shout, "Company, get on parade," and we would all march loosely forward to take our places to the left of our marker. There would follow a complicated series of drills until the ranks were properly formed, all in correct lines and spacing. Then he would command us to stand at attention before marching towards the officers, who would by then be strolling towards the parade. Addressing the Officer Commanding, he would report, "Company present, correct, and waiting your inspection, sir." Then, with a smart salute, he would stand aside.

The day following this first parade under the new regime, we were standing at the foot of the parade ground, waiting for the right markers to be called. Instead, Mr. Straight marched past the lot of us and then approached from behind. He stood behind the loosely formed rear rank, then threading his ebony staff to the next rank, he prodded our mail corporal in the centre of his back and growled. "Take the parade, corporal."

The corporal was Reg Kelly, an extremely good natured and popular chap. We were all more than surprised at this unexpected turn of events. Poor Reg marched to the head of the parade ground and started the procedure, commencing with the right markers. He got it wrong at the outset which drew a bellow from Mr. Straight, correcting him. Reg carried on to the end making one mistake after another. The poor chap was a shaking wreck. At work afterwards, the troops were muttering about it. "He wants to smarten up the junior NCOs," said our office sergeant. "It is a way of creating a disciplined unit. This chap means business."

The next day, gathered before the parade, Mr. Straight repeated his manoeuvre. This time I was the NCO chosen. I felt the prod between my shoulder blades and the order "Take the parade, corporal." I was a conscript and the last person to claim I was good soldier. However, I have been blessed by a good memory. Without having consciously thought about it, I was absolutely confident I could do it. My only concern was that being the soft-spoken person I was, I hadn't got a powerful sergeant-major shouting technique.

However, I relaxed, opened my mouth wide and the sounds came out like a solo singer, not a sergeant major bellow, but loud enough and clear. I never missed a beat. I ended the parade by addressing Major Bruen in the regulation way. And that was it. Mr. Straight took over organising the loading of the troops onto the three tonners. As he passed, he gave me a small grin and a nod of appreciation.

My stint as acting sergeant major on the parade ground was actually the last. There were no repeat performances probably to the relief of the many NCOs who were terrified that they might be called on next. I suspect Mr Straight had made his point: they needed paid close attention.

Mr Straight's office was three doors down from the kit stores office where I worked. If he had an important report, he would come in and ask if I would be good enough to type it for him. My reputation as a fast, accurate typist had spread. He never engaged me in conversation, but he clearly appreciated my help.

15th February 1952. The King is dead

It was the first anniversary of my being called up in 1951. We had no newspapers, TV or phones so we relied on our officers and senior NCOs to brief us. We were told that the King had died on the 6th of February 1952 while Princess Elizabeth with Prince Phillip were on holiday in Kenya. I can't remember how long it was after that date that a funeral parade was held in the garrison at Tel-el-Kebir.

The weather was mild (unlike like the following winter) so we were ordered to prepare our best khaki drill uniform with shorts, hose tops and puttees. To explain the bizarre dress in the army, I should explain that we were issued with regular short grey socks, 100 percent wool with no seams to prevent blisters. (Soldiers' feet were valuable and subjected to regular foot inspections.) These high-quality ankle socks were extremely comfortable. However, when worn with shorts, they looked untidy. Unfortunately, knee length socks of that quality were not available. So instead, we wore our short grey socks and pulled up over them, a pair of "hose tops". These had no feet but covered the top few inches of our socks and along with our lower leg right up to just below the knee. To cover the gap between boots and hose tops, we then wore "puttees", which were relics from the Boer and First World War. The puttee was wrapped neatly around the ankle starting below the top lace-holes of the boots and gradually wound higher. The end of the puttee, which was about six feet long, continued as a linen tape which then was wrapped round the whole ankle. The last few inches were wrapped around itself and tucked in to prevent coming undone. You can imagine what it was like to wear that lot in high summer. Thick woollen socks, then a length of hose top, finally covered by six feet of woollen puttee. At the end of the day, you could pour the sweat out of your boots. The overall appearance, however, was rather smart – dashing even. We felt more than a bit proud especially after months wearing denim overalls.

However, we Royal Ordnance Engineers, were in for a surprise when the detachments from the various cavalry regiments joined us. Even their simple khaki drill was adorned in various ways which were in-keeping with the traditions of their cavalry regiments and reflected their historical associations. They wore, for example, coloured belts instead of our regular khaki army belt. They had coloured epaulettes of different designs depending on the regiment. Other ranks wore swatches of chain mail attached to their epaulettes. Some had "georgettes", a small banana shape piece of armour worn on a chain round the neck to protect the throat. Coloured cockades attached to berets completed a very colourful picture.

After getting dressed up in our Sunday best, we then had to sit on the dirty floor of our three tonners to cross the desert to the garrison. Once there, we formed up on their central parade ground. A senior office stood on a podium and addressed us. I couldn't hear a word he said. Then we marched past him and gave an eyes left salute, and then we dispersed to our lorries for the return journey. All that spit and polish for such a dull event.

As 1952 wore on, it was still quiet with the occasional "noises off" but no real trouble at our site. We were still bumping across the desert in lorries to Tel-el-Kebir to do our day's work.

Then, to our surprise, we were offered the chance of a week's leave in Cyprus of all places. It wasn't free. The cost would be deducted from our pay. I thought it wasn't worth it for a week and adding to my (ill fated) savings account would be a better idea. The few who managed to get on the scheme came back all starry eyed about the wonderful time they'd had with the lovely Cypriot girls.

Military justice

I can't remember exactly when, but at some time before my final Christmas in 1952, I was suddenly told that I was on a charge and had to come before the officer commanding the following morning. I was duly marched in with the usual briskness and stood before a major I had never seen before.

"Prisoner and escort, caps off," roared the sergeant major. He peered at the paper on his desk. "You are charged, under Section 40 of the Army Act of behaviour prejudicial to good order and military discipline, whilst on active service. That at some time in last July, you lost your personal weapon, namely a .303 rifle." Silence. Losing your weapon in time of war was viewed very seriously. He didn't ask any questions; this was a preliminary formality before remanding to higher authority. "Remanded for CO's orders. Caps on, right turn quick march."

A few days later there was a repeat at Tel-el-Kebir in front of a full colonel, name unknown. The colonel had none of the strutting, bullying authoritative attitude of the major. I found my voice and explained nervously that I had been literally forced onto a stretcher and whisked off to hospital. My rifle had been the last thing on my mind. I remembered the Royal Engineer sergeant's words from all those months ago, "This is the army. Somebody is always in charge." And explained that, under the circumstances, I thought some senior NCO or officer would have taken over in my absence and taken responsibility for my rifle.

The colonel just smiled and said, "All charges dismissed." A rare glimpse of common sense from "them up-stairs".

Autumn came around and with it a flare-up of the troubles. The infantry regiments returned to have more stints in the front line. I didn't experience any combat, but we were told that we were a prime target for the terrorists who were making a base for themselves in Zagazig. This was a small town about fifteen miles further along the Cairo Road between the abandoned hospital and Cairo. Night after night we could hear bouts of gunfire, followed by the thunderous sound of our formidable 25 pounders.

The story brought to us by our friendly sergeant was that Zagazig had become so troublesome that a Regiment of Royal Artillery had been brought up to virtually surround the town. Some of our Arabic speaking officers were using loud hailers to warn the populace and to encourage the terrorists to leave otherwise the whole place would be flattened by artillery.

While the sergeant was delivering the shithouse griff, there was a loud ringing of bells. Three military ambulances roared in through the gates. Apparently, the drivers were not up to date. They believed we were still a functional hospital, and they wanted treatment for the stretcher cases filling the ambulances. I was standing by the first ambulance as the driver rushed round the back and opened it for our nearest officer to see. Bodies were stacked on stretchers three high in two rows completely filling the ambulance. In that brief glimpse, I recognised the pallor of the skin, bare skulls and bare feet of the wounded, and possibly dead. The colour brought back memories of the poor little lad on the canal side at Middleport Pottery.

Having discovered that we had no doctors or hospital facilities, the ambulances roared off again towards Tel-el-Kebir.

The bath house incident

I mentioned this earlier but didn't amplify. The old British Military Hospital lay five miles beyond the fortified depot of Tel-el-Kebir, in the direction of Cairo. It was the farthest west point of the Canal Zone therefore the British Military considered it to be at risk of possible incidents not only because of its geographical position but because of the vulnerable nature of its occupants: female nurses and sick or injured patients. The nurses were all British military belonging to the Queen Alexandra's Royal Army Nursing Corps. Each nurse was rightly given officer rank because of their responsibilities. but also to ensure proper respect from non-medical staff, soldiers and airmen patients.

Because of these concerns, the hospital was closed as soon as any hint of possible troubles was felt. The patients were transferred to the main British Military Hospital at Ismailia, and I was given to believe the nurses were then repatriated to the UK.

This small military hospital had been built years before the abdication of King Farouk and was not, at that time, considered to be at particular risk as evidenced by the single strand of barbed wire which formed and protected its perimeter. The dozen or so buildings on the eastern side were taken over by the army and allotted to the Armoured Replacement Group when it was transferred from Shandur, south of Suez.

The main reason for this was the lack of accommodation at. Although the depot was huge – an impressive complex of Ordnance Corps' stores, workshops, and parking for the vehicles – there was no spare accommodation. So, we worked all day at Tel-el-Kebir, but come evening, we were loaded into lorries and returned to the hospital to sleep.

At the northeast corner, a little away from our accommodation in the disused wards, was the bath house. It could more correctly have been called the shower house because it contained only showers. No baths. No hot water. In summer, hot water was unnecessary, and the winters were much milder than in UK. The bath house was a low single-story brick and concrete structure. Typical for that climate, there were no glazed windows. Instead, there were two long open spaces along the wall nearest the perimeter wire. These were above head hight and were enough to provide ventilation. Along this wall and below the gaps there wooden slatted seating benches which are typical of men's changing rooms.

One day we had just returned from Tel-el-Kebir and a bunch of us were taking a shower before tiffin. I had just finished dressing after my shower when I heard the unmistakable sound of gunfire coming through the glassless window openings. We all had our personal weapon with us; we even took them to bed at night. So we clambered onto the benches which were just the right height for us to poke our rifles or Sten guns through. We saw a few flashes in the dark which we took to be gun shots, and we started responding in kind.

At that moment, one of our company stepped out of the shower bay behind us. He was just a private soldier but older and far more experienced than us young national servicemen. He had been an infantryman during the war. He had found it difficult to settle back into civilian life after the war so, like several others, had re-joined the army as a basic trainee alongside the rest of us. It was fortunate for us that he had seen combat. He shouted, "Get down off those benches. If you poke your weapons into the window space like that, they'll see your muzzle flash and shoot right back at you. Pull them benches back a couple of feet and then get up on 'em and shoot through the gap. That way they won't be able to see where you are." We hurriedly did as he said but the terrorists had vanished in that short space of time. Just a quick hit and run job.

A short time afterwards, the officers inspected the area and deemed that the dump just beyond our side of the barbed wire should be cleared and the empty cans disposed of. This would deny the terrorists of one supply of possible Molotov cocktails. I didn't see the disposal, but the cans did disappear. I guess they were buried in the deep toilet dump in the remote centre area of the base.

The incident of the exploding toilet

That, incidentally, brings another memory to mind. Before and during the WW2 years when the base was a fully functioning hospital, there were few toilets in the hospital premises themselves. The lack of a sewage and drainage system had to be overcome.

There were small toilet blocks near to the old hospital wards that we ARG personnel had taken over. However, several hundred yards away in the centre of the base was a much bigger toilet complex which had not been used since the hospital was abandoned.

We were told that it was a "round robin" set-up. This consisted of a dozen or more wooden cubicles with a space between each one but joined to its neighbour by wooden spars. These were arranged in a semicircle around a central large hole. The idea being that if and when more cubicles were required, they would be added until a complete circle of cubicles would surround the hole.

The soldier or patient would enter a cubicle via its front door. Inside, a wooden bench spanned the width of the cubicle with the necessary hole in the centre of the bench-seat. At the back of each cubicle was a low trap door through which a huge iron bucket was placed so it sat right underneath the hole. At regular intervals the toilet attendants – Egyptian labourers – would empty these buckets into the massive hole behind the cubicles and then shovelled loose sand over the contents.

The hole was very large and very sandy and so had, presumably, served the hospital well for many years.

The emergency got into its stride in 1952 and one night, I can't remember when, but the summer had cooled so it must have been approaching winter. Infantry units taken from each regiment in turn at fortnightly intervals, were posted to guard the hospital. This was to give them a taste of the front line.

I remember being woken at about 2.00 a.m. by a very loud crump. The infantry was on duty. We could hear them swearing and swarming, so we left it to them, rolled over and went back to sleep.

In the morning, we woke to the most appalling smell. We could see the raffia thatched roofs of the old wards dripping with sandy covered gloopy excrement. It seemed that a group of terrorists had assumed that the strange semi-circular structure of cubicles was of great importance. They had got through the single-strand barbed wire perimeter and left a bundle of explosives near the centre and blown the old toilet complex to bits.

The mess was revolting. However, we had enough more than enough on our plates guarding our vehicle facility in Tel-el-Kebir, so we were spared the clearing up duties and cheerfully left it to the infantry.

Innocents abroad

Writing these incidents reminds me of the extent that we were just innocents abroad during our service. We in the Ordnance Corps, as national servicemen had received sixteen weeks of basic training, much of it square bashing, a necessary training to inculcate reasonable military discipline. We also got some lectures on the technical work that the Ordnance Corps provided, and basic weapons training. My squad had spent a whole day on the open-air firing range where we were trained in the use and maintenance of our rifles, Sten guns and our, shared, Bren gun.

The infantry regiments went on to become fully proficient in fieldcraft, tactics, battlefield first aid, and other skills. Despite the criticism from some quarters about the deficiencies of young national servicemen, the thoroughness of the infantrymen was revealed in a variety of skilled and brave actions. For example, the Gloucester Regiment at the Imjin River in Korea. Many reports revealed the exceptional bravery of that regiment which consisted of mostly young national servicemen. It just so happened that we Ordnance, Service Corps, REME national servicemen received training in basic self-defence but due to exceptional circumstances found ourselves in situations where we could have benefitted from more infantry training.

Fortunately, there were no injuries. However, if during the bath house incident the older comrade, towel wrapped around his middle, had not been with us, there could well have been.

Another Christmas approaches

Another Christmas approached. The terrorists were active somewhere, according to bits of information coming largely from infantrymen or the drivers of tankers collecting vehicles. However, after the bath house incident and Zagazig, things were quiet for us. The worst thing was the weather. The previous Christmas I had been surprised by the cold. This year it was even colder. Over Christmas we had lots of chilly rain and snow – which, fortunately, didn't stick. I kept scratching my head remembering geography lessons with Miss Adams at school who described the hot dry desert climate in Egypt. Something was wrong!

Then, some good news: a Royal Navy destroyer had rounded the Cape of Good Hope in South Africa, sailed up the Indian Ocean, through the Red Sea and reached Suez, carrying, amongst other things, cigarettes, tobacco, rum and canned beer of some foreign origin. I could never decipher the labels, but it tasted good after months without any. I was never a drinker, but an occasional beer was always welcome. I didn't smoke either, but it was good to see the lads enjoying these free goodies. I recall the cigarettes were Navy Cut, larger and of much better quality than the civilian versions at home. They came in a drum-shaped tin with a built-in opener on the underside of the removable outer lid.

We had a bit of a party that night and I sampled the free rum. I had never tasted rum before. It was good, not as fiery as whisky. This led me to sample a bit more than was wise. I staggered out of the corporals' mess across the short stretch of sand to our ward but never made it. I awoke next morning in the sand with an evil headache.

There was a tradition that the officers would act as waiters to other ranks on Christmas Day. So, we had our morning tea in bed! Then, later, Christmas lunch was served at tables by the officers.

However, no matter what merriment, our unit never relaxed its watch for terrorist activity. We had been alerted that terrorists could be aiming to attack while we were drunk or otherwise relaxed.

I was on guard on Christmas Eve 1952. I wasn't the guard commander. Things had grown serious enough to put sergeants in charge where possible. During the day my mate and I had two "stags" of guarding the water tower at the corner of the hospital. Someone had the daft idea to detail the two of us to climb the tower, more than sixty feet, and set up our Bren gun and a large wooden ammunition box full of .303 rounds. The armourers hadn't filled any of the magazines. My mate and I had four mags each which we needed to fill with 30 rounds each.

Nobody had had the foresight to survey the situation before deciding to position us there. The roof turned out *not* to be flat. It had four triangular sections rising as a gradual slope up to the centre. My mate, fortunately, was a great companion. He was a big Scotsman from the Highlands named Tom Paine. He was a national serviceman like me but four years older because he had been granted deferred service as he had been needed to keep his family farm going. Finally, the War Office insisted on calling him up.

As different from the poison dwarfs as you could wish, he was quiet, thoughtful and a tower of strength during any difficulties. Our first problem was the sloping roof. There was no guard rail at the edges of the roof. When Tom and I levered open the ammunition box, a large number of rounds spilled out and started slowly rolling towards the edges. We scrambled to retrieve them and set about filling the magazines with our frozen fingers. We eventually succeeded and waited for trouble. None came.

We lay on the concrete roof – for safety and to keep as low profile as we could against the cold wind. We could see for miles in all directions. Just desert and stones crisscrossed by the wadis that we had struggled with on our route-march. As I expected, the Egyptians could see that from our eerie we could spot any movement, so they, sensibly, kept away.

Dusk fell, we finished our stag on the tower, took four hours off and then were deployed to a slit trench at the foot of the tower. We each wore our winter battle dress: a scarf which doubled as "cap comforter". We were each only issued with one of these, so we had borrowed an extra one. These plus our heavy greatcoats kept us warm but, after a few hours of constant sleet and drizzle, they grew sodden with water and even heavier. .

We began to see flashes and the occasional report from rifles or shotguns. It wasn't possible to see the people behind them, but whenever we caught sight of a bright flash, we replied with a short burst from our Bren. There was no noise in response that suggested we'd or not hit anyone, so the night settled into watchful waiting. Our companions in the guard house could hear the shooting and decided it was unsafe to cross the open sandy area between them and our slit trench. That meant it was daylight before replacements relieved us.

By that time, the water in the trench was over our boots. But we were in luck: we had South African boots rather than the standard British Army issue. The British Army had run out of boots for all the new national service recruits, so they had procured a whole load of South African ones. These were brown and had to be dyed black as only officers could wear brown, but they were of far higher quality than the British ones. In particular they had a bellows tongue which sealed the lace holes from rainwater. So our feet stayed dry. .

On our way home

After Christmas things quietened down again and my thoughts began to turn to demob and home

The weeks dragged as I waited for notice of when I would get shipped home. February 15th, 1953. No news. A couple of weeks passed with still no news.

Then I was told suddenly to gather my kit, return my bedding to the stores and report to the guard room. There were six others there. I was confused: I had expected them to be the same chaps I'd travelled with from Shandur, but no, the Army has its weird and wonderful ways. We were loaded onto lorries without being told our destination. Hours later we arrived at what transpired to be Fayid Airport.

On so many occasions during my time abroad, civilian volunteers had been on hand with extremely welcome hot, good quality tea, sandwiches and cakes and here they were again. We were then led onto the tarmac to a waiting plane. I recognised it from my childhood when my brother and I kept outlines of all known planes, friendly or enemy. It was a York, a four-engine bomber, similar to the Manchester – a precursor to the Lancaster. The York, however, had, for some reason, a different setup for rear tail planes and rudder. It was distinctive because it was the only plane I knew that had three vertical rudders.

The plane had been converted from a bomber inot a passenger plane. The conversion had obviously been hurried and was incomplete. The bomb-bay had been emptied and rows of canvas seats had been installed looking like a rough version of a passenger plane. There were no windows, it had poor lighting and, worst of all, when it started, it was clear there was no noise insulation from the four engines. It was deafening. We took off, late afternoon then made a stop at Luqa airfield in Malta to refuel. We had to resort to sign language and lip reading when dealing with the steward as the noise of the engines had temporarily deafened us.

We took off from Malta into a bad weather system that, according to the steward, stretched north into and through Europe. The plane didn't have the power to reach a high altitude so when we reached the French coast and started to cross the Alpes-Maritimes, we hit a lot of turbulence. That was the first trip and only trip on which I have suffered with airsickness. I thought seasickness on the Empire Ken was bad, but this was far, far worse. The plane would drop like a stone then stop suddenly when it hit denser air. After a few minutes it would lurch back up again. The worst was when it dropped, halted then, instead of bounding back up it would drop again. It was difficult to brace myself against these unexpected ups and downs while holding onto my sick bag. It became so bad that the passenger in front of me, a captain in the

Royal Artillery, collapsed into the aisle. The steward gave him artificial respiration and he recovered enough to get back onto his seat.

After we had crossed the Alps, the flight was calmer with only slight patches of turbulence. As dawn approached, I could glimpse the English Channel from a tiny window some way ahead of me on my left. The pilot switched on his PA system for the first time, "We are scheduled to land at Stanstead, ladies and gentlemen. However, the storm has followed us north from the Med and is making it difficult for us to land. So, I am heading west down the coast to find an alternative landing site."

It seemed hours later when he announced that the weather had cleared over the Bournemouth area. After circling Hurn airport, the pilot eventually made a bumpy landing. We were walked down the ladder to the tarmac and a short way to the terminal building. I shouldn't have been surprised but nevertheless I was amazed to see a long trestle table set up, with small tables covered with snow white linen. Once again, those wonderful ladies from the WVS had turned up trumps again. Someone must have kept in touch with aircraft control and anticipated our arrival. My stomach had settled a little during the long detour down the English Channel, so the hot tea and sandwiches were most welcome!

After refreshments we went through customs. This was a novel experience. I couldn't understand the attitude of the customs officers. We felt like criminals. I could understand the need for some bags to be searched, but not the aggressive way it was done. I didn't smoke, but they insisted on repeating the same questions about how many cigarettes I had with me.

Eventually they were satisfied, and we all went through to buses which took us to a railway station and a special train which had been organised to take us to Waterloo and from there by lorry to Feltham in Middlesex, the site of the regimental depot for the RAOC. It was from there that troops were despatched abroad and were received back when returning.

I was still dressed in my Army Uniform with all my field service marching order packs plus kit bag. I was told to keep my army gear, because after national service, it was compulsory to stay on the Army

Roll and to serve three years as a reservist. This meant a fortnight every year doing refresher training to keep us ready for any conflict with the Soviets.

I spent an uncomfortable cold night at Feltham and, after an equally cold breakfast and hours filling in administration papers, I was taken back to Waterloo Station with a travel warrant to go to Stoke-on-Trent station. The train journey from London was slow – high speed trains were years away – and the journey took five hours. I couldn't help marvelling at the landscape as the train travelled north. It was late February and there were patches of snow by the track and in high spots in the fields. Despite this, the overwhelming surprise was the greenery. After nearly two years in the desert, I'd forgotten this "green and pleasant land" of William Blake. At Feltham, I had changed my few piastres into pounds sterling which turned out to be enough for a taxi to our house in Burslem. A blessing as I couldn't face the bus journey as I was tired, bewildered and loaded up with all my army kit.

I remember knocking on the door after midnight, hearing movement upstairs then Father coming down in his pyjamas to open the door. The end of an extra ordinary episode in my life.

Chapter 5: Return to Civilian Life and Starting Married Life

Prelude

National service was one of the watersheds in my life. The other was meeting, falling in love with and marrying my beloved Sheila. Here, I explain how that happened and how we embarked on our journey to carry our family from the working class to the middle class.

Disembarkation leave

I had a money order from Feltham to pay for a fortnight's disembarkation leave. I spent the leave at home, quietly getting used Mother's cooking, and adjusting slowly to the cold. Egypt had been, as I described earlier, had been much cooler in 1952 than in 1951, but the Potteries, with it's cold, wet and windy climate, took a while to get used to. Another thing was the hilly landscape. The Potteries is a collection of small hills, many of them steep. This came as a surprise to me. I'd become accustomed to the flat desert. The group of friends that I used to hang out with, playing tennis at the local courts, had all moved away.

Back to civilian, working life.

To this day, I can't explain what I felt or why, but I just couldn't settle down to civvy life. The work, which before call-up was interesting and full of cheerful chats with people on the "bank" and in the office, now seemed dull and pointless. After a couple of weeks, I handed in my notice and started looking for a different job.

The Midlands Electricity Board advertised a vacancy for a storeman at their Hanley depot. I sailed through the interview and started the following Monday. It wasn't an office job, I wore overalls, because occasionally I needed to handle, in addition to switches, cables and conduit piping etc. There was also the occasional delivery of bagged cement and plaster.

The other two storemen were jolly chaps, so it was a happy working environment. Apart from, on the other hand, the store manager. He was rather odd, wore a brown warehouse coat and rarely appeared out of his little office. He seemed to regard himself as some sort of Olympian figure, elevated above the reach of ordinary mortals. I worked there for three months and never exchanged a word with him.

However, boredom had overtaken me again. Also, I felt I needed to return to more civilised attire, with collar and tie. My father was disgusted with me for giving up a "respectable" office job. In their working-class world, he and always had an ambition that I would be "somebody", not just a working man. He and my mother viewed office workers as superior beings and the height of their ambitions for me was to be an "*office worker*".

Father had a chip on his shoulder because of the class distinction in those days. He felt condescended to by the office staff. I remember him complaining bitterly one day about the toilets and washrooms at his place of work. "Posh, scented, toilet soap for those who don't get their hands dirty. And, for those who do, crude bar soap fit for scrubbing floors."

One morning, before I got up, he came into my bedroom and threw down onto the bed a copy of the local paper, the Evening Sentinel. It was opened at the job vacancies page where he had marked an advert for somebody with experience in the export department of the tile company called H&R Johnson (known to everyone as "Johnsons") where he worked. It sounded "straight up my street" as the expression went in those days.

Finding my business niche

I applied, was interviewed by Bernard Keightley, the export manager, and I was set on at £5 a week – more than I was being paid at the MEB. There were other advantages over the MEB. For one thing it was good to get out of overalls and boots and back to wearing a suit and a nice clean shirt every day. "Workingman's" experience had proved interesting, and the change had snapped me out of my ennui that endured after the army. Also, I didn't need to travel by bus to Hanley in the centre of the Potteries.

The H&R Johnson factory and offices were in Tunstall, only a mile and a half walk away from home. This meant I could stroll home for lunch, crossing a huge "shawdruck" between Tunstall and Burslem. A shawdruck was a dump, usually belonging to one particular pot-bank, where broken pottery shards had been dumped. The factories that created that particular dump had gone away in the distant past, but the area was still used as a general dump. It didn't contain anything objectionable. It still seemed to be mainly masses of broken pottery, partly overgrown by invading grass and weeds.

The work at H&R Johnson proved to be interesting. Our little office was a separate closed office at the end of the main office. This main office housed home sales staff, general administration, and so on. At the other end of this main office was a short corridor opening onto the "typing pool", presided over by a very nice lady of extremely ample proportions. She had a number of shorthand typists and regular typists preparing order forms for the various production units, invoicing and other clerical procedures. In our export office, we were able to get on with our work without many interruptions. There was only Bernard, the Export Manager, me and three typists who prepared the various export documents involved with the customers' orders.

Home sales business was carried out by a lot of telephoning with some typewritten correspondence. Our export business was nearly all correspondence-based, except for the occasional order from one of the big international trading companies which had offices in London or Liverpool.

If Bernard or I wanted to write to a customer, shipping agent, insurance broker etc, we would pick up the phone and ask to be put through to Eileen Watson, the typing pool supervisor. She would detail one of her stenographers to walk across to our office armed with her shorthand notebook and an array of pencils. Because of the complexities of the export trade, and the different language expressions often used, Eileen would detail one of her better, experienced girls.

Business turns to pleasure

It wasn't until the second day that I needed to write a few letters. Eileen said she was sending someone and, a few minutes later, the door to our office opened and a young lady came in. Her name was Sheila Arrowsmith. As soon as I saw her, I was struck by something. I suppose it was her charisma. She was dressed in a simple, smart brown skirt, a woollen cardigan of the same colour, and a primrose top – what you would describe today as a T-shirt. She had short, blonde hair with a natural wave in it. She had large blue-grey eyes and a wide smile that, when she looked at me, lit up the whole world.

I wouldn't say it was "love at first sight", but her appearance, her voice and her general manner radiated a sort of happiness I had never witnessed before. She took down half a dozen letters in shorthand and I was struck by how skilled she was. She never hesitated, never asked me to explain my meaning or for the spelling of a strange foreign word. Later, when the typed letters were brought for my signature, I was again struck by the accuracy and complete absence of any eraser marks.

We chatted for only a few minutes before she took away the letters, nothing personal, just a few questions I had about Tunstall as I had never worked there before. I noticed she had a small diamond ring on her left hand. Later, I learned she was engaged. It was several days before I had the nerve to ask if she was interested in the cinema. I had spotted that she was no longer wearing that ring. It was a while until she told me the whole story.

She had harboured doubts about her fiancé and when she met me, apparently, she had also struck by a feeling that there was something different about me. So, the evening after she first saw me in the export office, she went home, saw her fiancé and broke off the engagement. Apparently, she didn't know whether I was the "one" destined for her, but getting to know a little about me, she realised that her fiancé was certainly *not* the one she wanted to spend the rest of her life with.

Later, we met in Tunstall one evening and saw a film in the one cinema in the town. After I walked her to the bus stop and waited until I saw her safely onto the Well's bus for Scholar Green where she lived, about four miles away across the border in Cheshire. I found it rather disconcerting that she stayed in my mind after parting at the bus stop and she was the first thought that popped into my head on waking the following day.

The Arrowsmiths

So started, our courting days. It turned out that her brilliant smile and her pleasant ways hid her unfortunate family situation. Sheila was the second eldest of six children. Her father had died when she was thirteen, following years suffering with TB. Her siblings were Martin, the eldest, (then came Sheila), Nancy, Leonard, Geoffrey and Audrey, the youngest who was six years old.

Martin and Leonard had both joined the RAF as regulars to escape the poverty of their existence. Geoffrey, the fifth child, had been diagnosed with type one diabetes. Like all the Arrowsmith's, he was extremely intelligent, so was trained into monitoring his own diabetes and injecting insulin as required.

One day, Hilda, Sheila's mother, had phoned their GP because Geoffrey had passed out. The GP came quite quickly and assembled his kit, preparing to give him an insulin injection. "No, doctor," Hilda tried to explain. "I have seen my boy like this before. He is in shock. He's given himself too much insulin." The GP brushed aside her protests and quickly injected Geoffrey with more insulin. They still couldn't rouse him, called an ambulance and, at the hospital, they found he was in severe insulin shock. The shock was so severe that it caused brain damage, so that he spent the rest of his short life in Parkside Mental Hospital at Macclesfield.

Every Saturday Hilda – Sheila's mother – and Sheila visited Geoffrey, so I accompanied them, travelling by train from Kidsgrove Station. Geoffrey always looked forward to our visits and his cigarettes, which they brought him. In appearance, it was impossible to see any sign of mental illness. Like all the Arrowsmiths, he was extremely intelligent – and an excellent card player, which kept him in extra pocket money.

I questioned Hilda about why he was being incarcerated in the maximum-security wing of the hospital. Actually, that sounded worse than it was – there were no violent patients there. Any such would be kept in a separate area. Access to Geoffrey's area was a little intimidating, however. We were accompanied by a male nurse when we arrived, who unlocked and then locked behind us a series of doors. Apparently, Dr Crowe, the superintendent, had explained that Geoffrey had "lost insight" and couldn't be trusted to control his food intake. Every scrap of food and drink he consumed had to be weighed or measured and entered into a log.

Dr Crowe had told Hilda that Geoffrey couldn't be held against his will. Under the Mental Health Act at the time, he was classed as a voluntary patient and, in theory, he could sign himself out at any time. Fortunately, he was quite content in his little world with his cards and cigarettes.

I need to jump forward in time so that I can complete the account of poor Geoffrey. Later, when Sheila and I were married, I bought our first motor vehicle, a Lambretta scooter. It was surprisingly powerful it shielded us from the worst of the weather. With two of us aboard, we could cruise through the Cheshire countryside at 50 miles per hour.

A few years after we were married, the Government made amendments to the Mental Health Act. It was relaxed even more for "voluntary" patients. This caused a lot of confusion at the hospital and Geoffrey was one of the many patients who signed themselves out. Hilda was not notified, and it was only when we visited the hospital on the following Saturday that we discovered he was no longer there! In fact he had absconded and was sleeping under hedgerows. Sheila and I hurried home on our Lambretta scooter and prepared a sheaf of notices with Geoffrey's photograph. We then returned to Macclesfield and distributed these in the major shops as well as asking passersby if they had seen this man.

Martin, Sheila's eldest brother who was living in Epsom in Surrey, came up to Macclesfield to join the manhunt and found Geoffrey, purely by chance, in a field near the hospital. Martin bundled Geoffrey into his car and drove straight-away to Epsom having phoned Hilda who consented to Geoffrey living with Martin.

Unfortunately, Martin wasn't as completely aware of the restrictions on Geoffrey's diet. A few days later they went out to a pub. Geoffrey got drunk, was sick in bed and drowned in his vomit. Poor Hilda was devastated, but put it, with the other setbacks in her life, behind her and just got on with things.

Accommodation problems

This all happened after Sheila and I were married. Before we got married, there was the problem of accommodation for Hilda, Sheila and Nancy, who had been living in a very nice council house in Scholar Green. Hilda was suffering from arthritis and the upkeep of the house became too much for the three of them. The house had a huge garden which had gradually become over-grown. As a result, they were evicted by the council.

Hilda went to live with her mother (Sheila and Nancy's Grandmother) in their spacious cottage in Alton (of Alton Towers fame). Hilda got a job at Elkse's biscuit factory in Uttoxeter and Sheila, with Nancy, went to live with Hilda's sister, Ida, in Sneyd Green. They were most unhappy there, but it was years later that I learned that their Uncle Vincent had been pestering both girls with unwanted advances.

By this time, Sheila and I had become inseparable and when I asked her to marry me, she accepted. I then started searching for somewhere for the girls to live.

Our combined income at that time, Sheila and me, was £10 per week. We had no possessions apart from our clothes and it was disappointing to read the adverts for furnished accommodation. They were completely out of our price range. We couldn't expect anything from our respective parents. Hilda, a widow, and my mother eager for any earnings she could get from me. I had already put my foot down and insisted on just paying my board, so I could have proper use of my wages.

Then, in the Evening Sentinel, I saw a small ad – that was listed in the properties section of adverts. The ad had been placed by a firm of solicitors offering a house to rent in Porthill. I phoned the solicitors' office and arranged to call there later that day. There, I was met by a youngish chap, a relative of the well-known Malkin family of potters.

Apparently, the family had tasked him with dealing with the house when one of his great-grandparents had died.

It was obvious to me that he had no familiarity with the property market, and he more or less admitted this to me. He explained that his main interest was not milking the property for its rental value, but to find a respectable tenant who would care for the house. We chatted easily and he soon said, almost apologetically, "Do you think £3 pounds per week would be reasonable?" I almost hugged him with surprise and relief, then confirmed I would be very pleased to be his tenant. He produced a blank "rent book'. "It's the law you know," he explained. "It is necessary to have an agreement in the form of this standard printed rent book with the necessary script in the back."

Next job, finding a method of payment. I had never had a bank account, nor a savings account, apart from my (now empty) army savings account. I went into the nearest bank to H.& R. Johnson in Tunstall. It was the District Bank, later to be taken over by the Westminster Bank and now, called NatWest. I have stayed with them ever since.

The Manager wasn't the typical dragon sort of bank manager of those days. He welcomed me and promised he would open a current account for me as soon as it became possible. He explained that, sadly, for some obscure reason connected with the fact that the country was bankrupt by the Second World war, I needed to be earning £10 per week to qualify.

(Later, after I was married, I got a small raise. This was added my wife's income. This got us over the £10 threshold. So, soon after we were married, we got a joint bank account and were soon in possession of our own cheque book. But, for now, I would have to pay cash.)

That very weekend Sheila and Nancy moved into the house. It was a solid Edwardian house at the end of St. Edmund's Avenue in Porthill. Porthill was, a few generations ago, a sort of "Nob Hill" posh area where the pottery owners and the senior management class built their homes. At first, these posh homes were built at the top of the hill, overlooking the valley below where the factories and lower classes lived.

As the years passed, the top of the hill reached its capacity, so newer avenues were built horizontally down the hill, until it reached the bottom avenue, St. Edmund's Avenue. It was still a rather posh, quiet and civilised area, with an air of slightly faded grandeur. As I said, the house was soundly built with high-quality fitments, and it was fully furnished in a quality style. Aunty Ida kindly donated some bedding and soft furnishing to the girls. I suspected she was glad to get the girls off her hands, even though they were both educated and behaved impeccably. I am more certain that the girls were relieved to leave. As I said earlier, it was many years after that I learned of Uncle Vince's behaviour.

I didn't move in with them. We were not yet married. The Potteries was always an old-fashioned area, so in the 1950's the moral and sexual standards and customs were well in force. All this was to change. We had rationing of some foods and fuel until after 1956. Then came the 60's with pop music and the social revolution it brought with it.

But all that was still to come. And so, meantime, I lived at home in Middleport, and spent evenings and weekends helping Sheila and Nancy get the house in order. But every evening I would walk home to Middleport. It was absolutely out of the question to even consider sleeping in Endymion, as the house was named.

Of course, unwanted pregnancies were a regular "misfortune" and many an unhappy marriage as well. However, both Sheila and I had been both brought up with strict taboos about such behaviour. This was born, in the case of my family, of their enforced marriage when Mother became pregnant with me. So, like well-disciplined Christians, we behaved with strict self-control, all the while skimping and saving every spare penny to be able to afford getting married.

For example, it was the custom in the office for the canteen trolley to arrive mid-mornings and the same in the afternoon with free tea and to-be-paid-for toast, teacakes and cream cakes in the afternoon. Sheila and I never indulged in the foods on offer and out of those years grew a strict savings ethos which served us well in later years.

At that time, the Government's income tax rules allowed a generous tax rebate to couples marrying before the end of the tax year (5th April). This meant all pay that year which had been taxed as a single person, would be re-calculated at a married person's rate. This surplus would be paid back to the happy couple in the form of a cheque. We had worked out (thanks to Sheila's brilliant and disciplined mind) that we could afford the big day in March 1955.

Up to that date, we didn't go out. The cinema had lost its appeal and we were happy to have a house which soon we could call home. The house, though old, was very well built so didn't need any repairs. That meant we didn't have to bother and wait for the landlord to fix things. It was, basically clean, but it was a large house with many lockers, or built-in wardrobes as you would call them today. There was a fair bit of clutter that the old lady had left, so Sheila and I, helped by Nancy, made a good job of clearing it up.

There was no central heating. That became a popular part of modern living many years later. There was a good old-fashioned Victorian fire range in the kitchen. The actual fire was placed about three feet above the floor – much better for sitting around than the more modern floor-level fireplaces in the other rooms. The fire was of a good size, so we had masses of hot water. We had to watch out when stoking it; coal was expensive at around £2 per hundredweight (50 kg).

The whole room made a cosy kitchen-cum-dining room with a small scullery where, in days gone by, the housemaids would have done the laundry, dishwashing etc. I was laughing when I pointed out the "call bell system" in the hall. It was mounted on a mahogany board with tiny bells labelled with "Dining Room" "Bedroom No.1" and so on. It was a changed lifestyle that we brought to the house. The whole place had an air of faded past history and we felt lucky to have it as our home.

Wedding plans

We, or be more precise, Sheila and Nancy, began to plan our wedding. Women are so much better at that sort of thing. Money had been carefully conserved. Sheila had a system of envelopes labelled "rent", "grocer", "milkman", "coalman", "house insurance" and so on. In those days, before we were granted the privilege of having a bank account, that was the way things were done. Such a contrast to today's cashless society.

Many people today, when I describe our wedding, seem to suspect that I might be exaggerating or embroidering things. Ours was a *do-it-*

yourself wedding. Sheila and Nancy worked wonders. They were so close, like twins, and shared the same styles of workmanship. For example, they were both excellent at knitting.

On many occasions, particularly when the children started to arrive, Sheila and Nancy would knit a garment together. Sheila would knit the front and back, lapels and buttonholes etc., while Nancy would knit the sleeves and cuffs. The style and tension of their knitting were absolutely identical so, when sewed together, the whole looked as though it had been knitted by one person. Sheila wasn't so hot on needlework. She could do it alright, but deferred to Nancy, who was more skilled in that area.

Sheila got hold of a wedding dress in a sale. It had been reduced because it was a little on the large size for those days of rationing. Together, Sheila and Nancy took it apart, re-styled, and added a beautiful veil and floral head-dress. I still have on my mantelshelf the professionally taken photograph of Sheila in that wedding dress, with lovely wide eyes, film star looks and dazzling smile.

We also decided that we would do the catering ourselves. The dining room at Endymion was large enough to hold all the wedding party, about twenty, with two tables together, covered by Sheila's collection of lace tablecloths and crockery. I'm afraid there was no posh bone china – sacrilegious in the Potteries, but, somehow, we coped. It was a cold buffet and, actually, it was extremely well done.

My brother, Bill, helped enormously with the preparatory work and as the hour approached, Bill and Nancy worked all night to finish the preparations. My mother gave us our wedding present before-hand. I might have forgotten to tell you, but when she was quite young, she spent some time "in service" where she was trained in French cuisine by the Mrs. Bates of the Grand House. The present was a whole ox tongue she had bought from her butcher who had pickled it for some weeks ahead.

I remember the bread at our house from Woods Bakery, a very well-respected baker in Porthill. His bread was the finest I've ever tasted, and he did us proud with a wedding cake. Nancy added her own baked hors d'oeuvres, pastries and also small cakes. A professional caterer couldn't have done better. I have always been so grateful to Bill and Nancy for their wonderful help.

Finances improving

Bill and Nancy grew very close that evening before Sheila and my wedding, and a year later they got married too. That made a great difference financially – we had four salaries from which to pay the rent and general housekeeping.

Things at work went well. The post-war recovery continued, and export sales grew with Bill Bennett, our senior export traveller, completing the first of his many round-the-world trips. He was a great character was Bill. Much older than he looked, very tall and handsome with blonde hair. I would describe him as an archetypal Anglo Saxon. Although he had oodles of charm and a quick wit, academically he was way down the league. But he brought in the business. It was some months after I started to work at H&R Johnson that he finished that trip and I met him. We got on like a house on fire. I was quick with figures and, as Bill put it, I had "fine turn of phrase" when a difficult problem needed explaining to an irate customer.

Unfortunately, or perhaps not – as it turned out all right eventually, Sheila got into a fierce argument with Joan Long, who was what you would call it a senior executive. Joan was engaged to Trevor Warrington, our company secretary, and rather took advantage of the relationship. This didn't faze my wife. Sheila was so happy and smiling, ready to help anybody in difficulties with her quick and able mind. She dealt with everybody the same way be it the chief executive or the office cleaner.

When faced with any hint of injustice she would, in contrast, be extremely fierce and eloquent in her own defence. I cannot remember what the argument was about, but Sheila was adamant. She handed in her notice. This caused consternation with the directors and senior managers. I remember, Trevor Warrington and my boss Bernard Keightley both trying to placate her. Her mind was made up, however, and she left.

Sheila had worked at H&R Johnson from when she left the City School of Commerce in the Wedgwood Institute and the upset at her leaving had made them realise what an asset she was, quick and adaptable with business and with people. On the plus side it gave her an opportunity to hone her skills at different jobs until we had our first baby, Gary, in 1958. She didn't go to work again until our youngest, Edwina, had left school when she was poached from home by H. & R J again.

Moving house

We lived with Bill and Nancy at Endymion until Bill and Nancy bought a new house in Kidsgrove. It was in a new, smart development in what was once Clough Hall Park. Sheila and I wanted to start a family, so we thought we it made long-term financial sense to also get onto the property ladder.

They were building new bungalows in Clough Hall, less than half a mile away from Bill and Nancy's house. Although Sheila and Nancy were so close, that hadn't influenced the decision. The bungalow we chose just happened to be so suitable and we could, with Sheila's careful money management, afford a mortgage. The bungalow had not yet been built, but it didn't take long before we moved in.

The only drawback was that the garden looked more like a building site. It wasn't a large garden, fortunately, but by no means a pocket handkerchief sort of plot. It had a gradual slope up from the back door and a level plot in the front of the house, where I grew a nice little lawn from seed. It was a lot of hard work for me preparing the back-garden. The ground was filled with builder's rubble, and it was heavy work clearing the heavy clay soil.

I bought from the council's building yard some old kerb stones and used these to create a series of steps at the centre, running up to where it levelled out before the back fence. Also, from the council yard, I bought some rockery stone and built a dry-stone retaining wall at the end of the lawn. The level of the lawn was about three feet above the pavement level, so it needed a wall to retain it.

I laboured like Hercules to sort out the garden and when all was ready, planted (with flowers and some salad vegetables at the back).

Our new house was three miles away from H&R Johnson in Tunstall, but there was an excellent bus service. The bus stop was about a quarter of a mile away, so all very handy. I decided we needed more independent means of travel, so that is when we bought the new Lambretta scooter that I mentioned earlier. I bought the scooter from a shop in Tunstall Square. It was a marvellous machine, with fantastic build quality., Its sophisticated transmission, with a fully enclosed gear box and shaft-transmission made it easy to drive and economical. When we travelled any distance, it would cruise, with both Sheila and me aboard, at 50 miles per hour.

I read later that the explosion in Italian light vehicles was an aftereffect of the War. Mussolini's government had invested heavily in developing an air force and an aero manufacturing industry to supply it. That, in turn, needed an expansion in technical education. Italy produced an army of qualified and talented aero designers to meet their strategy. However, it fared badly in the war and at the end there was a collapse of their aero building capacity.

This left an army of highly qualified engineers looking for employment. Some of the firms which previously had been building armaments turned their talents to designing and producing new types of vehicles. They had to be cheaper than cars, as the war-ravaged population couldn't afford them. So, things like the Vespa and Lambretta scooters, and smaller, cheaper cars were turned out into a European market hungry for means of transport. This accounted for the amazing quality of the Lambretta. It served us well for three years until, happy days, Sheila became pregnant with our eldest, Gary.

Before then, Sheila and I had a fortnight's holiday in a rented caravan at Abersoch, at the end of the Lleyn peninsular in North Wales. What an adventure that turned out to be. I bought an AA road atlas and worked out a route. The conventional route was to head northwest to Chester and from there to follow the coast road past Prestatyn, Rhyl, Llandudno, then turn south down the Aberglaslyn Pass from its head, high in the moors, down to Criccieth on the Lleyn Peninsula.

That journey on our sturdy and reliable Lambretta lives on in my memory as the most beautiful and scenic of routes. Down through heavy woodland, all variety of trees in full summer leaf. The road was deserted, and we could enjoy the intervals when, on our left-hand side, we could see the River Glaslyn as we followed its path down the mountain.

When we arrived at Abersoch, we found the caravan we had hired privately from one of Sheila's old school friends. It was more than we expected, smart, immaculate and roomy. The site we were on was called Blackrock Sands. Over the years it has been progressively developed as the up-market resort of Abersoch. With its dolphins, it became an attractive holiday destination for people looking for somewhere more sophisticated than the usual caravan park.

The weather was glorious. We drove around the peninsula on our Lambretta, enjoying the lovely quiet bays along and over the peninsula to the resort of Nefyn on the northern tip. On one of these explorations we found, a little way inland from Llanbedrog, an old people's care home for retired Polish ex-servicemen and their wives. I've searched my memory but can't recall exactly how we found it. Isolated from the nearest village, it stood alone. Perhaps we were looking for directions, however the place had tables and chairs outside in the beautiful weather. Sheila and I were invited to take a seat at one of the tables and helped to a welcome cup of tea.

The old people were so polite, warm and friendly and some spoke quite passable English. Most were ex RAF – I knew from TV documentaries that the Polish fighter pilots had earned themselves outstanding records for their exploits against the Luftwaffe.

It was such an enjoyable experience that in later years, when we brought out children to that part of Wales on holiday, we took them there to re-visit the Poles.

And those children were about to start arriving…

Chapter 6. Starting Our Family

Prelude

My grandchildren today live comfortable lives and drive around in cars that would have been an unbelievable luxury to Sheila and me when we started out together. Here I hope to give you an idea of what life was like as we started our family.

Baby number one

We were loath to part from our Lambretta but sometime after that memorable Abersoch holiday, Sheila became pregnant with our eldest, Gary. A bigger form of transport was going to be needed but a car was outside our reach. We started looking round and then heard from the insurance agent who had insured our scooter for us that he wanted to sell his motorcycle and sidecar in order to buy a car for his growing family.

It was a Velocette 350cc machine with a lightweight single seater sidecar. I tried it out and bought it. Velocette were famed for their quality and our bike certainly lived up to its reputation. I had studied books about vehicle maintenance and repairs from Tunstall Library and had little difficulty in doing all the jobs that were needed to keep our "combination" (the term in those days for a motorcycle and sidecar) on the road.

Our first child, Gary Anthony, was born on 7th July 1958. He was born into a new and very different generation. Sheila and I were children of the war. The conflict and its repercussions had affected so many people, even those who didn't actually serve in the armed forces. Sheila's father, Horace, was called up into the Royal Navy. He passed with the top mark, A1, at the medical fitness examination but, after only a few weeks in the training station, he was taken ill and diagnosed with TB from which he eventually died.

You have to remember that a chasm that existed between our generation and the one that followed. The pace of technology, medicine, social welfare development accelerated and along with them the rate of cultural change. Contraception and sex education were particularly impactful and led enormous social change. Our puritanical morality was rapidly eroded: strict chastity before marriage was no longer the norm.

The freedoms women gained meant that many more of them went out to work. One unforeseen side-effect was a variation on Parkinson's Law: prices rose to meet income. Previously, when wives had stayed at home to care for the children and the house, the family had to survived on the father's wage. However, as time passed and more and more women worked, the wives' earnings were a wonderful uplift to the family wealth and even allowed for a few treats. However, it didn't last. The cost of living simply rose until a double income became almost a necessity in many households.

Sheila and I, however, had been born on the cusp of this social revolution. She was a wonderful and dedicated mother and swore that her children would never be latch-key kids. They would be properly cared for until they reached school leaving age.

In 1958, the year our Gary was born, over a third of all UK births took place at home. This was an increase on previous years. But, as time went on, more and more births were in hospitals or maternity homes. I remember the fat information pack we received from Nurse Webb, the midwife in charge of Sheila's pregnancy and birth. She was a well-known and highly respected member of the Kidsgrove community. We considered ourselves lucky that Sheila was under her care.

Nurse Webb visited Sheila regularly during her pregnancy and coached her in many things, not just the newly developed ideas of natural childbirth, but in general infant care, diet, clothing. She educated us both on how to spot problems before they became serious.

The information pack gave directions on how to prepare the room and bed where the birth would take place and practical advice about hygiene, antisepsis, and the like. The instructions on preparing the bed were detailed: remove all bedding and cover the mattress (double in our case) with three layers of clean newspaper, then three layers of brown paper, followed by an old clean sheet which would be disposed of later.

I won't go into all the details of the birth. Our generation don't generally like to talk about these things. I was impressed by Sheila's sheer guts. It was obviously painful, but she didn't scream or had any sort of performance. However, it was clear after a few hours that there was some sort of problem. Nurse Webb had been called three times after the contractions started and, on the last visit, she exclaimed, "The head is coming, but it is stuck." The top of Gary's head appeared. But to my horror, it was blue-black.

Nurse Webb managed to wriggle her hands further in. "The umbilical cord is round his neck. You," she turned to me, "hold baby's head in position." She then produced a pair of surgical scissors and made a cut to the perinium that opened the birth canal a little wider. We were able to pull the baby out far enough out for Nurse Webb to manoeuvre the scissors around the cord and sever it.

"Made yourself useful then," she said. I remember her removing the afterbirth, wrapping it in layers of newspaper and placing it on the blazing fire we had in the bedroom.

Throughout the whole birth, Sheila had no pain relief. It had not been for want of trying. Two hours in, Nurse Webb had decided it was time Sheila had some gas and air to give her some relief from the pain. Unbelievably, after all the care and effort made in preparing for the birth, the gas and air machine turned out to be faulty. So, Sheila went through the whole experience without any pain relief.

Some hours later, our GP, Dr French, came and stitched up the scissor cut. These stitches should, apparently, be done as soon after the birth as possible when nature's endorphins are supposed to dull the pain. However, once again, not a complaint, wince or whimper from Sheila. She then settled down for a long and well-deserved sleep.

Gary was a big, healthy baby and grew rapidly. He was, however, a colicky baby and suffered long bouts of pain in the nights, drawing his little knees up to his tummy trying to seek relief. Even as he grew into a toddler, colic troubled him on and off until Dr French's younger colleague prescribed the old-fashioned remedy "tincture of belladonna in peppermint". This was a godsend. However, Gary's colic never fully disappeared until he was seven years old and he had his appendix removed. After that, he had no more trouble.

Will we have more than one child?

We had always hoped for more than just one child. Both Sheila and I came from large families, where we both experienced occasional frustrations with our siblings. However, these ups and downs were more than compensated for by the camaraderie of having brothers and sisters around us. We didn't want Gary to be an only child, so we were delighted when, nearly two years after Gary's birth, Sheila became pregnant again.

Unfortunately, she miscarried at three months. She was taken to North Staffs Royal Infirmary for dilatation and curettage and general examinations. She spent a week there and was discharged after being pronounced clear of problems and in good general health. Six months later she had another miscarriage and had to go through the same treatment and overhaul.

When we visited Dr French, our GP at the time, he told us about the report from the hospital. They had ascertained from talking to Sheila, that she had experienced severe morning sickness during the first trimester when she was expecting Gary. However, during the two pregnancies for the miscarriages, she had not been sick at all. This, they felt, supported their view that she had a deficiency in one of the hormones involved in maintaining a pregnancy.

They proposed that in the event of her becoming pregnant again, she would benefit from a course of a hormone product called Primulat Depot. So, when she found she was expecting again, she had to visit Dr French and his able colleague, Dr Hickson, weekly for the required injection.

I remember going with her on these weekly visits. Walking back to Clough Hall, past the park railings, she would be overcome with spasms of nausea and vomiting. She would hang onto the railings retching until the waves passed.

Baby number two

The hormone did the trick. Kevin Michael was born at home, just like his big brother had been. Dr French congratulated Sheila on her successful pregnancy but said kindly, "You have two lovely boys but, in view of your hormone problem, it is doubtful if you will be able to enlarge your family any further."

Kevin was healthy and although slightly colicky to start, he was never as severely afflicted as Gary. Kev was an adorable baby. He was precocious like Gary but not in a physical way. He was a late walker and shuffled around on his bottom until well after his birthday. Just as Sheila and I were getting a little concerned and considering consulting our GP about it, Kevin suddenly got up and walked. None of toddling and tumbling that most babies do. He just up and walked like a three-year-old.

The same with talking. He was obviously bright with a highly developed sense of knowing his own mind, so he created his own sort of sign language, pointing and gesticulating when he wanted something or needed help doing something. Sheila was on his wavelength, so he progressed along happily in his own way until he was two years old. Then, as with his walking, he just began to talk. No baby language: he just talked. We decided he had his own unique approach to life: watching and observing until he had mentally assimilated all that was necessary to behave in a particular way. And then he would just do it.

Baby number three

Because Dr French had told us further children were unlikely, we felt that birth-control precautions were unnecessary and dispensed with them. Soon after, when Kevin was only three months old, we found Sheila was expecting again!

Dr French asked Sheila, "How are you feeling? Are you having morning sickness?" She was, in fact, violently sick – just as she had been with Gary.

The doctor's response was, "Good, carry on. The moment you start feeling better, don't delay, come and see me so I can start treating you!" Sheila's terrible morning sickness continued unabated for three months. But after that, the pregnancy continued without a hitch until the baby was due and contractions started. This time Sheila's labour was so short that the midwife grilled me on the phone when I begged her to come quickly. However, she agreed to come and have a look. Lifting the bed sheet, she exclaimed, "Oh, baby's head is fully out." After, a few moments, our third baby was born. A beautiful, healthy little girl born just a year and two days after Kevin. We named her Edwina Lyn.

She began to cry furiously as soon as the nurse had gone. Our hearts sank at the prospect of another colicky baby. However, I got into bed alongside Sheila and, half sitting, placed Edwina on my chest. She slept the whole night through and thereafter we never had the slightest trouble during her infancy. She was a remarkable baby, seldom crying and never waking to be fed in the night. She slept soundly and throughout her early childhood she was a healthy and extremely energetic little girl.

Chapter 7. Family School Days and Early Careers

Prelude

My mother wasn't keen on education. She felt that "too much learning would addle your brain", and that education past the age of fourteen "wasn't for the likes of us". However, like most parents today, Sheila and I were determined to get the best education possible for our children. But then as it is now, that wasn't necessarily straightforward. Here, I explain how we tried to get the best for our children.

Our children start school

I should retrace our steps to Clough Hall. All three children were born there. They were all born without any pain relief and their childhood was progressing comfortably. Sheila and I discussed education. This was a subject close to Sheila's heart and she was very clear about what she wanted. "All our children are bright and healthy. I want them to have the best education so they can use their talents and get good jobs with a secure financial situation." She continued, "I don't want them to skimp and save their way through life. I want them to be happy at school. I want them encouraged but not crammed."

Clough Hall was in the town of Kidsgrove which was situated in the county of Staffordshire. We knew that the Potteries and Staffordshire in general didn't have an exceptional reputation education-wise. Cheshire, however, was considered to be a better prospect. Also, Sheila had a hankering for Scholar Green, her childhood home. Unfortunately, looking through the property pages in the Sentinel didn't reveal anything suitable for us.

The only property available was a little cottage in a lane called Little Moss, situated between the Macclesfield Canal on one side and the Manchester/London Railway on the other. Not crammed between them but it was a pleasant location. Actually, it was the cottage where Sheila grew up. Although small, it had three compact bedrooms, and we had decided our family was not going to increase. The important thing was it meant access to education. A bidding war followed, cottages were much in demand and after several phone conversations I put in the highest bid of £1,000.

As with our house in Clough Hall, the vogue for central heating hadn't yet arrived. The cottage had coal fireplaces but, because it was small and partly insulated by the adjoining terraced houses, it was comfortable and cosy.

Gary was the first to be enrolled at Scholar Green village Church of England school. It was the actual school where Sheila and her siblings had their early education. A sturdily built little school in the Jacobean style of architecture with a neat asphalt playground on the A34 road to Manchester. It still had the same two classrooms and the same two teachers who had taught Sheila as a child. Miss Mould taught the lower class for children just starting at school and Miss Woodfine taught the follow-on year as well as being the headmistress.

I remember one day, shortly after Gary started at the school, going with Sheila to pick him up near the end of the school day. Miss Mould asked us into the classroom and Miss Woodfine joined us. "Of course, I remember you!" said Miss Woodfine, "and Martin, Leonard, Nancy, Geoffrey and Audrey." She went on, "And yesterday, I came into this classroom and noticed straightaway this young chap sitting at his desk with a reading book, his elbows on the desk and his hands over his ears to keep out the clamour of his classmates. I turned to Miss Mould and said, 'He is an Arrowsmith. His uncle, Martin used to sit exactly like that.' All the Arrowsmiths were known for their outstanding intelligence."

When Kevin started school, he followed his basic style of learning – keeping quiet, watching and observing until he could recognise the name of the game. Then he would suddenly join in as though already experienced. Before he started to school, at only three years old, he would pick up the newspaper and climb onto Sheila's knee with it and demand, "Show me how to read. "I have to read so that I can go to school." So, like Gary before him and Edwina after, he could read a newspaper at four years old.

Unfortunately, it turned out to be bitter-sweet when Kevin started school in Miss Mould's starter class. After Sheila had collected him from that lovely old School, he sat down to his tea. After a while he said to Sheila, "That was good. I've been to school, what do we do next?"

Sheila realised then that in the previous year or more, when he had talked about going to school, he didn't realise it was an on-going business. He had no conception that he was expected to go to school every day except weekends and holidays. It was a rather upsetting moment for all of us when the realisation sank in. Strangely, he hadn't noticed that Gary wasn't at school all day and that he was missing during school hours.

This advanced reading age was something of a problem for all three children. At school, Miss Mould introduced all the children to the educational series for young children. I seem to remember it was called the *Janet and John*. Sheila had already bought the whole series, and all our children had gone way beyond that. They would read the Daily Mail and popular comics like Dandy and the Beano, which we had delivered along with our newspapers.

When Miss Mould realised that Gary had read all the books in her class, she talked to Miss Woodfine and then started him on the "upper class" books. Gary went through those in short order too.. To avoid boredom, the school borrowed other books – from where I never knew – but they managed to satisfy his need for reading until the time came for moving on.

On from infant school

Sheila had been planning ahead and urged me to join in the search for ideas. After Miss Woodfine's class, usually the next step was to attend the junior school at Rode Heath which was a good couple of miles away. Sheila had gone there as a child. There was no such thing as the school bus in those days. She and her brothers and sister walked to school and back along the country lanes, regardless of the weather. She remembered being so bored at Rode Heath School that she was transferred to the village school at Mow Cop which was farther away with steep hills to climb.

Looking further ahead, we looked at options for secondary education. After the eleven-plus examination, if the boys passed, there was only one grammar school for miles around, namely Sandbach Grammar School for boys. We visited the school and discussed things with a helpful teacher. He understood our wanting the children to have a grammar school education and that, as Scholar Green School didn't provide for children over eight, the only possibilities were Rode Heath or Mow Cop.

He made us aware of something at Sandbach School that we hadn't heard of: they had a "junior school" for children for the three years before the eleven-plus. However, it was a "private" school, and we would have to pay for them to attend. If, after their time at the "junior" school, they passed the eleven-plus, they would get priority in getting a place in the grammar school itself. However, failing the eleven-plus meant having to attend a secondary modern school like Rode Heath, or to continuing to pay for their education in the grammar school. It wasn't just a matter of paying for this junior education, there was an entrance examination.

The day of the exam arrived. It was held inside the quite imposing building of Sandbach Grammar School. A colleague of mine at H&R Johnson had a son the same age as Gary who was also taking the exam. It was a two-hour exam. Each boy was examined individually. Gary was called in first. We had an anxious wait as, although we knew Gary had done well at Scholar Green Infant's school, this was his first experience of formal exams. We just hoped that he didn't have any nerves.

To our horror, after an hour, the teacher who had taken him into the exam room came out holding Gary's hand. "I'm so sorry," she said. Our hearts sank. Then she continued, "Gary is bored. He has completed the whole exam, and, for the past half an hour, he has been asking us what is next." I thought Gary must have raced through the exam and not given answers in sufficient depth. We needn't have worried, however. The results were announced at the end of the morning. Gary had passed and my poor colleague's lad had failed.

Two years later, Kevin passed the same exam but with no drama. This was no surprise, because both boys had the same Arrowsmith quick intelligence.

The Junior school at Sandbach was a great success. Both boys enjoyed it except for periods of boredom when covering subjects that they had learned at home. I should stress that they had *learned* not been *taught*. They were avid readers and were able to satisfy their curiosity with books at home.

The eleven-plus came, and both passed and went on to the senior school, in the same building with the same lavish sports grounds and facilities.

We had to face up to the approaching problem with Edwina. After she had passed through Miss Woodfine's second year class, she left the infant's school. As it happened, the education authority had built a completely new school in Scholar Green, for children from starting school age up to age eleven.

Fortunately, Edwina's teacher was a keen young woman, Miss Ashfield. She recognised Edwina's precociousness and, as Edwina had already read all the reading books set for her age group, she borrowed books from the higher classes. There was no problem with maths either. Miss Ashfield was able to get more material for that subject too.

The only problem – if you could call it a problem – with Edwina was a slight speech peculiarity. She had difficulty in pronouncing sibilant sounds and pronounced "s" as "th". This was compounded by her quick speaking and more so when she was excited. Sometimes, at home, even Sheila and I couldn't understand her. The only person who could was Kevin, so we would ask Kevin to translate for us.

I remember one morning, Edwina rushed into the house and said to Sheila and me, "Der gardent full of tluckt"

"The garden is full of slugs," said Kevin nonchalantly.

Edwina's best friend at school, one of the local newsagent's daughters, also had speech difficulties. They were so different from Edwina's that Miss Ashfield and the headmistress didn't believe they were a copycat problem. They recommended speech therapy. Edwina's friend was quickly referred by her GP her to North Staffs hospital.

Sheila was firmly against the idea; another example of her intuition proving to be right, just like so many other times in our life. She was convinced that Edwina would grow out of the problem. "Mark my words," she said, "Susan (Ed's friend) may be helped, but I suspect that being continually being made aware of the mistakes in her speech could have an inhibiting effect. It might improve her speech, but the therapy could have effects that last much longer." Time proved Sheila right. Susan's speech problem improved, almost to the point of disappearing, but she was left with an odd hesitant manner of speaking.

We, or more correctly Sheila, had overcome the problem of getting a grammar school education for the boys. Now Edwina's eleventh birthday was approaching. Sheila searched for the equivalent to Sandbach for girls without success. There was no advanced secondary school in South Cheshire, but there was a school in Stoke, St. Dominic's school for girls. This was what the locals termed "a convent school". It was a Roman Catholic school, but Sheila discovered there was no actual stipulation that students must belong to the Catholic faith.

Sheila resorted to going to see our GP, Roger Raby, and discussed the problem with him. "Roger, Edwina is extremely capable and highly competitive. I suspect she feels at a disadvantage to her brothers, and she won't be satisfied with the next school lined up for her, Rode Heath Secondary School. I fear she will feel this disadvantage for a long time."

Roger sympathised with our problem and wrote to the local education authority for Cheshire expressing his concerns that there was a strong possibility that this lack of opportunity could affect the mental health of his young patient. The result of Roger's kind intervention was a letter confirming that, providing she passed her eleven-plus, Edwina would be accepted at St. Dominic's.

Our family doctor

At this point I must record how fortunate we were to have Roger both as a GP and a family friend. As a GP, he didn't look the part. He was a big man, though athletically built, with large, strong, features and the largest hands I have ever seen on anyone. He was good with these hands; his hobbies were practical things like carpentry and iron-work. He responded to friendly jokes about his size, "I think I would have preferred being a blacksmith to being a doctor."

As a doctor, he always listened carefully to what we had to say before carrying out any examination (except in an emergency). He spotted things that the hospital people had not noticed. For example, as I already explained, a paediatrician had diagnosed Edwina's motion sickness as a form of migraine, saying she would grow out of it at puberty. When she started with appendix pains, Roger had examined her and called an ambulance. But it was Roger who alerted her surgeon that there was something unusual about this appendicitis. And perhaps it was that that caused the surgeon to find and remove that benign tumour.

Roger was a family friend because his two children went to the same village school as ours and, in the early days, Sheila or I would meet him and other parents outside the school to collect the children. As I have already mentioned, Roger was a keen and talented Badminton player. And Sheila, who before we were married was a mean tennis player, also got involved in Scholar Green and Rode badminton clubs. With Roger's and Sheila's talents, the club was promoted at the end of the season to the next level in the county league. This happened again the next year and again the following year. Sheila was invited to play for the county but declined. Family commitments came first.

Roger was a popular figure in the community. He always played the part of Father Christmas at the yuletide fair, held in the village hall. I remember when Kevin was about four years old waiting in line to get his little Christmas gift from Father Christmas. When he arrived at the head of the queue, we could hear his loud clear voice, "That isn't Father Christmas. It's Dr Raby. Look at his big hands." Very little got past Kevin and, as always, he was prepared to make his views known.

Sheila's ear

I talked earlier about Sheila's stoicism in the face of pain. She was to be put to the test again when she suffered a series of abscesses in her left ear during the years when the children were at school. She had been deaf in that ear since infancy. It had started when she was a toddler with a bad cold which lingered and developed into a secondary, bacterial infection. This was years before the development of antibiotics, so the infection spread to the inner ear and became a chronic condition.

Years later, when we were married, she had a repeat of these painful abscesses in her ear. It got so bad that she was referred to an ENT consultant at North Staffs Infirmary. He had a reputation of dealing with stubborn conditions and took a keen interest in Sheila's problems. (You will notice that I refer them as "problems" – it was many years later that the movers and shakers in our society introduced the word "issues". It had the effect of minimising problems so complaints often could be taken less seriously.)

Mr. Kapur, who was the ENT surgeon in question, recommended an operation. We agreed, not knowing just how bad the problems were. Sheila, after the surgery, spent a week in the hospital heavily drugged with pain killers with huge wound dressings over her left ear.

After a further week in hospital, she was allowed home. Mr. Kapur said he would like to follow up her case and would we call at his home in the Westlands, Newcastle-under-Lyme. In the manner of some upper-caste Indians, he had a peremptory manner. He opened the door to us with, "Take off your shoes." and we followed him along a thick cream Indian carpet.

After a while, he explained that the operation had been complicated. The underlying condition had been going on since childhood. The ear drum and the ossicles (the tiny hammer, staple and anvil bones in the ear) had rotted after being soaked in a chronic infection for years. The infection had also spread to the mastoid process, the bone behind the outer ear.

During the operation he had cleaned out inside her ear and opened and drained the mastoid. Then, he had replaced the ear drum with one grafted from tissue elsewhere in the ear. After that he had implanted a set of artificial ossicles. The procedure was successful in that she never had a repeat of the ear infections. However, he hadn't been able to fully restore the hearing in her left ear. But Sheila was no longer stone deaf in it. She could pick up indistinct sounds only, but this helped with her ability to sense the direction of sound sources.

Gary at grammar school

Gary did well at school, particularly in the sciences. Maths, physics and chemistry were his favourites. He had no problems with homework. He sat down after his evening meal and did it in pretty short time.

Gary also enjoyed music. We bought him a good acoustic guitar and paid for private lessons with a lady in Newcastle-under-Lyme who was well known by the staff at Sandbach. However, after a few months, when we collected Gary from her house she said, "I'm sorry but Gary has gone through my entire range of theory and techniques. He is extremely talented, and he needs and deserves somebody beyond me who can take him further."

After our chat, she came back to us a few days later with the name and address of a retired jazz musician, Mr Lancaster, who was interested to hear about Gary's talent. He was prepared to take him on. When we called to pick him up from his home, the musician asked us if we would mind if Gary could stay for an extra hour, without charge. He explained that he and Gary were enjoying a jam session, and it was a long time since the teacher, who had retired from his professional musical career, had the opportunity to enjoy a free and easy jazz session where both could improvise. "Gary is extremely talented," he said. "He could make a successful career in it."

We needn't have feared about music interfering with Gary's love of science. He made it clear that he was making the sciences his priority. Although, that was to change later.

Kevin at grammar school

Kevin's schooling turned out to be different. He had always been a precocious child with an extremely quick wit. He sailed through the junior school entrance exam, like Gary had done, and went on to easily pass his eleven-plus. He also did well at the senior school, and he cropped a high number of highly rated results in his O-levels.

As he went on to study for his A-levels, we were a bit surprised on the annual school visit, when his form master said, "Kevin is extremely intelligent. He did remarkably well with his O-levels, which he achieved largely by 'native wit'. I'm afraid, however, that won't be the case with his A-levels unless he knuckles down and works hard at his studies."

He was right in a way. Kevin worked at things that came easily to him. His A-level results were low, not enough to earn him a place at a good university. Paradoxically, because he had a flair for languages and enjoyed them, He studied Latin and got the highest grade possible. He just loved the logic and mental discipline that Latin required.

Ed at grammar school

Travel to school was no problem for the boys: Cheshire Council provided a school bus for pupils attending Sandbach School. In Edwina's case, we were anxious about transport. St. Dominic's stood at the top of Hartshill, near the North Staffs Infirmary. Hartshill was on the road from the town of Stoke to Newcastle-under-Lyme. She had to travel by train from Kidsgrove Station to Stoke-on-Trent Station. She caught the bus from Scholar Green to Kidsgrove. Our concerns about the train journey were eased when it turned out that there was a crowd on St. Dominic's girls joining Edwina on the train every day.

Edwina was always a supremely self-confident and capable child. But, despite this, Sheila and I did actually have some concerns about how Edwina would fit in with the disciplines of a convent school. And, on the other hand, how a convent school would be able to handle such a supremely confident and self-willed girl. We needn't have worried. Ed loved the convent school and, after she left school, she said to me that the nuns were the only people who could properly discipline her with actually no harsh practices.

The head mistress, Sister Mary Edward, was quite a character. Without any exaggeration, she stood only four foot six inches tall, always in full clerical habit. A gentle smile and a quiet voice hid an iron authority. She set the tone for the whole school. I remember when the time for leaving school arrived, and the arts (lay) teacher organised a concert to be performed by the school leavers.

The evening culminated in a musical revue by a selection of girls. Sheila and I were innocently unaware of the preparations for the finale. It ended with a group of girls dressed and coiffured in the 1930's style.

The music started for this finale: it was the orchestral backing for a Shirley Bassey number. Then, to my horror, Edwina appeared centre stage, dressed in a slinky full length black, shoulderless evening dress, wearing a Gainsborough hat and evening gloves, elbow length.

She was singing *Big Spender* in the style of Shirley Bassey. As she sang, she slowly slipped off a glove and, after whirling it once around her head, she flung it into the audience. I never found out whether the nun's had previewed the performance or were, like me, watching in sheer suspense wondering what was the follow the glove. I was sitting some way to the side and behind the teachers and nuns on the front row. They sat with stony faces throughout.

Medicine and music

Meanwhile Gary after some searching, he found a university that suited him. He chose Nottingham, not only for its excellent reputation, but because it had a more rural campus on the outskirts of the city. He was always a bit of a country boy having been brought up in the village of Scholar Green. Sheila and I took him to London to visit St. George's Hospital and the Royal Free Hospital, both of which had famous medical schools, but found the city environment stifling. Also, when Sheila took him to see Leeds University, he disliked the crowded tower blocks everywhere.

So, Gary went to Nottingham and enjoyed his medical studies. He came home for a weekend occasionally and brought with him a load of washing, including his lab clothes worn during his dissection of cadavers and stinking of formaldehyde. He carried on and obtained a good degree in Medical Sciences. However, he had exhausted his enthusiasm for medicine and decided he wouldn't go on to the next stage, the long course that would culminate in him qualifying as a medical doctor.

By this time Kevin had finished at Sandbach School. He went to stay for a while with Gary at the nice flat he had taken after his first year at Nottingham. The boys were always close and during that stay they cooked up a scheme to form a group and try out performing music. They found a drummer and started.

Gary bought a good PA amplifier, and I put my lessons at evening classes to work on building him some heavy cabinets from a professional set of drawings to house the speakers he had obtained. I also made a wooden reel with sockets and a good length of cable to set up on stage.

I'm sure they enjoyed themselves enormously and the experience introduced them to the world of entrepreneurship. They hired a studio and produced an LP record, doing everything themselves from writing the songs and music to even designing the extremely smart album cover with its striking image of a great white shark. It eventually came to the attention of John Peel of the BBC who played it repeatedly on his radio program.

I'm not sure exactly how it all ended. I remember they found the business side of the enterprise demanded more time and money. If they wanted to make inroads into the music market, they would need capital.

Kev seemed unhappy at this turning point. He had been reflecting on his academic career which had been put on the back burner, so to speak. Eventually, he decided he would get himself a university degree. After a two years gap after his disappointing A-level results, he looked for a course that would interest him and should be straight forward without too many special skills.

Sociology and socialising in Hungary

He chose Nottingham University's psychology and sociology course and eventually got a good degree. Talking to me years afterwards, he said he found psychology not to be so useful as a practical career tool. Sociology, on the other hand, was a complete surprise. It fascinated him, and apart from its sheer interest, it turned out extremely useful when he took up a career in sales and marketing.

At the end of his course at Nottingham, the university announced their annual exchange visit for graduates to spend a month with a university in Hungary. They had links with this university going back for decades. The university was in Debrecen, a large city on the far eastern side of Hungary on the border with Romania. Kevin, relieved from the pressures of his studies, enjoyed the visit enormously. He found some great and interesting characters in Hungary.

It wasn't long before, at one of the regular musical events there, that he met Andrea, to whom he has now been married for many years. I think it was *coup de foudre* as the French say about "love at first sight". They became inseparable. Andrea took Kevin to their family home in Szolnok, a pretty city on the Riva Tisza in the centre of Hungary. Sadly, they had to part when Kevin returned to the UK.

Kevin came home to stay with us for a while. Andrea had a lot of end-of-term vacation, so she and Kevin arranged for her to come and stay with us for a month. As soon as we saw Andrea, it was obvious they were well matched. Andrea had the same quick intelligence as Kevin and shared his taste in music, politics and life in general. She returned to Debrecen at the end of the month.

We learned that they would like to get married. There was an obstacle, however. Kevin had graduated from Nottingham University with a good degree in sociology. Andrea, who had started her university course at the same time as Kevin, was now only halfway to her final examinations. This was because Hungary, at that time, was a communist country and was heavily controlled by the authorities in Moscow.

The Russian education system was a fine one, contrary to the popular opinions in this country. They were progressive in many areas. For example, they recognised that throughout the world the English language dominated many fields. So Russia decided to fit in. The science subjects, for all students from the age of eleven, were all taught in English and the textbooks were printed in English too.

And the excellent education standards meant that Andrea's course was longer than Kevin's and had not yet completed. This meant that, if Andi wanted to leave Hungary, she would lose the opportunity to graduate in her chosen subjects – predominantly linguistics.

Kevin's reaction on learning this was, "Don't worry, I've got my degree. I'll move to Hungary while you finish your education." He was confident that he would find a way to earn a living."

From playing music to selling medicine

Gary was hoping to find a source of short-term finance so he could take his music business further. He applied to a number of recruitment agencies. He wanted a job that would pay well so he could build up some capital. For example, he considered a stint working on an oil rig which, because of its privations, was extremely well paid.

He wasn't successful at that – it turned out to be over-qualified. The agencies all kept on at him saying that, with his degree, he would be snapped up in an instant by a pharmaceutical company which were eager to recruit salespeople at that time.

Gary agreed eventually and, to his utter surprise, found he was very good at selling. He worked first for a small German company called Sanol Schwarz and rapidly progressed to Regional Sales Manager. At an off-site training course at Lane End in Buckinghamshire, he met his future wife, Karen. By one of those coincidences in life, he and Karen now live about a mile from the conference centre where they met.

Gary took to business like a duck to water. He joined the (then) large American pharma company Smith Kline and French, where he climbed rapidly through the ranks. Then, a vacancy for a General Manager of their large Saudi Arabian business arose.

Cutting short a long story, after three years in Riydh with Karen and their two children, they had accrued a handy nest egg. This was because of their wise financial outlook, aided enormously by the fact there wasn't much you could spend your money on in Saudi. So, he and Karen decided it was time to return to the UK.

Gary didn't move straight back into business. Instead, he took a year out to take an MSc in Management via a Sloan Fellowship at London Business School coming top of his class. Then, he secured a job as Head of Global Marketing at the respiratory medicines pharma company, Fisons.

After that, he became Director of Marketing at a biotech company, British Biotech. He laid all the plans for the launch of their drugs in development. But development was delayed, and Gary used the time to plan for him and Karen to launch their own business.

Eventually, British Biotech's development compounds failed completely. He and Karen used his payoff and their savings from Saudi to found a pharmaceutical forecasting and pricing agency.

From school straight into banking

Edwina didn't pursue an academical path. With her vigorous, adventurous spirit, she wanted to grab the world by the scruff of its neck. She got good grades in her O-levels but opted to leave at sixteen years old. She had the same gift for maths and a logical outlook as the boys. They all resembled Sheila in that. I like to think they got their aptitude for art, music and literature from me.

There was another set of abilities that I think the children inherited from both of us – performance skills. Sheila had been an enthusiastic member of the amateur dramatics society in Scholar Green called "The Rode Players" and, later, she coaxed me into joining. Presumably, the name came from their patronage from the baronet at Rode Hall, located in a beautiful area mid-way between Scholar Green and Rode Heath. Unforgivably, I can't remember the name of the notable residents at Rode Hall, but the Players were fortunate in having their support and that of the local church, Odd Rode Church, which provided places for rehearsals and to store scenery, props, etc. I remember well the one-time rector who was a keen dramatist and loved to participate on-stage and off.

However, I digress. Back to Edwina.

She gave a lot of thought about a possible career path. She decided, with her aptitude for maths and her love of interacting with people, that banking would be a good outlet for her. She set to with a will applying for jobs. It was a time when the country was going through one of its intermittent recessions, so jobs were scarce. It was a very difficult time for school leavers. It was in an age when home computers were a distant dream, so Edwina wrote her letters in clear longhand, every single letter. She wrote to each of the banks in our region within a radius of twenty miles. She wrote not only to the banks' regional offices, but also to every single branch.

129

After what seemed an age, she was called in to the nearest branch of Barclays, which was in Kidsgrove. The manager was impressed by her character and set her on.

Many years later, I was at a function held by local employers. That was when, after a period of relative prosperity, the country had sunk into yet another recession. I was at a later stage in my career – which I'll come onto later – when I was setting up a new project to support school leavers in gaining employment. I found myself chatting to the one-time manager of Kidsgrove Barclays. He was pleased to meet me and told me the story behind Edwina's start in banking.

Apparently, he was at a meeting with the branch managers from Barclays for miles around. They were discussing the unemployment crisis for young people. One manager showed them an excellent letter they had received from a young girl, keen to get started in the banking business. Another manager recognised the letter – he had received the same letter, and others chimed in saying they had received the same letter too.

The Kidsgrove manager was so struck by Edwina's determination and keenness in starting in the banking world that, even though he hadn't actually got a vacancy at that stage, he offered her a job. A decision he never forget because Edwina had steadily risen through the ranks, working at different branches including a ten-year spell in their Cardiff branch. She studied at home and passed her banking exams followed by further promotions until she became a regional director for the whole north London stock-broker service.

A major re-organisation of the whole of Barclays should have given her an opportunity for an even higher appointment. However, this was before the days of "#Me Too". A lack of opportunities for women and the glass ceiling for female employers prevented further progress.

Edwina opted to take early retirement. With her pay-off, she decided to join her husband, Kelvin, who was a self-employed work process consultant. They don't have children but enjoy their work together, undertaking many extremely interesting projects in this country and abroad.

Chapter 8: Recollections on Married Life

Prelude

Every family faces its travails. Although society and technology were so different in our day, I think many of the challenges Sheila and I faced were not so very different to those that married couples face today.

Houses

As I was typing up these notes, I began to recall the different houses we've lived in. We lived in a total of nine different houses including our first home, Endymion, and our final home here in Grosvenor Avenue, Alsager.

Financially it has been a good thing. Since we were married, property prices have outstripped the cost of living. On each of our moves we made a profit and, in most cases, moved to more expensive properties. The motivation for the moves varied. A number of our moves were driven by Sheila's "itchy feet", as one estate agent remarked.

The first move from Endymion was motivated by our – mainly Sheila's – desire to own our own property. We were happy at Endymion. It was a very respectable area. The house was sound and warm. We had good neighbours and, a bonus that it was within walking distance from our workplace in Tunstall. In bad weather we would take a bus. But Sheila wanted us to own our own house. She considered it a non-investment to pay rent.

At the beginning of our married life, I managed the money, arranged a bank account and a savings account with the TSB (Trustees Savings Bank) which paid a fairly good rate of interest. I became increasingly aware, though, of Sheila's quick intelligence and thinking ability. We progressed to working together on keeping the accounts and budgeting.

Gradually, Sheila took over. She had, from the outset, handled the housekeeping. (And I told you earlier about how she allocated money to individual envelopes for each of the tradesmen who needed paying.)

After three years at Endymion, we learned of a new housing development at Kidsgrove. Like Endymion it was still in Staffordshire. They were building on Clough Hall Estate. This was a large area which had previously been the land belonging to Clough Hall, long demolished. It was just outside the centre of Kidsgrove, next to the well-kept public park.

We had a meeting with the agent for the developers and chose a detached bungalow, with two bedrooms and a boxroom (big enough for a child). It hadn't been built yet, but we put down a deposit after securing a mortgage. When the bungalow was ready and completely decorated by the builders, we moved in.

We carpeted it and furnished it out of our savings, no hire-purchase or other debt (except the mortgage of course – an unavoidable method of financing).

The house had a coal fireplace in each room, except the boxroom. In the kitchen we had our first gas cooker. This was a boon after Endymion, where Sheila cooked everything on the coal fired kitchen range, which had an oven built into the side of the fireplace. The only drawback was that the building site of a garden, and I related earlier how I channelled so much youthful energy to sorting that out.

Then Sheila became pregnant with Gary. She worked for only a few more months before retiring from work. I described earlier Sheila's determination that our children would never be latch-key kids.

Our little bungalow was well built, so, when the fires were lit and kept burning, it was a warm enough. The fires went out at bedtime; coal was so expensive we didn't keep them burning all night. Gary, as I said earlier, was a colicky baby, and would spend hours in my pyjamas, carrying him about the bedroom. He was well-wrapped, fortunately, because during the cold spells the windows would ice over.

Transporting the little ones

Anybody reading this will have to excuse me bragging about Sheila's abilities. If I thought she was a wonderful wife, she turned out to be an even more wonderful mother. Kevin and Edwina, born just year apart were more like twins, so it made sense we should buy a twin pushchair. Sheila insisted, however, that we find a tandem model. She had seen mothers with the side-by-side models, and she could see they were clumsy and awkward to get through shop doorways and up and down steps.

Before his fourth birthday, we had bought Gary a small, two-wheeled bike. He was so quick and adaptable. In no time at all I had removed the little out-rigger wheels intended to be a learning aid. We bought him a little white plastic helmet. We couldn't find a proper safety helmet to fit a child, but we thought the plastic would offer some protection. In the event he never had a crash.

Each week, Sheila made the trip to visit my parents in Middleport. The children really enjoyed this. She would set off with Kevin in the rear section of the pushchair, Edwina in the front where she could be easily reached by Sheila. She walked to Kidsgrove Station, which was in between Clough Hall and the centre of Kidsgrove. Gary would be cycling carefully along with them.

Sheila told me how much fun it was for all three of them to climb into the train. They were all compartments in those days. The open carriages hadn't been developed yet. There was always a friendly, helpful porter available to help Sheila lift the pushchair onto the carriage. Quite often, when there wasn't a completely empty compartment to hold the four of them and the pushchair, the porter would suggest they might like to travel in the guard's van. There were seats for Sheila and Gary and plenty of room for the pushchair. Strangely, she was never asked to pay extra for the pushchair.

After the (steam) train chuffed its way out of Kidsgrove Station, it was only a short distance before it entered the Harecastle Tunnel. This tunnel was three miles long, burrowed through the big escarpment that surrounded the Stoke-on-Trent valley. Children were always excited by the tunnel, the sudden darkness on a bright sunny day and the muffled sound of the engine reflected from the tunnel wall. The tunnel ended a few miles before Longport Station. The pushchair and passengers were unloaded and set off to walk to Middleport, a distance of exactly one mile.

"Those were the days" the song goes. We were at the start of an era when the economy boomed. Businesses grew and with some of them, their profits. The trade union movement also grew in strength which all meant that wages increased to the point where, to stave off strikes, some industries found efficiencies to enable them to assuage the union demands. These efficiencies were found in some cases by automating some operations. Others were found by simply reducing staff so that the same wage pot could be used to pay fewer people. H&R Johnson's management adept at doing this. This, in my view, has resulted in the current situation where costs are being contained by avoiding the use of labour. Many firms won't employ staff to man the telephones, so customer service suffers. Some firms even remove any reference to telephone numbers and e-mail addresses from their documentation.

Sorry for the digression into an old man's rant about modern efficiency.

Passing sports interests

Our little house-hold's prosperity grew, and we could afford the boys' education and demands for sports kit etc. And our children toyed with a number of sports.

I recall the sudden rise in popularity of judo. All three children were attracted to it, perhaps because of the character of the Shaolin monk cplayed by David Carradine in the Kung Fu TV series

We found a club in Tunstall. All three children were enrolled, and we bought them the required outfits, even a tiny one for Edwina. They enjoyed it, but, like children generally, their enthusiasm didn't last long. Gary was the last to lapse, but not before he had become quite proficient at the sport. This served to be an asset in his teen years.

Gary's enthusiasm had shifted to music, and I have mentioned elsewhere how he progressed at it.

Kevin played football in the playing field at Scholar Green. He was a joy to watch. His natural poise, speed and accuracy made him a popular playmate. One of the adults watching him said, "He plays like a miniature Franz Beckenbauer", the famous German player.

Children's enthusiasms wax and wane, and Kevin had a friend at school whose father played golf at Astbury Golf Club. Kevin was invited to learn there, and he so impressed the club professional that they offered to take him on without fees so his natural talents could be taken further. Fortunately, in my view, his enthusiasm for golf also waned. I had read about youngsters being coached in sports like swimming when it virtually takes over their lives. Sheila and I didn't like the thought of that. We didn't interfere, we allowed his keenness to fade until he left the club.

Edwina, horses and health

Edwina was very fond of animals. A family friend at Lawton Heath End had a number of horses and gave riding lessons to youngsters. We took Edwina along to see the horses and she was delighted. She started lessons when she was only five and took to it quite quickly. Her tutor was impressed by her natural ability. She was, apparently, sitting the pony like an adult, using stirrups and reins in a completely relaxed way.

After a few weeks, she had progressed to jumping her pony over small barriers. We were hesitant about her progressing to full jumping. Sheila's intuition was strongly against it. It so happened that we had to withdraw her from horse riding. She developed motion sickness when she was on a horse, and after only a short time in the saddle the sickness began. She was so disappointed. At that early age she had difficulty in understanding how a horse's motion could make her ill.

She took after Sheila in that way. In later years, crossing the channel on our car holidays she was so sick that on one occasion, in a gale, she was taken into the sick bay, injected with anti-emetics and kept in bed until some time after we had docked.

We took Edwina to the GP who couldn't find why any sort of travelling brought on bouts of vomiting, so he referred her to a paediatrician. The problem wasn't life limiting, and the paediatrician thought it was a form of migraine. "It sometimes manifests itself in a different form from the usual headaches," she said. "As she reaches puberty, she will probably grow out of it."

A few years later, Edwina developed a severe tummy ache, so we called out our GP. I am jumping ahead a little here and by that time we had moved to Scholar Green and our GP was Roger Raby. Roger lived at his surgery in Scholar Green and was a family friend. By that time Sheila had relaxed a little about caring so closely for the children. They were older now and had developed extremely capable life skills. Sheila and Roger were in Scholar Green's badminton club. Always keen to participate rather than just watch a sport, Sheila became quite a good player. More about that later.

Roger came to our house and examined Edwina. "It is appendicitis," he said. "I am definite about that, but there is something different about it. I don't know exactly what it is, but we have to get her to hospital quickly."

A short time after we made the 999 call, an ambulance took Edwina to the North Staffs Infirmary. She had the operation the same day. "Everything in order now," her surgeon said. "But there was a small, benign tumour. Removal was straightforward and she should recover quickly." She did and, curiously, just as with Gary's colic, Edwina's motion sickness "migraine" improved to the point of almost disappearing. If she had a rough sea trip, she was seasick but not violently. It was at the level of most sea passengers. At puberty the paediatrician's prediction proved correct so no more health worries.

Ed and dancing

I previously related how Edwina had to give up her horse riding because of motion sickness. It was then that Sheila found Edwina an alternative hobby which involved learning a physical skill without the sort of motion which would affect her like the pony riding. She discovered the Lynne Cox School of Dance. Lynne held lessons in the Alsager Institute, near to the library. Sheila enrolled her for all three dance types that Lynne offered, namely ballet, folk dancing, and tap dancing.

Edwina loved all three. She would practice at home from time to time. Lynne had not required this, but Edwina was enthusiastic about it all. We bought her the necessary kit – not a lot as was the case with some sports: a leotard, ballet shoes, and tap-dancing shoes with steel plates at toes and heels. By that time, our house had fitted carpets which were unsuitable for tap dancing, so I fashioned a stout plywood board that she placed on the kitchen floor and gave the best sound "feedback" for her when tap-dancing.

We were going through early teens with all three at this time. The boys were as thick as thieves when creating games and activities. They mischievously had a way of "aggravating" Edwina by surreptitiously pointing at her. At the dining table, they would hold their knife with their forefinger stretched forward while smiling at Edwina. The result was that Edwina would protest angrily, "They're pointing at me, Mum."

She soon, however, found a highly effective revenge: tap dancing. The "tap,tap,tap" would reverberate throughout the house, and she would pointedly grin at the boys as she danced. This had the effect of winding them up until they claimed it was interfering with their homework. It was reduced to more reasonable lengths of practice, fortunately. Oh. the joys of having teenagers!

Edwina was enthusiastic about dancing, and we feared she might emulate one of her schoolmates, who also studied under Lynne Cox. She qualified as an entrant to the "Ballet Rambert" and went away to study at their college in Manchester. Sheila and I never either encouraged or discouraged her about this. We just kept our fingers crossed that she would pursue a normal course of education. She did. St. Dominic's was a perfect school for her. She was happy there until she left at sixteen. Then began her long career in banking.

Children's health problems

Gary had a problem with his eyes. Edwina had the motion sickness abdominal migraine. Kevin had nothing other than the occasional cough or cold.

Sheila first noticed Gary's eyes when he was only five months old. She took him to Dr French who examined him. His response was, "It is

137

too early to tell if he has a problem. Babies' eyes don't settle down until well after they are six months old. Don't become over-anxious about it."

That evening Sheila and I discussed the matter. I shared Sheila's concerns about Gary's eye. Anybody other than his parents would not notice it. It was discernible only occasionally and was difficult to describe. It looked as though one eye was almost imperceptibly smaller than the other. We both felt he should be referred to a specialist. This presented problems with the NHS. We didn't believe we could compel Dr French to refer him. The other alternative was to pay privately for his examination and probable treatment.

By then, we were both determined, so we went together to see Dr French. We told him of our utter conviction that things weren't normal and asked if he would refer Gary to the consultant surgeon, Mr. Murray. (I had already researched and found people who gave us good reports about being treated by him.)

So, after a couple of weeks, we were in Mr. Murray's chambers in Newcastle-under-Lyme. As soon as he clapped eyes on Gary he said, "He has a slight "convergent" squint. This is fortunate. The other type of squint is a "divergent" squint, where they eye is looking outwards rather than, as with Gary, looking towards his nose. It is not uncommon and, when he is a few years older, we can carry out an operation to correct it. Before then he will need glasses (spectacles) with a special lens covering the 'good' eye. This is necessary because, if the squint is neglected, the affected eye can become a lazy eye and lead to its blindness. Thank you for being so observant and acting promptly. I shall write to Dr French telling him not to delay when confronting this problem, no matter how young the patient."

I then turned to the question of finances. "Can you give us an idea of how much all this will cost us?"

"Don't worry," he said. "I shall send you my bill for this private consultation. But any subsequent treatment will be carried out by the NHS. It doesn't make much difference to me; the NHS will pay me the same as you would." I can't remember how much his bill was. It wasn't cheap, but we paid it with a great sense of relief.

By this time, Gary was nine months old. Mr. Murray referred him to the hospital optician, and he was given his first pair of spectacles. The spectacles and the hospital treatment were both free. In those days, the rising cost to the government in running the NHS. had not yet forced them to introduce charges for prescriptions and things like spectacle frames. (The lenses were subject only to the prescription fee.)

Gary was so good about his glasses. He wore them without any complaint. The hospital optician was amazed on subsequent visits that he'd not thrown them away or broken them like other infants. When he started school, Gary said to Sheila, "The other boys keep calling me 'specky four eyes'. Why?"

"They call you that because they don't have a pair of smart blue glasses like you. Just ignore them.", she replied. Her advice worked; his indifference to their remarks caused them to die away and we had no further problems.

Later, the hospital explained to us that it was to be expected that a child with a squint would tend to use his other eye more than the affected one. This would cause the affected eye to become "lazy" which, if allowed to continue, would result in the loss of sight in that eye. The technique for dealing with this was to apply a sticking plaster over the good eye to force the "lazy eye" to work harder to restore sight. After a couple of months with his left eye covered, the right eye had recovered to normal forward vision.

Unfortunately, his left eye now had a slight squint. The optician explained that this was normal and, unfortunately the procedure had to be repeated to restore the focus of the left eye. This reversed the situation to our initial problem. The right eye had, again, a slight squint. This procedure was repeated. Each time the squinting eye recovered more quickly until at the end of this regime, at home we removed the patch from the latest eye to be covered.

As we did this Gary said, with some surprise in his voice. "Oh, I can see two Daddies." I found this a heart-breaking had great difficulty not bursting into tears. Gary was so very good about the whole series of treatments. By this time, he was still only four years old, and we were anxious about the next stage in treatment.

This time he was examined by Mr. Murray who told us, "He is now at the stage where we can operate."

So, it wasn't long before he was admitted to the Haywood Hospital in Tunstall. In those days, North Staffordshire was one of the country's major coalfields. There were so many miners suffering from nystagmus, called locally, the miners' blindness, and industrial injuries from this hazardous occupation that the Haywood was largely reserved for their treatment.

I have no words to describe how brave and composed Gary was about the whole business. He listened, and obviously understood, Mr. Murray's explanations, and he was calm and collected when he was admitted to the special "optical" ward. He understood the explanations that, after the operation, his eyes would be bandaged over for a few days. Gary was the only child on that ward full of injured or blinded miners.

It was a harrowing for Sheila and I waiting for news. We were allowed to visit Gary the day after the operation. He lay in his hospital bed, his head covered with bandages. The miners had sort of adopted him and were constantly visiting his bedside laughing and joking with him and generally supporting him.

The miners came to us when we entered the ward. "He is such a wonderful lad. He hasn't complained a jot."

Two days later, his eyes were uncovered. They looked fine. And he could see normally! He was discharged to out-patient status, and we said goodbye to the miners who had been so good to him.

At his next out-patient visit, we were told that the operation had been a partial success. The registrar was very good in explaining the situation. "Dealing with a squint means shortening fibres in the small muscles that hold the eye during its movement. We have to err on the side in shortening them too little rather than too much. Too much can result in the eye squinting outwards (called 'wall eyed') and that is very difficult to deal with. There is another factor which the lay man is usually unaware of, that the mechanism of the eyes is linked, mechanically and neurologically. This means that to correct a squint we sometimes can operate on either one of the eyes to correct things. In

Gary's case we want to operate, now, on his left eye to add to the compensating measure we have taken on his right eye."

To cut a long story short, this meant a repeat spell in the Haywood Hospital. The second operation cured the squint but, they explained, he would need special lenses for his glasses for a while from then on.

While we are focussing on medical matters, I must mention the next hospitalisation: Kevin. With all three of our children Sheila was determined to breast-feed them. Unfortunately, it turned out to be increasingly painful for her. However, she was determined they should benefit from the colostrum before switching to the bottle. Each time the doctor prescribed tablets to dry up the milk supply. Later, we went through the same rigmarole when Edwina was a couple of weeks old.

Unfortunately, I had an accident with Sheila's medicine bottle. I had placed it on the mantle shelf above the fireplace while I checked the safety guard surrounding the fireplace. We had not invested in the conventional mesh-guard which was like a wire-mesh bowl stood in front of the fire grate. Instead, I had bought a well-built guard made of chain link fencing. This was like a rectangular box which surrounded the whole fireplace, including the hearth. I had screwed eye bolts in the wall to hook it in place. Kevin was in the process of trying to walk and he was shuffling along on his bottom. He was amazingly fast in his movements.

As he approached the fireguard, I hurriedly placed the bottle on the fire-place surround while I checked the guard was securely hooked in place. I accidentally knocked the bottle, and its contents of milk-withdrawal tablets spilled onto the hearth rug. With his characteristic speed Kevin was onto them like lightening. He must have thought they were sweets. Looking back now, I'm convinced that he hadn't swallowed any. I had swooped down and swept them up and into the bottle.

Being an over-anxious parent, I couldn't be absolutely sure that Kevin hadn't swallowed any, and I imagined I saw his jaw moving. I immediately rang 999. The paramedics were there in no time. The ambulance must have been in the neighbourhood when the call went through. They wrapped our wriggling one-year old in a blanket and whisked him off to North Staffs Royal Infirmary.

A telephone call later, "We've given him a stomach-pumping. Nothing injurious found, but we shall keep him in over-night for observation."

Next day I visited the hospital. Kevin was in a cot. Standing with his hands on the top rail and jumping up and down happy as Larry, pointing to a box of toys he wanted to get his hands on.

The doctor said, "He's fine. He hasn't cried or complained. I think he's enjoyed the experience."

So, parental anxiety assuaged, I took him home to Sheila.

The only other emergencies were Gary's and Edwina's appendicitis episodes.

Moving for better education.

The children were growing, and my job was progressing well at H&R Johnson. The annual salary reviews felt rewarding.

All three children had been born in the bungalow at Clough Hall Road. School age was approaching, and Sheila had been pondering education. From friends and colleagues at work, we had gathered the impression that Stoke-on-Trent and Staffordshire generally were not as well served educationally as Cheshire. Cheshire, and particularly southeastern Cheshire, had always had snob appeal. It was much more of a rural county than Staffordshire. And Stoke-on-Trent, with its working-class environment and some slum-like areas, didn't have the same appeal.

Don't think this was snobbery. I, particularly, had nothing to feel snobbish about. Although my childhood home in Albion Street had been demolished as part of Stoke's struggle with slum clearance, I never considered it a slum. The neighbours were all decent, hard-working people who kept their persons and their houses as smart as they could afford. There was, literally, no crime that we experienced or heard about. We closed the doors at night and although, in addition to the latch, there were mortice locks, we never used them. I don't know, but I suspect from the peacefulness, that the neighbours didn't either.

Every street had at least one pub. Every four streets or so there was a thriving fish and chip shop (more chips than fish), until the swinging sixties, when the whole country suddenly became more prosperous. This prompted Harold MacMillan, the Prime Minister, to make his famous remark, "You've never had it so good." It was true. Clothes changed from war and post-war drab to more colourful and smarter "Carnaby Street" styles.

I digress, I was talking about the children's education and how this caused us to think more about Cheshire - Sheila particularly, having spent the main part of her life there, until we were married and living in Endymion. Sheila was remembering the village school at Scholar Green, where she and all her brothers and sisters had started their schooling. So, we began to search the newspapers' property pages, trying to find a house in that general area.

Things happen in the strangest ways. After weeks searching for a property in Scholar Green – or reasonably close – we hadn't found anything. Then, in small print at the foot of the property pages was an advertisement for a cottage in Scholar Green. Knowing how property was so scarce in that area, and in particular cottages, I phoned the chap advertising it. Of all places, it was the very cottage where Sheila and her family had lived in her early childhood, before moving to the council house in Meadow Bank, Scholar Green.

The cottage was in a small area between the Macclesfield Canal on one side and the LMS London-to-Manchester railway line. The small terrace of three cottages ran down across this area down to the canal. The only other properties in Little Moss were a house at the end of this terrace, actually on the canal-side and, further along, a farm occupied by the family of one of Sheila's school friends, Bunty Jones. The farm and its farmyard stood at the head of the plot between the canal and railway. Their fields were all located on the other side of the railway. A wide track lay under the railway to these fields.

To get to Little Moss Cottages we drove along the A.34 towards Congleton. Then, opposite the Bleeding Wolf pub, we turned into Little Moss Lane, which ran for less than a mile, ending in a wide dirt track which then crossed on a canal bridge and carried on at the other side of the canal and alongside the railway. This track ended at the small, cobbled yard facing the cottages and before the farm entrance.

There was a separate, asbestos sheeting, garage next to the railway. This belonged to the middle of the three cottages, which was the one we were to buy. I got into a bidding war on the telephone with other prospective buyers. Uncharacteristically, Sheila left it to me to negotiate, although she was much better at it. I thought, in retrospect, she was so emotionally worked up at the prospect of returning to her child-hood home that she left it to me.

The bidding finished with me offering £1,000 for the cottage. It seemed a lot for a small cottage, but I knew Sheila was absolutely determined to find a foothold in Cheshire and, consequently, secure a solid education for our three children.

I had consulted before entering the bidding with the solicitors who had handled our purchase of the bungalow at Clough Hall. They were Hollinshead and Moody. Their office was in the main square in Tunstall, very convenient for me to slip out of the office at H&R Johnson and walk up to the square. They had recommended a new, small building society who were just setting up in business when we bought our bungalow, the Tunstall Building Society.

The manager at the solicitors' office was a young chap, only my age, Mr. Wood. (He remembered me subsequently when I renewed the mortgage when buying subsequent properties.) I asked Mr. James how to approach an estate agent to sell our bungalow. Now in 1964, the U.K. property boom had only just started. Estate agents were few and far between.

"Don't bother with estate agents," Mr James was emphatic in his advice. "It is we solicitors who do all the work whether you use an estate agent or not. They are an unnecessary intermediary adding to everybody's costs and inconvenience. Just put an advert in the Sentinel advertising your property. Don't advertise a price. When people come to view your property, show them round, answer their questions except for price. When they show that they are interested, give them my address and telephone number and tell them, 'Please see my solicitor with your offer.' Do the same with any other interested buyers. I will sort things out and negotiate on your behalf."

Because the boom in property movement had just started, we quickly sold our bungalow and were ready to move into Little Moss. Mr.

James's advice was sound and practical for those early days. However, householders wanting to sell or buy were, generally, not as inclined as I was to deal with things themselves with only the aid of their solicitor. So, estate agents began to get more and more involved until we reached the stage that it was no longer a practical proposition to sell by yourself.

They day quickly came for "flitting", as moving house was and still is called in the Potteries. We found a removals firm, avoiding the large national operators – we had learned about their exorbitant charges. A little chap from Kidsgrove did a careful job at a reasonable price.

Then Sheila took over. She, like most women in my experience, had a better idea of where to put the furniture and effects and the best way to utilise the space. The cottages, because of their setting, looked small. In fact, they were a bit like the Tardis with a surprising amount of space, if you used it carefully.

We had two bedrooms upstairs. Sheila and me with Edwina in her cot in one. The two boys had the second bedroom. Downstairs there was a living room, a small dining room, a separate kitchen and a small bathroom. Also, separated by part of the cobbled yard, was a separate outside toilet. Sheila did a great job, organising things. The fact that it was part of a terrace meant the houses on either side contributed to keeping the place warm. We had one fireplace and, even in winter, it was cosy.

There was one issue concerning living in those cottages which Sheila had forgotten to warn me about. The main railway line was about two hundred yards away from the cottage. This never bothered us, but on the first night, at 11pm when we were tucked up in bed, the whole house shook as the late-night express from London roared past. As Sheila reassured me would happen, after a couple of weeks it never bothered us, we always slept through it.

The other potential problem was the canal which ran down the other side of the property at the bottom of a steep slope beyond the end of our long back garden. The hedge was a really thick one and the canal was not visible without determined effort to climb the hedge, so it never posed an actual problem.

Sheila's mum and a living space crisis

In those days we still had the occasional need to help Hilda, Sheila's mother. After they had been evicted from the council house at Meadowbank, Sheila and Nancy had gone to live with Hilda's sister, Aunty Ida, at Sneyd Green.

Hilda had gone to live with her mother and father, Granny and Grandad Bridden, at Alton (the village near the famous Alton Towers theme park). Hilda had an unfortunate gift for not getting on with people. As a result, the day came when she had to leave Alton with nowhere to live.

Big-hearted Sheila stepped in. "Come stay with us. We'll cope."

I mentioned earlier that the cottage, being built in an age before fridges were invented, had a large walk-in larder just off the kitchen. I cleared out its contents and dismantled the shelving (and transferred it to the garage). We then bought a single bed, bed-side cabinet, a small carpet, bedside lamp and a small chair. It all fitted in OK. It wasn't spacious, but neither was it too cramped for comfort.

All the time, Sheila had a strategy in mind. "When the children are a bit older, we can buy a bigger house. In the meantime, to be able to cope with my mother, we can apply for a council house, on the grounds of serious overcrowding."

Sure enough, Hilda and the rest of us adjusted to the new living arrangements. It was surprisingly comfortable and relaxed. However, we had an eye on the children getting older and bigger, so we started to look for a bigger house. There were few properties locally, and none that would accommodate us comfortably. So, we fell back on Sheila's plan and applied to Cheshire council for a council-house.

A housing inspector called on us quite soon after receiving Sheila's application in which she described our sleeping arrangements. I was at work when he came. Sheila told me about his reaction: "He was horrified that so many people were living in such a small cottage. At the same time, he was full of admiration for the way every inch had been utilised so successfully." After this compliment he promised to act quickly. We would go up the housing list and be dealt with as a priority case.

True to his word, after a couple of weeks we were invited to view a council-owned, detached, four-bedroom house in Mount Pleasant. This wasn't so far away, just up the road leading to Mow Cop but on a level road which ran like a terrace across the lower slope of the Mow Cop Mountain. It promised to fit our needs and was on the school bus run for the boys and not a long car drive to Kidsgrove Station for Edwina's later needs.

We were reluctant to depart from our long-term plans to rise up the property-owning ladder, but we reasoned we could move from the council house when circumstances changed.

As it happened, Hilda had already had a council housing application lodged while she was living with her parents in Alton. The council found a small house on the road from the A.35 towards Talke Pits. She accepted this and one part of our problem was solved.

Move to Portland Drive

While we were still deliberating about the house at Mount Pleasant, a semi-detached house came up for sale in Portland Drive. It was unbelievably close to where we were living. A short walk through Jones's farmyard, over a canal bridge and down a short leafy path and we were at the head of Portland Drive, which ran up from the A34. The asking price was realistic. We accepted and moved in quite quickly. It was a very short walk from the village school and was on the main bus route to the town of Congleton in one direction, and to the Potteries in the other.

There was a small problem in that it had a shared drive with the next-door semi-detached house. This was owned by Mike Cotton, a lecturer in motor body work at Stoke Technical College, and his wife, Margaret. She and Sheila knew one another quite well. Her parents lived quite close to the cottage we had just left at Little Moss. Mike and Margaret were a few years younger than us, but we got along well with them. They were excellent neighbours and so sharing a drive was never a problem.

Extension tensions

After a few years in our semi in Portland Drive, Sheila developed itchy feet again. She thought we needed more room even though our two bedrooms and a large box room were adequate as we had decided that we wouldn't be enlarging the family any further. The basic problem that remained, however, was the shortage of houses in the Scholar Green area.

In the end we decided to have an extension built onto the house, after discussing it with Mike and Margaret next door. They were happy with our outline of what we planned because the extension wouldn't impinge on their space or on their view.

Again, another one of Sheila's Badminton pals was brought into play. Elaine Hargreaves was a nursing sister at the Haywood Hospital. Her husband, Peter, was a self-employed quantity surveyor. We knew the family; their children were the same age as ours and had started at the same village school. For a reasonable fee, Peter drew up plans for a two-storey extension. Also, from his many connections within the construction industry, he recommended a pair of chaps, still young enough to be enthusiastic, yet having the skills and experience to do a good job.

Another coincidence in our life of many coincidences, one of this partnership firm of two was our ex-neighbour from our time at the bungalow at Clough Hall Road. Alan and his lovely wife Ursula were still living there. We got on so well with them, and they did a brilliant job with the extension. Sheila's father and uncles, who had been skilled artisans at the top of their trade, would have been proud of it.

Our builders went to a lot of trouble to search for a supply of bricks to match the rest of the house. Also, everything was finished and clean when they announced it completed. The children were approaching their teen years, so we reckoned we needed to make sure we had ample supplies of hot water for the new bathroom. We had a new boiler installed and, as a backup, we specified an immersion heater to be fitted into the hot water cylinder.

The two builder-partners, Alan and Bob, were both bricklayers. They did most of the construction work themselves but sub-contracted with the electrician and the plumber.

To cope with our demand for a plentiful supply of hot water, they removed the old, galvanised tank from the loft and replaced it with a modern, black PVC model. It was circular, like a garden pond. I remember them getting it up through the ceiling trap door into the loft. To do this they folded it so it could be squeezed diagonally through the opening.

To complete the job, I re-wallpapered downstairs and painted the woodwork. The whole place was ready just before Christmas. I was feeling pleased with myself as I had done the decorating by myself, including papering the ceilings. I had researched the DIY books in Alsager Library and decided on a method of pasting a length of paper for the ceiling.

I needed Sheila's help for this. She was a natural at manual skills. Must have been in the genes as all her uncles were at the top of their trades. She would paste a length of paper and feed it to me and between us we would fold it in concertina fashion with the wet side inside the folds. The pasted section was placed along the bristles of a household broom. Then, holding the broom in my left hand with my paperhanging brush in my right, I stuck the start of the piece on the ceiling then brushed it out, feeding it gradually from the folded length on the broom, all the time carefully brushing it into place and eliminating any bubbles.

It is only necessary for me to detail the work involved because of a later event. We were all ready for Christmas, fridge packed with food, parcels all wrapped underneath the new Christmas tree with its electric fairy lights. The house was toastie warm with the new boiler. The children went to bed, and Sheila and I relaxed before the fire with a glass of sherry. It was a late night for us, and we were relaxing after a lot of pre-Christmas activity.

I should mention that it was a bitterly cold night. We were just discussing going up to bed when we suddenly heard a roaring noise. We looked around in alarm trying to figure out what was happening, when the noise reached a crescendo and the whole downstairs was enveloped in a dense fog of steam. Boiling water, black with loft dust, poured down the walls. The newly papered ceiling bulged, and a torrent of hot water poured out of it. The strange thing was that the electric lights still worked. We had a ceiling light like an inverted bowl. This filled with hot water, yet the electric bulb, half immersed in water, still shone. The light switches on the wall and the power plugs had hot dirty water jetting from them. Then the noise stopped as quickly as it started.

At midnight on Christmas Eve there was little we could do. I found the emergency number for Saga Insurance. It wasn't manned, but a voice machine recorded my message as I reported the incident, describing the damage and asking for tradesmen to fix things.

On Christmas Day, I phoned Bob, and he quickly came to the house. He went up into the loft and reappeared with the news. "The new PVC cold water tank has split from top to bottom. There is a little water remaining, but it is not cold, its warm."

Despite this set back, we had a good Christmas day. Miraculously all the gift-wrapped parcels were untouched. They and the Christmas Tree were in a far corner of the room where the water had not reached. I re-examined the damage and was surprised to see that the dirty water streaks on the walls and ceiling had disappeared. Presumably, after rinsing through the loft insulation, the last few gallons had consisted of clean water that swept away the suspended dust.

The heating system was unaffected, and in the warmth of the house, things dried quite quickly. The bulges in the wallpaper disappeared and, to my amazement, even the ceiling paper, which had been hanging down in huge sheets, had contracted and dried back into place without needing any work at all. The hot water had disappeared through the carpet into the under-floor space and even the carpet, looking neat and clean, was drying into place. After a couple more days the whole house was pristine clean and almost dry.

An anxious Bob and Alan called in again to check if we were alright and began their investigation into the cause of this near disaster. Their conclusion was that the fault lay with the new immersion heater. The thermostat had failed to switch it off when the water in the cylinder reached the required temperature. There was a vertical expansion pipe from the top of the cylinder leading up into the loft where it emptied any surplus water from the cylinder into the cold-water tank (our new PVC tub). At the bottom of the tub the outlet pipe led down to the base of the cylinder to keep it filled.

When the immersion heater failed to switch off, the contents of the cylinder kept on heating, pushing up to the cold-water tank and the whole thing happened like a cycle action, progressively emptying boiling water into the tank until the whole system was filled with boiling water. The PVC tub was designed to hold cold water only. The boiling water caused the fold, where the tub had been forced into the loft, to split causing – it must have been approaching fifty gallons of – boiling water to pour onto the loft floor and on downwards. As the tank emptied, the ball tap, fortunately, switched off, preventing any more water from reaching the tub.

The aftermath was a dispute between the contractors, Bob and Alan, and the sub-contractors, the plumber and the electrician. I wasn't involved in the discussions, but I gathered that the electrician blamed the plumber for forcing the tub through the loft opening, folding and thereby weakening it. The plumber said that, despite the fold, the tub was safe while holding what it was designed to hold – *cold* water. The root cause was the failure of the immersion heater. Eventually the poor electrician lost the argument and paid for a new immersion heater which he then installed. By this time there wasn't the slightest sign of water damage, in fact the house looked cleaner. So, I phoned Saga and withdrew my insurance claim.

Chapter 9: Our Married Family Holidays

Prelude

During the recent Covid pandemic, holidaying in Britain became popular again. It even acquired a name – a "staycation". When I was a child, every holiday was a staycation. A working-class holiday was, at best, a trip to the British seaside. But, by the time we were raising our family, the country was much richer. The height of middle-class sophistication then was a "continental holiday". The continent in question was Europe. It was a daunting prospect, both financially and culturally for Sheila and me. But this is the story of how we progressed from staycations to continental holidays.

Our first family holidays

When Edwina was old enough, we took our first family holidays. We stayed in Torquay in a static caravan park, which had been built in an old quarry. Also, we had a similar holiday in Tenby, which was in Abergele in North Wales. I used to tell Sheila about my enduring memories of our wonderful childhood camping holidays in Talacre. Life, viewed through the rear-view mirror of childhood experiences, often turn out to be a completely different experience in adulthood. I hadn't realised this when describing my childhood experiences, so Sheila gradually accepted that the children would enjoy a similar holiday.

Family transport

Before that, a word about transport. I've described our first vehicle, the trusty little Lambretta scooter, and, when Sheila was expecting Gary, the Velocette 350 motorbike with its single seat sidecar. This served us well, me riding the bike, Sheila with baby Gary in the sidecar. We took the motorbike and sidecar for a lovely holiday at Penmaenmawr in North Wales, just beyond Conway on the coastal road, which continued to

Llandudno and beyond. We had rented a caravan which was privately owned and stood on its own in a neat little field just off the coast road.

I remember it was the season for Welsh spring lamb, and Sheila found a little butcher's shop in the village. Sheila cooked us lamb most evenings in the caravan. I remember, it was delicious.

Gary still had the occasional bout of colic. It usually happened in the evening. We found a way of settling him off for the night, however. He loved riding in the sidecar and the velvety thumping of the single-cylinder engine produced just the right rhythm to cause him to relax and drop off to sleep. It was quiet in the evenings, the traffic was almost non-existent, and we drove the four or five miles to Conway and back, catching glimpses of beautiful sunsets. A holiday to remember.

After the Velocette, Sheila was expecting Kevin, so I bought a second-hand "Ariel Square Four" motorcycle with a child-adult sidecar. The motor was 1,000 cc so it pulled the full load effortlessly. The sidecar was completely enclosed and weather-proof, and it held Sheila and, after Edwina was born, baby Edwina and the two boys comfortably. I had a proper motor-cycle suit of waterproof PVC, and with my crash helmet, I was dry in the heaviest downpour. The boys found it amusing to grin and wave at me from the side-window during the rain. They obviously didn't realise that, though I might have looked uncomfortable, I was completely warm and dry.

As the children grew, I traded in the Ariel for a brand-new Morris Mini-Minor. Our first car, and it was wonderful. Although the Mini was a small car, the designer, Alec Issigonis, had done a clever job in placing the engine sideways at the front and creating quite a spacious interior. After three years, it developed a fault in the transmission, so, instead of going to the expense of having it repaired, I traded it in for another brand-new car, a Volkswagen Beetle.

This was an absolutely superb family car, so easy to drive, warm and comfortable and completely free of ever having any mechanical faults. We kept that for a couple of years, and we would have been happy to run it for much longer. However, as the years progressed at H&R Johnson, I had had a number of minor promotions, but I was suddenly promoted to the level of senior management and was given a company car.

It was a Morris Oxford, a much bigger car than the Beetle. It held the whole family in comfort and, with a huge boot, was ideal for venturing onto the old dream of a camping holiday.

Camping

So, we bought a tent. Because we were inexperienced, and didn't want to spend on something that later might prove unsuitable, I found a second-hand one. It was in good condition, but after our first holiday we found it wasn't as modern as the newly developed "frame tents", with their vertical walls and windows plus separate bedrooms. It served us well enough, however.

Our first holiday was at Talacre. In the same field at Williams's Farm, that I had camped in as a child. Although, it was a younger Mr. Williams, the old man's eldest son, who ran it. The years hadn't yet changed the place and Mr. Williams the younger, was as helpful and welcoming as his father had been.

Things didn't work out quite as well as my remembered holidays. We stayed for a week. The children enjoyed the wildness and the freedom just as I had at their age. The weather served up a number of wet days and Sheila tried to keep a cheerful face on things, but she confessed it wasn't her idea of a holiday. Getting up in the morning and walking to the farm toilet through long, unmown grass, which was soaking wet, wasn't her idea of fun.

So, we went home and gave the matter some thought. Sheila and I happened to meet one evening with a couple we had known casually for a few years, Robert and Jill. They sympathised with Sheila's view of the camping experience. They were a little older than us, and it turned out they had enjoyed camping in France and in Spain.

"It's a completely different world on the continent," said Jill. "Particularly in France where camping has been taken to a different level. The climate is better, for one thing, as you travel South. The campsites are not grassy as in Britain. The sand-based soil is dry and easy to pitch on, and what grassed areas there are regularly mown. There are public camp sites in most towns, run by the local authority. They are alongside the local public parks. They have smart toilets and shower blocks with hot water, all very civilised and ridiculously cheap. As you get further South, you find private sites which are quite luxurious without being very expensive."

Our first touring holiday abroad in France

After our experience in "wet and windy Wales", as Sheila always called it, we quite fancied a holiday in the sunshine, so we started planning a camping holiday in the south of France. There was no internet in those days, but by scouring the travel agents, I found a few brochures describing campsites in France.

Because it was our first trip abroad, and without any experience of camping there, I took the precaution of buying one of the excellent Michelin maps of France, showing the complete road network. I studied the brochures and thought, in view of our lack of experience, we ought to book a campsite in advance. I didn't fancy the idea of landing on the Mediterranean coast in high summer and finding the campsites were all full.

I found an advert for a site called Yotel Cogolin. Yotel is short for yachting hotel. Cogolin was a small area next door to Saint Tropez. It had all the facilities I was looking for, and, for a site in that area of France, it wasn't ruinously expensive. I had been studying French, not very successfully, at evening classes, so I was able, after some effort, to compose a letter. A reply came quite quickly, requiring only a modest deposit, which I despatched. I didn't book at the sites on the way down to the South. For one thing, I didn't know how far we would be able to travel in a day, and I was sure, in emergency, our budget would run to a hotel for the two or three nights it would involve.

Sheila looked after the equipment side of things, apart from a cool box (on which, more later). I concentrated on getting the car ready. I had to fit the headlamps with yellow beam deflectors to comply with French regulations, which I had gathered were extremely strict. The French cars all had yellow bulbs, so the fact that the deflectors were yellow solved that. They also helped to cope with driving on the right-hand side of the road. British headlights, when switched to dipped beam, actually deflected the beam, not only down but to the left, and this would be into the path of oncoming cars in France. I found, by experimenting around Scholar Green at night, that these deflectors almost cancelled out the beam, rather than merely deflecting it.

So, I made a firm decision not to drive at night in France. I would take care to halt for the night well before dark. There was an international driving licence required, and I joined the AA overseas rescue service. Then I got the car serviced, and carefully checked so that it complied with the French regulations. I then worked out a route, and then booked travel insurance and the ferry crossing.

I had read that a great many French people took the whole month of August for a holiday, and that travel on the routes to the Med would be crowded. So I had booked for the last week of August and the first week in September at St. Tropez. I had learned, from colleagues at work, that the holiday traffic eased towards the end of August, so I hoped to avoid any huge traffic jams.

My final task was to create a way of carrying perishable food stuffs. The whole operation was turning out to be expensive, and Sheila wanted to cook on our excellent multi-burner and grill camping gas cooker. Dry goods and veg. were neatly packed, but we had butter, bacon, eggs, cheese and other perishables. It is hard to believe it, but, in those days, cool boxes for private use had not been invented.

So, using my woodwork skills, I took care in making a box out of plywood. I then scrounged some polystyrene insulating sheeting off a builder's merchant for a few coppers. I cut pieces to size to fit the bottom and sides, gluing them in place. Then I glued a piece to the underside of the lid. It didn't need to be hinged. I cut the polystyrene to size that would fit inside the side of the box making a nice tight fit. On the morning of our departure, the local fishmonger gave Sheila a small block of ice that fitted on top of the food. Actually, that cool box was an excellent device as the days following proved.

We were all so excited when we set off on our adventure. The weather in the UK was glorious, and it continued to be so throughout the whole fortnight. The children were enjoying the different new experiences. The Channel crossing on a ferry was new to all of us. The crossing was calm, a relief in view of Sheila's and Edwina's motion sickness difficulties.

It was a change driving on the right, but the excellent road signage system in France made it a quick business adjusting to a foreign system. Actually, I found that driving a right-hand drive car on the right side of the road had, at times, an advantage. The road signs were closer to the driver and consequently easier to read.

Despite the warnings from drivers who had driven in France, I had no problems with the "priorite a droite", which meant giving way to traffic coming onto your road from the right. We were driving mainly on main roads, and the road signs made it clear when you had priority. Roundabouts also were OK. We gave way to traffic on the right, just as we did in UK.

The only difficulties we experienced were the road works. From memory, it was 1966. There were no motorways as far as I could tell. No signs to "autoroute" as we found in later years. France had undergone a massive re-building following the Second World War and in 1966 it was entering into another phase. They were building a network of autoroutes throughout France. Every few miles we came across huge earthworks where long stretches of the fields had been bull-dozed and a series of roads and bridges were being built. Consequently, we were faced, at frequent intervals, with the sign "Deviation".

Unfortunately, these signs didn't include any information about where the diversion would take us. To add to our problem, I found that all the main roads in France seemed to radiate from Paris. This meant that these diversions were taking us closer and closer to Paris, and I dreaded the prospect of coping with that city's traffic problems.

We paid close attention to our Michelin map and managed to avoid this "black hole" effect. Our general idea was to travel in a southerly direction. Avoiding the earthworks and the routes to Paris meant we were heading south but drifting eastwards. Until we got past Paris and found the main route the N.6 (called ominously by the French "La Murderesse" because of its appalling accident rate), we struggled to navigate our way.

I was aiming for the largest city in that Region, Troyes, from where we picked up better and better ways south. At the end of the first day's driving, I had driven, including the journey to Dover, a total of 474 miles. I remember well seeing the number on the trip recorder. At that point, we arrived at a town called Sezanne. Road signs directed us to "Le Camping".

We arrived at the public camp site, which was built beyond the public park. It was an extremely large camp site, so spacious with loads of room to pitch one's tent. We learned that France, the largest country in Western Europe, was so different from Britain, and one difference was the spaciousness in the suburbs and public places. We pitched our tent on a lovely patch of grassed land. It sloped gently down to a large open air swimming pool.

The sun was still high in the sky. It was to hot, so, while Sheila busied herself with preparing an evening meal, Gary and I found our swimming trunks, and ran down the grassy slope to the pool. There were several people spaced out around the pool, sunbathing and picnicking, but nobody was swimming. I carried on my run down the slope and made a running dive into the water. It was like ice. It was clean and clear, and by the look of things, it was fed by a local stream. It was too cold for a leisurely swim, but the short dip across and out of it was so very refreshing. Gary ventured into the water too, but like me didn't stay in too long.

The next day we packed up our gear, paid the amazingly small fee for the night's camping, and headed on to Troyes. It is an historic, medieval city with a beautiful cathedral, but we were not tourists, we had a destination to reach, so we ploughed on.

After Troyes, the roads in that open region to the east of Paris were less busy, actually it was a pleasure to drive them. We made good progress, all the time finding it easier to avoid the "vacuum cleaner" road system, which sucked traffic towards Paris. The weather was pleasantly warm but still a northern European climate.

We stopped at a little town where we had passed a small, smart looking restaurant. We parked just beyond it and made our way inside. It was nice to get into the cool, shaded dining room out of the warmth and the glare of the sun. The proprietor sat us down at a nice table which he called an "en famille" table. We all had delicious, iced lemonade then chose a whole Chateaubriand to share among us. The waiter smilingly brought our steaks. The people there seemed happy to see a young English family. The waiter then brought a massive, polished steel bowl filled to overflowing with "frites" and a smaller bowl of salad.

We enjoyed our meal, there was so many frites we couldn't eat them all. Sheila and I finished with a delicious coffee in tiny cups. We learned later the request that English visitors used was for "café grande" or "café double" to ensure we had a large English-style cup.

To my surprise, having been told about the cost of things in France, the bill was so reasonable. I can't remember the actual sum, but, certainly, we wouldn't have been able to get a meal like it for the same price in England.

After our long, tiring drive the previous day, we stopped early for the following night. This time we had reached Macon, just short of Lyons on the River Rhone. We followed the ubiquitous signs for "Camping Municipal". It was on the north side of the city. We were prepared for another large, spacious site, but were absolutely amazed when we entered it. I'm not exaggerating, it was like a tent township. Our car was met by a group of students, dressed in white uniforms, riding white bicycles with the sign printed on the frame "Camping Municipal Macon". They escorted us to our site along little avenues with lawns and low hedges marking them out. As I said, like a "tented town".

Our plot was next door to a Swiss family with a large Mercedes estate car and a grand frame tent the like of which I had never seen. It was so large and so smart. The side was opened and spread out like an awning. Inside camp furniture, chairs and a table laid with china and sparkling Champagne glasses. I felt a bit like a peasant with our old-fashioned ridge tent with its wooden tent pegs. However, we had the hedge for privacy, and we enjoyed a restful evening and a good night's sleep before setting out the following day.

This time, the road headed south, straight as a die and we made good progress. We passed Lyons using the excellent by-pass with its "Toutes Directions" signs guiding us past the city itself. The road broadened with excellent views as we followed the wide River Rhone on our left. A little way to the right was a line of hills. Also, on the left, on the other side of the river, a long high rocky escarpment. At intervals along this ridge were the ruins of old buildings. They looked very old. They didn't resemble castles to my mind, but, from my meagre history readings, I guessed they were the remains of old Roman forts.

As well as the other interesting sights, I pointed them out to the children. One ancient structure stood on an impossible height. "Look," I said, "another Roman ruin."

At this, a little voice piped up from the back, "Daddy, how did the Roman's manage to get up there to ruin it?" It was Edwina, not yet five, who had been listening to my "commentary guide" and pondering what it meant.

"We'll talk about it tonight, when we pitch camp again," I said.

The next day, after another of Sheila's wonderful and quickly prepared breakfasts, we made another early start. We still had a massive journey before us, and our excitement was growing by the hour. I began to notice that the climate was changing even as we travelled. The lush green of north and central France was gradually becoming drier with patches of herbage among the drier soil. It changed from being pleasantly warm to becoming drier and hotter.

By then, we were at the beginning of the N7 (La Murdereusse). I could see why it got the name. The road was a three-lane highway, so traffic overtaking had to take the middle lane. Given the rate at which the French drivers travelled, collisions were not as frequent as I had imagined, but the sheer volume of traffic travelling down south and returning on this major route amplified the number of accidents.

Experienced drivers explained to me later the reasons for the great majority of accidents. Firstly, drivers were driving fast to keep up with the traffic and to get to their far destinations quickly. Secondly, overtaking made it necessary to use the third lane at the centre of the highway. This required fine judgement if you are to avoid vehicles travelling towards you, at speed, overtaking cars in front of them. Also, the roadsides were occupied by closely spaced, large mature trees. This meant there was no way of deviating to the road verges to avoid traffic.

At the eastern side of the road, we came upon fields filled with the rusting wrecks of cars. The lack of space at the roadsides made the road authorities hesitant about widening it, particularly as, and as noted earlier, the whole country was building a network of new autoroutes which would possibly replace the major N roads.

It became so hot, and our old-fashioned British Leyland car had no air-conditioning. So, after a break for a picnic lunch, Sheila and I discussed our plans and decided to stop early for the night. By this time, we had passed Chalons sur Rhone and we could see the city of Macon ahead of us on the map. As soon as we hit the northern outskirts, we saw a huge roadside advert for "Camping Macon". Shortly after this, the entrance appeared on our right.

This time it was a private camp site. It had a slightly more luxurious air about it, with a large supermarket, laundry and hardware shop. They had plenty of room. The charge for the night was more than the municipal sites, but, even on our budget, it seemed extremely reasonable. We ate at the camp site's cafeteria that evening, then spent a comfortable night.

Another start and we re-joined the N7 traffic continuing south. The road was busy, but we didn't encounter any traffic jams or accidents, so we made good progress. At lunch time, we again stopped for a picnic at a roadside picnic area, typically French, clean with smart toilets. Tables with fixed benches were generously spaced, so there was plenty of room to get out the gas cooker and brew hot drinks. The weather had become even hotter so, with the aid of a bag of ice and orange squash from the camp site, the children could have plenty of cold drinks.

We were finishing our lunch when Sheila and I got into conversation with the driver of a Mini and his wife. They were returning from a fortnight's camping on the Mediterranean. They were Scottish, a very pleasant couple who were still brimming with excitement about their holiday, even though they were on their way home. For years afterwards, Sheila and I recalled that encounter several times and the boys would imitate the little Glaswegian's accent.

"From here onwards," he said, "the weather gets warmer and more Mediterranean. You will see fruit stalls at the side of the road as ye goo doon. The fruit is wonderful and so cheap. Stop and buy some. You'll really enjoy it." Sure enough, we stopped and bought a melon, then a whole tray of peaches and plastic bags full of juicy grapes. The children thought they were in heaven.

Unfortunately, there was a down-side. The August heat was becoming intense, and the sunlight was dazzlingly bright, reflecting on the limestone scattered at the road verges. Sheila began to get a migraine. She has had only four migraines in our whole married life, and this was the first one. She was never a complainer, but it was obvious she was suffering. So, at the first opportunity I stopped the car.

There was an opening at the side of the road leading onto a clearing with a hedge and a massive plane tree in the middle of it. I unpacked one of our folding beds, erected it with a sleeping bag for Sheila to lie on and an ice water handkerchief over her eyes. It was cool in the shade of that tree. The children and I sat on some handy flat rocks and passed the time chatting about the sights we'd seen, while Sheila slept for four hours. After that she felt a lot better, so we piled back into the car.

The sun was still high, but the intense heat was easing, and on that straight road, we made good progress until we hit a crossroad. The N7 was crossing a new Mediterranean highway that stretched east and west just above the hills bordering the Med. This road led west to Toulon and Marseilles. To our left it headed east to Nice and Italy. We continued ahead but it was no longer the N7; it had degenerated into a more minor road that zig-zagged across the hills and down to St. Tropez. No navigation problems, however, and I found the road to Cogolin, which had been a little fishing village about ten kilometres east of St. Tropez.

The camp site (the Yotel Cogolin) was only about fifty metres from the beach, surrounded by a dry-stone wall with a gap leading on to the beach. The ground was flat with a firm sandy soil that was perfect for pitching our tent. The site was almost full, but we found a spot where we could set up camp without tripping over our neighbours' guy lines. We quickly set ourselves up, and Sheila, with a great sigh, settled down for a good night's sleep.

The next day, her migraine had completely gone, so we had breakfast, donned our swimming gear and set off the short hop to the beach. Our tent was close to the dry-stone wall. Standing there by the entrance to the beach was a farmer's cart, set up like a fruit stall. I learned later that it was the time of the "vendange" i.e. the time for picking the grapes at the local vineyards dotted all around us. The cart was laden with mainly grapes, which for some reason were surplus to requirements for wine making, either because they had literally grown too many or, perhaps, were the wrong variety.

They were excellent grapes, however. A large card advertised, "Des Raisins – 1 Franc per Kilo". A franc at that time was worth about ten pence in today's money. They had so many grapes, they were selling them off cheap. We each got a big brown paper bag containing a kilo of delicious red grapes to take onto the beach. Edwina loved them and eagerly tugged us to the stall every morning for her bag of grapes. When we got back home, she kept asking for grapes, she loved them so much, but they weren't always available in the UK, and the price was enormous. Poor Ed. We bought some whenever they were available, but she was so disappointed.

The site was absolutely perfect for young children. The beach was surprisingly wide for a Mediterranean resort. Clean golden sand with loads of space despite the number of August holidaymakers. The sea was an inlet from the Mediterranean, a large lagoon. This meant that even when the wind picked up there were no waves. The water was shallow, and even at two hundred metres from the beach the water was only about a metre deep. Because it was so wide and shallow the water was warmed by the sun.

Gary, Kevin and I have fair skin. The sunshine was constant and strong, but Sheila had planned well for this. The boys had long sleeved T-shirts so they could play and swim for hours without burning. Sheila sat under our huge beach umbrella with sunglasses to help prevent another migraine. Edwina, although blonde, had a strong thick skin which needed protecting only when sun was at its height. I watched her playing with the boys, and she began to tan before my eyes. It might seem hard to believe but it was almost like a piece of bread under a grill gradually turning into toast. This was repeated on every holiday we had on the Med.

I remember the end of the first week. The month of August ended on the Saturday. Very early in the morning, I was awakened by a murmuring sound with occasional bumps and bangs. It was still dark, so I went back to sleep. When we woke up at our usual early breakfast time, I unzipped the tent to find that the whole site was almost deserted. From being comfortably occupied – not crowded – there were only three other tents and ours still standing.

It turned out that the main crowd were French and had packed up and set off north to their hometowns. At first, it seemed strange after the bustling atmosphere of the first week. The site supermarket and laundry block were still open and, fortunately, the vendange farmer had his cart still loaded with delicious grapes, still at one franc per kilo.

The local roads were peaceful and quiet, so we drove into St. Tropez just to see what the famed resort was like. It was a small fishing village really. Most of the bars and restaurants, which catered for all the "beautiful people", had closed, so it was just a normal seaside small town. There was nothing special for us to see, so in the afternoon we returned the few kilometres to Cogolin for a late session on the beach.

On the Monday, we drove in the other direction to Nice. I had read about the "Riviera Corniche" roads, which travel writers claimed to be the most beautiful sights in Europe. They were not wrong. We drove along the Higher Corniche. The weather was glorious, and to our right the sea was like a sparkling blue diamond. The steep slope down to the sea was heavily wooded with gaps opening onto tiny little bays with golden sands. There were wildflowers everywhere, and their scent, mingled with the tang from the many pine trees added to the overall beauty of the area.

We arrived at Nice at lunch time. It was a surprisingly large town. Everywhere was well maintained and scrupulously clean. The large villas gave onto the promenade with its row of opulent hotels. Uniformed doormen with their smart top hats seemed to be everywhere. All the hotels had deep frontages with space for parking of the guests' cars. I have never, before or since, seen so many Rolls-Royce cars. They were not like the Rolls we saw occasionally back home, clad in sober black or dark blue paintwork. These were painted in bright two-tone colour schemes with women and girls pouring out of them dressed as though they were arriving at a Buck House garden party or Ascot. Ferraris, Maseratis and other sports cars added a bit of variety. I never saw a single motorcycle.

I couldn't see any car parking on the crowded front, so I escaped up a side road which was wide with loads of room for me to park. As we all got out of the car, we found I'd parked near to a "hole in the wall" style of ice cream parlour. Naturally, we all had a giant cone apiece. The variety of colours and flavours was breathtaking, and the ice cream was not expensive. Also, it was delicious.

We strolled the short distance to the promenade and viewed the beach. We had no desire to swim or sunbathe, but there was no opportunity if we had. Each section of beach belonged to the hotel it fronted. Large awnings advertising the name of the hotel and the beach seemed so wide, stretching down to the sea with tables and chairs, then beach loungers, all with gaily coloured beach umbrellas. Each hotel's area was separated from its neighbours by a two-strand wire fence stretching down to the sea. All very exclusive, though attractive to view.

We spent a couple of pleasant hours strolling along the prom and stopping occasionally for a rest on one of the many smart, comfortable benches. On our return, we found a pleasant wide lay-by, where we had a picnic lunch with beautiful beef tomatoes and salad veg, which Sheila had brought from the camp supermarket.

We arrived at the camp in time for an early supper, which Sheila rustled up so quickly. I never discovered the secret of her "lightening-speed cuisine". At the end of it, Sheila showed me our cool box. We had consumed all the eggs, cheese, butter and bacon, and there was still a small piece of ice surrounded by meltwater, remaining from our original set-up.

Next day, we stocked up at the supermarket. No great surprises except the price of butter. I can't remember in detail, but it was much more than twice the UK price. No British-style bacon, but their alternative, more like cooked ham, was acceptable, so were the cheese and eggs. We had already bought our daily baguettes there, and for a change we bought a huge "peasant loaf", which was equally delicious. Finally, their freezer held large bags of ice, so Sheila placed the unopened bag on top of the food, which kept everything cool and dry.

The second week flew by, and it was time to settle up with the site office and set off on the long drive home. It was about the fifth of September and, fortunately, it was somewhat cooler. There was a strong wind blowing from the north (the mistral, I believe). This was quite alarming. The low hills which we had to climb through on winding roads up to the N7 were thickly wooded and prone to forest fires at that time of the year.

As we were driving away from the camp, we saw large columns of smoke arising from the foot of the hills. Fortunately, the fires were a few kilometres to the west. We had to give way frequently to fire engines on their way to the scene, but we were able to forge ahead on the road we had descended a fortnight ago.

It was a long journey up those wooded hills, and we stopped for a picnic half-way up. After we'd cleared away our debris, I noticed that the clearing where I'd stopped led onto a wide driveway heading a short distance through the trees to chalet advertising "Mediterranean Souvenirs". Inside were shelves and benches covered with the most beautiful ornaments and utensils all carved out of olive wood. We bought a few, among them a wooden nutcracker made of a carved lump of wood with a wooden screw entering into a hole where you placed a nut. We used that cracker for years. I don't know where it went to in the end. Also, we bought a beautiful salad bowl, with fork and spoon included, all beautifully carved in olive wood.

We set off again only to find another chalet just before we reached the main road. There we bought a coffee set in brilliant brown and green glaze. We kept that set also for years but as an ornament in our China cabinet.

Once we hit the N7, we made good progress to our first night's stop. For once, my memory has failed me. I cannot remember where we camped that first night. It must have been uneventful as we continued north, making good progress.

We camped for a second night near Lyons, but this time at a small municipal site. By the third night, we had passed to the east of Paris, this time without hindrance from the "Deviation" signs that had be-devilled us on our southward journey. I remember Sheila and I felt satisfied with our progress. We hadn't got much of a stretch ahead of us to Calais, but instead of ploughing on and catching an earlier ferry, we decided to find a campsite, so we could have a steady un-rushed leg to the port on the following day.

I couldn't find a site, which was unusual because normally camp sites were everywhere. So, I stopped and asked a group of teenagers sitting at the roadside with their bicycles. "Le Camping, certainment. Il y a un petit moulin pres d'ici. Suivez moi." So, they mounted their bikes and led us down a narrow side road where we descended into a little valley by a small river. Sure enough, there was a watermill and built onto it an extension with the sign "Café" pained on the wall.

It wasn't actually a camp site, but the proprietor welcomed us extremely warmly and showed us a patch of grass not too close to the river. It was well mown and level. He didn't speak English but made it clear we could camp here. He then took us to the pathway to the side where a small well made of stone stood. It had a wooden lid and a post with an enamel jug chained to it. He removed the lid and pointed to the jug then to the water. "OK," I said, "Je comprend."

Sheila made one of her quick, hot dinners and we brewed tea from the brilliant clean well water. As it was still early, I suggested we all stroll to the café to see what was on offer. It had been a mild, sunny day, but we opted to sit indoors after our long alfresco holiday. The café was part of the old watermill building, completely unspoilt by the fashion for modernised restoring. It was quiet. Only two of the tables were occupied by elderly men, who had the out-doors look of farmers. They smiled and raised a hand in welcome.

The proprietor came and asked us what we would like. Since we'd just eaten our late afternoon meal, we ordered the pastries he offered us. To drink, coffee for Sheila (she never took alcohol, it disagreed with her). A bière blonde for me, and I asked for lemonade for the children.

"Et pour le petit M'sieur?" he gestured to Gary. "Peut etre un boc de bière?"

This was a surprise after the strict licensing laws in England. "C'est possible?" was my question.

"Certainment," he grinned. Gary was obviously guessing what was being said. He smiled enthusiastically.

The proprietor came in with our pastries, then very shortly afterwards, with a tray of drinks. He whipped off the head of froth on our beers with one of the wooden knives that they used in French bars.

Gary really enjoyed his "little beer". The old chaps at the two tables smiled at us and, pointing to Gary, they said, "Sante."

None of them spoke a word of English. We were in a rural part of France, where it seemed that life proceeded at a gentler pace. We had diverted from the main route north when we followed the teenagers, so I guessed the locals had little contact with tourists. We made our goodbyes as best as we could in our limited French and retired to our tent for our final night in France.

After breakfast, we packed everything up, stowing everything neatly in the car as the proprietor walked across to us. We expected him to produce his bill for the ground-rent, but no, he'd just came to say goodbye. When I asked him how much for the camping, he just laughed and said, "Non. Merci pour le visite et bon route." It was another example of the kindness and friendliness we had encountered in France once we were away from any large city.

The people in large urban places generally seemed to be in a hurry. I remember asking a gentleman as I walked on the pavement near Paris where I could find a boulangerie. "Plus bas, plus bas." He snapped without stopping.

I learned the following year, from a fellow British tourist, that in a shop, for example, Brits would approach the counter and simply ask, "Une baguette, s'il vous plait." And perhaps they would be surprised at the cool response of the shopkeeper.

It was explained to me that it is the custom in France, before anything else, to greet the lady or gentleman behind the corner with, "Good morning. How are you?" before placing your order.

I have never had the opportunity to practice this in a city, but in all the rural places we visited afterwards I always followed his advice. The change was remarkable. Instead of cool indifference, I was always treated to a pleasant smile and a goodbye afterwards.

Our second touring holiday abroad in Spain

Soon after Christmas that year, Sheila were chatting about the budget and plans for the new year. "Where are we going for our holiday?" she asked. I felt that after the relatively expensive holiday in France we should conserve our funds that year and spend a holiday at home.

I should point out that our holiday in France was relatively expensive for us at the time. In fact, looking back, it was an extremely inexpensive holiday for an overseas vacation, thanks to the reasonable costs of ground rent at French campsites and to Sheila had cooking nearly all of our meals. We decided to defer any decisions and see how the year's expenditure panned out.

As August loomed, Sheila broached the question again. I still insisted we should avoid the expense, and the idea was postponed again. Finally, at the end of July, Sheila put her foot down. "It doesn't matter what expenses we have to forego; I am determined that the children should not be denied the chance of another holiday like we had in France. It wasn't a holiday so much as an adventure. How many families have the chance of the kind of holiday we had? They are at an impressionable age and they will carry those memories with them for the rest of their lives."

I gave in. I spent some time studying my maps. By then, I had a small collection of Michelin maps of France in different scales. The same for Spain. Also, I had a superb large version of their map covering the whole of Europe.

"I've heard from folks at work, who have had package holidays in Spain, say how good a holiday destination it is." I said to Sheila, who wasn't one for studying maps. She just went on my information and agreed.

So began a frantic week of preparation. Because of my hesitance, we'd left it rather late. The usual breakdown and travel insurance. International driving licence to be renewed. Ferry crossing booked. The car serviced. New tyres all round. And finally, a tent.

Instead of our second-hand semi-ridge tent with its wooden pegs, we bought an expensive ultra-modern frame tent. It had a separate interior tent with three "bedrooms." I also bought aluminium folding camp beds and new superior sleeping bags.

I also thought about clothes storage. I never liked the idea of living out of a suitcase, so I found a light-weight clothes rack from a firm of shop-display specialists. It had rails and a plentiful supply of coat-hangers. It fitted the end of Edwina's bedroom. It kept our clothes neat and free of creases and also off the floor. Added to the folding kitchen we already had; it meant we could live more like a household instead of constantly grabbing things off the floor.

We still had the Morris Oxford. Although heavy to handle – no power steering with heavy gear lever, clutch and brakes – it was fine for the European open roads. I planned a route. Because Spain lay in a more westerly direction, I booked an over-night crossing from Portsmouth to Le Havre and picked out roads by-passing Paris on its western side. I will refrain, this time, from giving a blow-by-blow account of our journey. To summarise: the Channel crossing went well. The roads were busier than on our more easterly journey, but the roads were good, and we had the benefit of the auto route toll roads which, by now, had been added. This was an extra expense but not ruinously so.

We camped at a little town near Nantes. After a little difficulty finding a way across the Loire – there were so many bridges in Nantes taking us over subsidiary channels. The following night, we treated ourselves to an enjoyable hotel stay. The proprietors were so helpful. Then we camped in an isolated village, then the following day joined the heavy traffic travelling from France to Spain by the coastal route instead of attempting to cross the Pyrenees.

Although heavy, the traffic kept moving, and we soon found ourselves at the Spanish border and on our way towards Barcelona. We were travelling south on the Costa Brava. The road was similar to the Corniche road at Nice. It ran along the top of a high ridge, with beautiful views of the wooded slopes descending on our left to the unbelievably blue Mediterranean. Mid-afternoon I spotted a sign to "Camping" on the left-hand side of the road. The entrance was immediately below the sign. A lovely set of wrought iron gates and, immediately on our left, a small "bodega" (a wine bar with restaurant) with a booking chalet attached to it.

As soon as I drove through the open gates, a chap came out waving at us. "Sorry, we are full, no camping plots left," he said. After our lunch, the children all felt sleepy, so Sheila had folded down the back of the rear seat. This opened onto the floor of the large boot. As this was empty of luggage – we had everything stowed on the roof-rack – it was almost as big as a double bed. Sleeping bags folded to make a mattress and a lightweight blanket to cover them, the three children were fast asleep.

At that time nobody had told me about the way the Spanish absolutely dote on their children. The chap stopped mid-sentence as soon as he saw the children asleep in the back. "Ah, los ninos," he said, signalling me to follow him to an empty plot nearby.

The campsite was a smart set-up, created from a disused quarry. We were at the top of a natural amphitheatre facing the sea. A roadway descended in the middle to the beach in a bay. The ground had been landscaped into a series of terraces descending the slope. Each terrace was marked out into separate plots, each boarded with a hedge of flowering shrubs. We had a great week at this site. The sea was clean and clear with a sandy bottomed stretches for the children relieved by rocky outcrops which, like a reef, were crowded with fish and other sea-life.

At the camp shop, the boys and I kitted ourselves out with flippers and facemasks. I also bought a small elasticated harpoon gun for spearfishing. Nowadays I regret this, and I resolved not to deliberately kill another creature. On our first snorkelling swim around the rocks, I failed to spear a fish but pierced what turned out to be an octopus. I swam ashore and worked to detach it from the spear. As I was struggling, a Frenchman with his little family came over to help. I made to return the octopus to the sea and the French man appealed to me with his eyes to let him have it. He ran with his children away up the slope and vanished. That evening, looking over our low hedge to the terrace below, I smelled a delicious odour of onions, garlic and tomatoes. There before me was the Frenchman with the octopus, cut into portions, frying it up for supper.

The campsite was great, and every evening we would stroll to the bodega for a coffee for Sheila, a beer for me and lemonade for the children. The proprietor and his wife obviously adored children, and I guessed it was a change for them to entertain British people, all the rest at the camp seemed to be French with a scattering of Italians. They used to sit Edwina on the bar so they could chat to her in between serving drinks. They made a fuss of the boys too but were entranced by Edwina with her sun-bleached, blonde hair and lively chatter.

On the Friday evening, Sheila said, "We've had a lovely week. It's a beautiful spot, but it's becoming hard work climbing up and down the "amphitheatre" with our beach gear" (and an inflatable boat the children loved to sail around the little bay in).

I consulted my trusty Michelin map and suggested we return a little way north to the coast before the Costa Brava hills started. We paid up and made our farewells to the proprietor and his wife and headed for the town of Rosas, which was less than thirty miles away. It was a wise choice. The coastal area there was unspoilt, almost wild. We followed a narrow road leading off the main road and found ourselves at a campsite. It was right on the coast, despite the fact that, after leaving the main road, I had guessed mistakenly that we were heading inland.

The whole campsite was deserted despite having a shop, restaurant etc and a bath/shower/laundry complex that was the last word in luxury. The firm, sandy ground was level, perfect for pitching our tent. Then, metres away, was a row of very low sand dunes, and beyond that was a perfect beach, absolutely deserted. The weather was calm, yet the sea had a constant range of waves perfect for body surfing. At night, we fell asleep to the lullaby murmuring of the surf only fifty metres away.

We found we could take a pleasant walk along the road on which we'd come into the town of La Escala. It was a lovely, unspoilt fishing village with a small restaurant, spotless with superb food. We had steaks, sauté potatoes, salad, finished by fresh fruit salad and cream. The whole experience was wonderful. Afterwards we pottered around the ancient ruins by the sea. Aeons ago, it had been a port settlement of the Greeks, followed by more precise structures added by the Romans who had conquered it from the Greeks.

We found a small river that emptied into the Bay of Rosas less than half a mile from our tent. We were walking back from the river one evening and were passed by some of the locals (peasants from their appearance). Each one carried a long pole across his shoulder. Hanging from the pole was a dozen huge carp, spaced along the pole, half the load hanging behind him and the other half in front. Later, we examined the river. Astonishingly, it was crammed with carp. It looked as though you could walk across the river on them.

That second, final, week was a superb stay, difficult to compare with the more commercialised Costa Brava site. The second site was a complete contrast, peaceful, wild, with unexpected sights. All in all the perfect "two centre" holiday.

As before the return journey to England wasn't a chore, with memories of our exciting holiday lingering in our minds. We passed through great places. I remember making such good progress that we had time for a leisurely lunch break in Provence at the town of Montelimar, the home of the famous nougat sweets. We couldn't believe that so many shops were given over to selling exclusively this delicious sweetmeat, made of egg white, honey, fruits and a variety of nuts. The children had a huge bar apiece and really enjoyed it. So much nicer than the poor imitation we had bought in the UK.

We stopped again in the afternoon and had coffee and soft drinks outside a lovely little café in the town square. The square wasn't paved; it was so old fashioned. The locals were playing "pétanque" or boules on a dirt pitch. All the on-lookers were so excited, and we got caught up in it from our ringside seats outside the café. Everybody was so well mannered and friendly.

Later in the afternoon, we had another of our delays in finding a campsite. We were passing along a stretch of the N7 which was quite sparsely populated. Once more, teenagers came to our rescue. A group of them, with their ubiquitous bicycles, said, "Suivez moi," and took us down a deserted country lane for a short distance. By then, it was later in the day, and the sun was lower on the horizon, so we couldn't get a good sense of where we were. Suddenly, a tall stone wall appeared, and we were led down the side of it where a good clear patch of rough lawn stood between the wall and an area of poplar trees on the other side.

It was quite spacious, but there were no tents. However, we pitched up, Sheila produced her lovely quick dinner, and we spent a quiet peaceful night. Water would have been a problem except that we always carried a stout white five-gallon container with its own tap.

In the morning, after breakfast, we looked for a toilet. No luck, so Sheila and Edwina entered the poplar copse. The boys and I were desperate by then for a wee, so we walked to the stone wall and relieved our bladders against it. The wall had changed height when it reached this "lawned" area, so while I stood before it I had an uninterrupted view of the grounds at the other side.

Suddenly, a face appeared before me on the other side of the wall. Clad in a black and white habit, it was the smiling face of a nun. I finished my wee while smiling in return to the nun and her companions, who by then had joined her. They didn't speak English, so I indicated as best I could that we were grateful for le camping and were about to leave.

As I drove the car to where the wall began, I saw the large open iron gates and realised it was the entrance to a large Abbey. The dozen or so nuns lined up by the gate and shook hands with each of us, indicating that there was no charge and wishing us "bon voyage".

For the last night, we treated ourselves to a stay at a little old-fashioned hotel. It was clean and comfortable, though we had a slight difficulty in understanding the way the beds were made. There were no pillows. Instead, there was a long "bolster", I think it's called, which stretched the whole width of the bed. The bottom sheet was longer than ours at home. The bolster was rolled into the end of the sheet to form a pillow. I've not seen that arrangement before or since.

After the usual French breakfast, we motored off to Le-Havre and caught our overnight ferry to Southampton.

Other holidays

There were other holiday experiences to follow, a couple of them at the "Cros-de-Mouton" site at Cavalaire, between St. Tropez and Le Lavendou, an absolutely delightful area of France. It was always quiet, despite being only 15 kilometres to the west of St. Tropez.

When Gary had passed his A-level exams and was preparing to go to university, we thought about our next holiday. By then, I had been made a junior director at the firm, so we didn't need to spend our holidays camping in order to reduce avoid the cost of a package tour.

Also, Sheila said, "This will be our last holiday as a whole family together; it's time we lashed out on a package tour, without all the driving and self-catering. Also, it will be a special treat for the children."

So, we booked a Thompson's holiday at an hotel in Malgrat, near to Gerona in Spain. It was on the Bay of Rosas where we had spent such an adventurous week previously. I regret to say that, although the hotel was good and the food and facilities excellent, it was a great disappointment to the youngsters. They missed, so much, the freedom of our camping holidays and, as teenagers, particularly the social life they enjoyed with other youngsters from different countries.

At the Cros de Mouton there had been a lovely restaurant with an outdoor dance floor. It was well made out of quality hardwood, surrounded by tables chairs and table lamps, perfect for them to mix with the German, French and Italian teenagers for a drink and a dance. They missed also, the sense of adventure, wondering where, on the journeys south and back, we would be spending the night.

I can't resist finishing this account of our family holidays with a little anecdote that illustrates the marvellous serendipities that can occur on a semi-planned touring holiday. We were travelling back from Spain on the coast road. We were at an international bottleneck, with the Pyrenees on our left and the Med on our right. In all our travels, it was the only time we were held up by traffic. I don't know what caused it that year, but it was so bad. It took hours to reach the French border, and the crawl continued beyond.

We were making for the N7 to take us past Carcassone and north towards Paris. After more hours spent crawling forward, I took out my Michelin map and plotted a diversion which would take us up in the Vosges mountains, then westward to pick up the road north. The road we took was quiet, and we made good progress. I stopped at the first mountain village where, fortunately, there was a campsite. It really was a wild, isolated area, surrounded by steep mountains. We took a stroll through the town. All the shops seemed to sell clothing, guns and equipment for "les chasseurs".

France, being such a big country, had plenty of natural countryside, and hunting, shooting and fishing were popular in such areas. It was such a contrast from Spain, where it had been dry and hot. Here there was a light mist that went everywhere. The hillsides were steep and heavily wooded with northern types of trees. The campsite wasn't perfect, it stood on a slope by a fast-flowing river. As we settled down for the night, we could hear howling from the mountains around us. We all thought it didn't sound like dogs, as there was no barking. The animals seemed some distance away and just howled. I still think they were wolves.

We ploughed on the following day, picking out roads which ran north and west until, later that day, we did eventually hit the N.7. We had cleared the traffic bottleneck and now made good progress north.

Amateur dramatics as a cure for empty nest syndrome

So, with that holiday at an end the family matured, the children got married and flew the nest. Sheila and I adjusted, in the end, after feeling the initial departure of the children. They had been the centre of our attention as parents, and we felt the loss keenly until time replaced those feelings as we grew accustomed to our new lifestyle.

Sheila resumed her badminton and amateur dramatics. Rode Players, however, had become a shadow of its former self, but one of Sheila's old friends introduced her to Basford Players. They used the Church Hall at St. Mark's Church in Basford. It was a small neighbourhood on the road between Hanley and Newcastle-under-Lyme. I went, to accompany Sheila, to the rehearsals and offered help with scenery, props and general odd jobs.

It was a lively company with a talented and enthusiastic producer/director. The first play they put on after Sheila's arrival was *A Tomb with a View* by Norman Robbins. It was a dark comedy (well suited to the roles that Sheila had played in the past). Fearing it might be a bit of a challenge, our director suggested we all take a trip to see the "Leek Players", who were about to open with it. This would either strengthen or allay our fears and give us a taste of the atmosphere the play created.

The Leek performance was first class and the whole Basford troupe came away extremely impressed. It would be a challenge, but we all felt that, with thorough preparation and rehearsals, we would be able to produce it.

One of the problems that seemed to bedevil amateur dramatic groups was to be able to fill the male roles. We had a number of men, like me, who liked to help but not so many who were prepared to appear on-stage.

At the first of our preparatory meetings, the eyes of the director fell on me. "You are just the right age, physique etc. for the role of 'Lucien'." – actually the leading part. I was horrified and made my excuses, but in the end, more out of sympathy for their shortage of male players, after a couple of weeks indecision, I took the part.

Sheila was a great help, coaching me in voice projection, techniques for memorising lines and, most important, disaster planning in order to cope with miscues. A fellow actor, in the middle of Act 2, would give you a cue from the middle of Act 3 and it took some presence of mind to be able to get the pair of you back on track.

I won't bore you with the rehearsals or the performance other than to say the play was successful. Sheila brought the house down with her portrayal of "Dora", the sister who was the villainess of the play. Dora was a loopy character, required to sing about the bodies buried under the roses. Because of her ear problems from childhood, Sheila had absolutely no ear for music.

At rehearsals the director asked her "How do you manage to always portray somebody who is mentally deranged and is singing off key?" Sheila took no offence and calmly explained that her "Dora voice" was actually her own singing voice.

For anybody contemplating a stage appearance, I would say that it is like I am told you feel like after a successful parachute jump: tremendously exhilarating. However, I didn't take on another role after "Lucien".

Chapter 10: My Early Life and Childhood Relatives

Prelude

Today, we hear so much about culture wars and the battle between progressives and conservatives. It is hard to appreciate that even today's most conservative conservatives are extremely progressive compared to the society that I grew up in. Here, as I introduce you to some of my relatives, you may get a feel for just how attitudes have changed.

My childhood relatives

My Mother and Father had to get married because my mother was expecting me. Father was unemployed, as it was the time of the Great Depression. They went to live with Father's mother and father in Albion Street, Burslem. Albion Street led downhill to Middleport on the canal side at the bottom of the hill, a distance of less than a quarter of a mile.

I don't remember any of those days. I just have memories of my father telling me that I was a precocious child. I walked at nine months and was talking fluently before I was two.

Paternal relatives

The Staffordshire Giant

Father's father was named Harry Johnson. He and my paternal grandmother lived in Armitage, south Staffordshire, where he was employed by Armitage Sanitary Ware, the forerunner of the large company it became with the new name Armitage-Shanks.

Father told me he originated from Newcastle-on-Tyne and had made his way south looking for work. His job title was "cod-plaicer" a play on words for the man who was in charge of the plaicers. Their job was to carry the loaded saggars from the finishing shop and place them into the bottle kilns (ovens).

It was skilled work. Inside the kiln, which was as big as a large room, the saggars had to be stacked vertically and securely to avoid any crashes during the firing process, which took three to five days until the fireware was cool enough to be "drawn" (unloaded from the kiln). The walls inside the Kiln were like the inside of a bottle, finishing near the centre of the domed top. This meant the pile of saggars were leaning inwards slightly. Bigger pieces of sanitary ware, too big to be contained in saggars, helped to secure the columns of saggars.

The workers who placed the unfired ware and also "drew" the finished ware from the kiln were called plaicers. They were not employed directly by the Armitage Co. Harry was what you might call a "ganger", paid for the job of dealing with a kiln. The plaicers themselves were then paid by Grandad. There was no PAYE or anything like that, just cash payments.

Harry had something of a fearsome reputation. He was a big man physically, with flaming red hair and a Victorian "spade" beard. Father once showed me a black and white photograph of Grandad in the backyard at Albion Street. Must have been before he retired with lead poisoning. My father, who was six feet tall, was standing beside his younger brother, Sid (my Uncle Sid), who was about six feet two inches tall. Standing behind them was my grandfather, towering head and shoulders over his two sons, with shoulders almost as broad as the two of them combined.

Father told me a few tales about him. He had a fierce temper, ready with his fists to discipline the workers in his gang or anybody else challenging him. Father insisted he was called "the Staffordshire Giant" in the local newspaper. Apparently, the Chairman of Armitage held an annual fete with sporting events as part of the entertainment. The chief event was the walking race over a course stretching for twenty miles around the town. It was a popular event, because the people of south Staffordshire were known for their dogfighting (hence the Staffordshire bull terrier) and other crude ancient sports. The Chairman's wife (Mrs. Cornes) had offered a cash prize and a pair of kid-gloves to the winner of the walking race.

A lot of bets were placed against Harry, because the majority of the gamblers reckoned he was too big, not the slim athletic type. However,

Harry won the event decisively. Mrs Cornes could not find in any of the local outfitters' shops a pair of kid gloves big enough to fit Harry's huge hands. But she honoured her pledge by sending off his measurements to a smart firm in London who made them specially for him.

I was told that my grandad, despite his fearsome reputation as a volatile "fighting man", was very fond of me. Father told me that, when I was an infant, he would sit me on his knee, smile and hold up a finger, not being able to talk – because of lead poisoning from unfired ware. I quickly responded by raising my forefinger too. This amused Grandfather and he seemed happy to be able to establish some sort of communication.

Grandmother Johnson

I mentioned earlier that Grandmother Johnson had a total of eleven children. At mealtimes, from my father's account, Grandad sat by the fire after returning from work. Grandmother laid the table, and when dinner was ready, instead of moving to sit at the table, Grandfather would reach over and grab the table with one hand, raising it and drawing it to where he was sitting. He and Grandmother would then eat their meal together. Meantime, the children all sat on a bench at the side of the room until the adults had finished, when the children would be called to bring themselves and the bench to the table.

Grandmother baked her own bread. She would knead the dough then place it into a large "joule" while it "proved". A joule was a large fire-clay bowl, which must have weighed several pounds without its load of dough. She would ask Grandfather to carry the joule down into the cellar to wait until she was ready to bake it. Grandfather would pick it up with the thumb of one hand in the inside of the joule and the fingers on the outside, in the way that normal size people might carry a pudding basin.

I have no direct memories at all of my paternal grandmother. Father always talked of her with great fondness. Apparently, she was a quiet but strong personality. She had borne eleven children. One, a boy – I think he was named Frank – died before he was school-leaving age from tuberculosis of the bowel. Grandmother died too, of cancer when

I was still a toddler, followed quickly by Grandfather. This left mother and father as tenants of the house in Albion Street, number 20.

Father's siblings

I can remember some of my father's siblings. Uncle Sid was the only brother, apart from Frank who had, as I said, died when young. The others were all girls.

Sid was a lovely gentle person. He and his wife couldn't have children, so they adopted quite a large family and cared well for them. Father however, inherited some of Grandfather's temper, although he was never violent. He regularly cautioned me about losing my temper. His favourite admonition which must have been dinned into him, was "He who loses his temper rides a wild horse without a bridle."

Auntie Mary was a lovely lady. She and her husband, Uncle Albert, were caretakers for the Wesleyan Chapel in Dalehall, about half a mile away. They had rooms in the chapel. And, as it was a big chapel, it was a full-time job for them both.

Auntie Mary, until she died, sent me a postal order every year, on my birthday. She did this only for me. Apparently, she had a soft spot for me in her affections.

Auntie Ethel lived in Sneyd Green. She had two sons who, like all of the Johnson clan, were extremely tall. The youngest had polio as a youngster which left him with his right leg in irons. However, he was able to earn a living as a cobbler.

Auntie Edna, I never saw. She had married a Yorkshireman and gone to live in a village near Sheffield. I didn't ever visit her, but Bill, my younger brother, went one year to stay with them for a week, enjoying the time he spent with his cousins. I never saw them either.

Auntie Betsie lived in High Lane, on the top of the ridge which runs above the Potteries. I saw her very occasionally.

Auntie Elsie, the youngest of the sisters, lived in Burslem. She had two daughters, Vera the eldest, and Violet. Violet had suffered with "Saint Vitus's dance". This was the explanation for her behaviour. A nice girl but constantly fidgeting or standing up then sitting down.

There were other aunts, but I never learned anything about them.

Maternal relatives

Grandfather Gaskell

Mother's Father – can't remember what his name was – from vague recollections of what Mother told me when I was a child, was a gentle kindly man. All I know other than that was that he was a "pottery artist".

In the days before underglaze painting and lithographs on glazed pottery, the decorations were started by skilled, experienced paintresses in the decorating department. They would paint the outlines or significant features of decorations. The less skilled paintresses would then complete the work by, for example, free-hand painting leaves (in a stylised manner in which they were trained by the skilled artists) or flowers, all in the same style to create a matching dinner or tea set.

Grandfather Gaskell, however, painted complete pictures on things like teapots or ornamental vases. It was skilled, time-consuming work and was reserved only for "special lines" sold at high prices. He must have made good money at it for he was able to buy the house in Orford Street, the first of the avenues climbing up Port Hill (the local "Nob Hill" in those days).

Grannie Gaskell

My maternal Grandmother was named Mary Gaskell. She too lived in the family home, that very nice house in Orford Street. As I say, it was the first of the avenues climbing up Port Hill. Below it was a stretch of low grassy embankment along the LMS (London, Midland and Scottish) railway. Beyond that was a wide stretch of grassland up to the Trent and Mersey Canal with its pottery factories on its far side, including Middleport Pottery where I spent my early working years. Grannie Gaskell's children all lived in the Potteries except for Auntie Lucy, the eldest girl.

I don't know why but Mother and Father weren't up for relatives visiting. I can only guess it might have had something to do with the shame of having to get married and being poverty stricken. It must be hard for young people, several generations on from this, to grasp how the almost puritanical values of that era affected attitudes and behaviour.

As I said earlier, churches and chapels were well attended. I remember my mother when I said I was to become a choir boy at St. Paul's Church, (opposite my school of the same name), she said, "It is a very large church with a balcony with seating for scores of people. At Easter and Saint's Days, the church was full, and latecomers had a struggle to find a seat in the balcony. All the pews in the nave were packed."

The culture at the time held it to be sinful to have sex before marriage. Actually, stronger in the belief than it was in secret practice. Natural instincts can be suppressed but never denied.

Uncle Wilf

Back to my maternal relatives. The eldest of all, Uncle Wilfred, was a very nice, cultured gentleman. He was a veteran of the First World War (the Great War, his generation called it). He had been gassed but not so severely that it had crippled him, as it did for so many unfortunates. He didn't describe the actual actions that he was involved with, but he told tales of companionship and some of the really decent people in the trenches with him.

I remember he fascinated us with an anecdote involving a German prisoner they had captured and taken back to the field station just behind their lines. The action he was involved with had been successful and in the shelter of this forward HQ building a supply of beer and rum had been produced and it developed into some sort of a party. The young German joined in their singing, and everybody quietened at the sound of him singing. Apparently, he had a beautiful alto tenor voice. The crowd remained silent until he finished the song when they began to applaud. However, one of the British soldiers, at this point, raised his rifle and shot the German dead. The way Wilfred told the story showed how deeply he had been upset by the war; the heroism mixed with savagery.

An aside on the impact of the Great War

I can't continue at this point without talking about the effect of the Great War. As a young child, Mother would take me with her to Burslem for shopping in the market hall. Burslem was a busy town in those pre-war years. The local economy was healthy, despite the unemployment, basically because it was a local economy. There wasn't the same level of national businesses and, of course, no internet. Even mail order hadn't reached the level of popularity it later achieved when neighbourhoods or groups of employees at a factory had someone running a catalogue.

However, in Burslem as we walked through High Street or Queen Street, the main thoroughfares, we passed veterans of the war with missing arms, legs, or eyesight, holding a piece of cardboard against their chest saying, "War Wounded", "Gas Victim", "War Blind". Some of them had simple cardboard trays, held against their chest by a string around their neck, holding boxes of matches for sale. I also remember at school, one teacher with only one arm and two with bad limps. I never knew whether they were amputees or not, but I suspected they were.

At the age of eleven our PT teacher took us to Burslem Swimming Baths once a week. This was invaluable help to me. The baths superintendent had the bearing of an ex-military man, and he was an excellent swimming instructor. We were taught the proper techniques for breaststroke, crawl (free style it is termed today) and back crawl. In addition, we were taught rescue techniques and artificial respiration.

One of the rescue techniques taught us how to approach someone in the water who would grab hold of his rescuer with the risk of pulling them both underwater and drowning. We were instructed to approach from the victim's front and if he held onto you, to put the outspread fingers of your left hand onto his face with two fingers pressed each side of his nose. Then put our right hand onto the small of his back, pull him or her close and push up with the left hand until their head was bent back, continuing until the victim's head was under-water. It was surprisingly effective. Pity, although I had a number of occasions to help people in difficulties in the water, I never had to use this technique.

However, sorry again for digressing, I was talking about war wounded. Being a keen swimmer, I walked up to Burslem Baths once or twice a week, in addition to the school visits. I always went early, while most people were enjoying their evening meal. So, the baths were almost always empty, just me and one other swimmer who always arrived ahead of me. I never spoke to him – he was always busy doing his lengths. I don't know if he was a war veteran, but he had only one leg.

His left leg had been amputated from high up his femur. In other respects, although getting on in years, he looked extremely fit. What was so impressive, however, was his swimming ability. He swam up and down the pool with a steady, graceful style of crawl. He covered the distance effortlessly with his right leg moving up and down without the company of his left leg to balance the stroke.

Back to Uncle Wilf

Uncle Wilf, who lived in Waterloo Road, Burslem, had a wife, Auntie Edna, who was a cripple. A strange story behind that. Apparently, she was using a sewing machine when the needle pierced her finger, penetrating through the nail and the bone and out the other side. Must have been an industrial sewing machine. From what little I knew from the later years of my childhood, helping my mother to thread and re-spool her sewing machine, a domestic model couldn't possibly cause such an horrific injury. However, and remember this was years before the discovery of anti-biotics, she developed septicaemia. It spread throughout her body and left her partly paralysed. She wasn't a chatty person. Just kept in the background.

Aunty Lucy and Uncle Jack

Auntie Lucy, the eldest of Grannie Gaskell's children, had married Jack who, after returning from the Great War as one of the many wounded, walked with a slight limp. That it was so slight was quite remarkable considering the wound he had suffered. The only occasion we talked about his time in the army was when I was approaching national service.

He described advancing in a great line abreast at the battle of Verdun. Unusual in a way, because the Allied force at that battle were nearly all French. One of their worst defeats I gathered. However, Jack went on to tell me he stepped on a mine. The explosion knocked him unconscious and when he came round his left leg was broken at the knee. He looked at in astonishment for it was bent to his left at right angles from his thigh. The stretcher bearers recovered him quickly and he was operated on, obviously by a skilled surgeon, since he recovered well and was left with little pain and only a slight limp.

He and Lucy were tenant farmers. Their farm, Stapeley Farm, was about five miles out of Nantwich on the main road to Woore and Newcastle-under-Lyme. They were very good to us, and for several years during the war and after, they had us over for a fortnight's summer holiday. My father never came with us. He carried on working.

Those holidays were idyllic for me. I loved helping, feeding the chickens with grain – I was allowed to go into the barn, next to the shippon (cattle shed) and gather the different feeds from the various hoppers.

They had geese too. These are excellent "guard dogs". Apparently, the ancient Romans used them for that purpose. The head goose – the gander – seemed aggressive, until Auntie Lucie showed us how to face him down. He would rush at me with wings outstretched and head lowered, honking and hissing. "Just stand your ground," said Auntie Lucy. "Look him in the eye and stamp your foot at him, he'll give in if you do."

Auntie Lucy in looks was like a twin, but older, version of my mother. Although identical in appearance Lucy's character was very different indeed. Mother was extremely shy and timid. She would never speak up for herself. Lucy on the other hand was a tower of strength at the farm with her positive, firm, manner. She could deal with all sorts of visitors, being positive, yet still pleasant, with tradesmen or neighbouring farmers who wanted to, for example, borrow a piece of Uncle Jack's machinery.

Uncle Jack and Lucy had worked extremely hard and saved determinedly to get the farm, and they had built up a small fleet of equipment. Their tractor was a Fordson. It had two fuel tanks, a small petrol tank, used to start the engine, then a large tank of TVO (tractor vaporising oil) would kick in. This was, effectively paraffin, sold to farmers during the war and strictly rationed. It was coloured to help Customs and Excise spot any used for purposes other than farm tractors.

He had a plough, a harrowing machine, a "Tedder" to pull behind the tractor to gather up and turn over the hay as it dried in the fields. He had a seed sower and other devices. These all enabled him to operate with a lot of independence. Farmers did a lot of borrowing from one another depending on their types of machinery. This was done for a fee and Jack was independent of this until, in later years, combine harvester machines were invented.

These were huge, complex and expensive outfits, used for harvesting wheat, barley, oats and other grains. The machine didn't only mow the crop it would thresh it to gather the grain which then poured out of a conveyor onto a trailer running alongside. The straw remaining after threshing was compressed into bales, bound tightly with twine and deposited onto the stubble behind the "combine".

I've skipped a bit. I should have mentioned when, in the early years of my visits, the power source on the farm was a beautiful, huge shire horse. His name was Tom, and he was a double for the LMS horse of the same name, which I grew to meet and love. Uncle Jack was very fond of Tom. The horse was a strong and willing horse. He knew how to haul the different types of machinery. When ploughing, he carefully trod to the right of the last furrow he had ploughed and he knew, when harvest time came, to back himself in the "binder" which was the forerunner of the far more sophisticated combine harvesters which came years later.

Tom had a beautiful chestnut coat, glossy with a white nose blaze and white forefeet.

Although a capable and willing worker, Tom had an inbuilt clock. At the end of the working day, he would act up a bit stubbornly – he knew when it was time to return to his warm, cosy, stall and his feed. Uncle Jack was always careful to give him a fair ration of oats during the working season. In the short period between ploughing, harrowing and the hay mowing, then teddering and corn harvesting, he had a short holiday when he was a shorter ration with fewer oats.

Apparently, it was necessary to watch a horse's diet and to match it with his work output. Basically, the corn, peas, turnips, mangelwurzels, kale etc. which Jack grew was for winter feed for his herd of cattle. The herd comprised 25 head, a small herd by today's standards, but the milk from the twice-daily milking provided a living for Jack and Lucy and their three daughters that remained after Frankie's death. They were able also to buy a house for each of them: Lily, the eldest, Doreen, (for some strange reason they pronounced it Dreen!) then Bertha (named after my mother). It must have been a headache caring for the girls as they grew up during the war years.

American troops arrive near Auntie Annie's farm

From 1942, American troops started to arrive in UK. They were stationed at newly built camps throughout the country. One such camp was located somewhere near to Woore, a few miles up the road from Stapeley Farm. The troops had a reputation for being extremely forward with British girls and, as you might imagine, they left a fair crop of unwanted pregnancies behind them. A lot of the girls seemed to welcome their advances, a change from the more reticent British men. Also, most of those British men were away serving in the forces in distant places.

The contrast in appearance was also quite marked. Although only a youngster, I noticed how much bigger and well-fed they looked. Their uniforms made of expensive material made them all look like our officers. Our "other ranks" uniforms were thick, rough "serge", not so smart and expensive looking as the Americans. This added to the glamorous aura surrounding the yanks.

Their troops seemed very fond of children. I remember standing with other boys outside the farm when lorry loads of American soldiers were passing on their way to the camp at Woore. They would throw sweets, chocolate bars and packs of chewing gum out at the children at the roadside. In those days of severe rationing, this was a real treat for us. However, I didn't like the habit that grew among some of our young boys who, when meeting yanks in the town, would ask "Got any gum chum?" Where this behaviour came from was a mystery, but my brothers and I all thought it smacked of begging and not the right way to behave.

Auntie Carrie and her children

My mother was the youngest of Grannie Gaskell's children. Many years the youngest. Auntie Lucy was the oldest. Next came Auntie Carrie. She lived very near to Middleport Park, in easy walking distance from our house in Albion Street. She and her husband, Uncle Edgar, lived there with their three children, Edgar ("Cousin Eddie"), William, ("Cousin

Bill") and Caroline – named after her mother. (She was "Cousin Carrie").

Edgar was a remote figure. I only saw him once, at their house when I visited one day. I wasn't introduced. Children in those days were to be seen not heard. I got the impression of a lone, miserable sort of chap.

Eddie was much older than me. He was a bricklayer.

Bill was about eight years older than me. He was a joiner who worked for the Canal Operating Company, soon to be nationalised into the Railways and Canal Transport Network. His work shed was on the canal-side where narrow boats were built and older ones repaired or overhauled.

Bill was an excellent swimmer. This was fortunate, because one day, at work, he saw a young lad, a non-swimmer, fall into the canal. Bill unhesitatingly dived in and rescued the lad. A big fuss was made of Bill. He appeared in the local Sentinel and was awarded a framed certificate from the Humane Society, commemorating his bravery and skill in saving a life.

Auntie Carrie's youngest, Cousin Carrie was a very pleasant, generous soul. She was some years older than me, but I was, apparently, her favourite. We were quite close, and I remember her kindness after I suffered an accident at home. I must have been about three years old. Auntie Carrie, with cousins Bill and Carrie, were visiting us. The tradition was to offer a cup of tea to visitors as soon as they arrived.

Father made the tea for everybody and served them up in mugs. We didn't have cups and saucers. These mugs were placed on the kitchen table. I reached up eagerly – I can remember the incident today, calling out, "Is this mine.?" I grabbed a mug at the edge of the table, but it was heavy and tumbled down onto my right wrist/forearm. It was scalding hot and very painful – I still have the faint scars today.

Huge blisters appeared. I was screaming a lot, so Dr Shields was called. He lived quite nearby so came and plastered me with a bright yellow lotion and bandaged my arm. He left a supply of the lotion with instructions that the dressing should be changed daily. Apparently, I must have been a bit of a "mard-arse", because I screamed if anybody attempted to deal with the dressing. All except for Cousin Carrie. She came every day for a week or so to change the dressing. To my embarrassment, I am told that I screamed and hid under the table if anybody other than Carrie tried to help me.

Eddie served in the Army during the last years of the war.

Bill was too young to serve during the war, but, as conscription was still in force, he was called up into the infantry immediately after war's end. He was posted to India and served there at the time of partition, when the country was divided into India for the Hindus, Sikhs, Jains etc. and Pakistan in the northwest of the sub-continent, for the Moslem community.

It was a dreadful time. Although, from the many accounts I've read about it, the British authorities had tried to avoid partition and did whatever they could to avoid violence, the country descended into chaos. Hindus and Muslim's generally hated one another. As the date of partition arrived, there were mass migrations of Hindus from the north-west into India, and Muslim's from India into the newly designated Pakistan.

Gangs of activists from each side roamed the country, attacking migrants on their journeys and even breaking into the other side's homes. I can't put a figure on the death toll. I can remember Auntie Carrie showing us one of Bill's letters home describing, where he was stationed near the River Ganges, the hundreds of funeral pyres along the river and the smell of burning bodies.

Carrie was spared military service; women were not conscripted, although many volunteered, like Princess Elizabeth, to serve in the WRAC's (Army), the WREN's (Navy) or the WAAF's (Air-force). Many joined the Queen Alexander's Nursing Corps or the Women's Voluntary Service, that wonderful organisation, un-remarked on but always on hand, like the Red Cross, to provide good hot tea, sandwiches and cakes to servicemen in trouble, or when travelling en masse. I was greeted by them when I landed at Hurn Airport, Bournemouth on the way back from Egypt, where the first thing I saw when we entered the airport building, after an exhausting eight hour journey, was the trestle tables, neatly covered with lovely white linen table cloths and loaded with refreshments served by those smiling, kind ladies. We were not in a bad state like the survivors of Dunkirk, but it was a smaller version of the reception they received at Dover etc. before continuing on the trains for their onward journey.

Uncle John (I think)

There was another sibling, an uncle – I seem to remember his name was John. I'm not sure but I have the impression he was a bit older than my mother. I was told he was a shy sort of man. As a teenager, he fell ill with scarlet fever. In addition to its usual side effects, strawberry tongue and peeling skin (which disappeared after recovering from the disease), it caused John to lose his body hair. He was completely bald, no eyebrows, no eyelashes either. Apparently, he was teased about his appearance and must have become depressed. He gassed himself. Don't know at what age.

When Grannie Gaskell got old

As Mary (Grannie Gaskell) grew older, she became, allegedly, unable to care for herself. For some years, Auntie Carrie and Uncle Edgar had her living with them in their house near Middleport Park. Eventually, they got fed up coping with her and her eccentric ways, so they persuaded Mother and Father to take a turn having her living with us in Albion Street. There were four of us children in a two-bedroom house. This was before Mavis, the youngest, was born.

The problem of having three boys plus Barbara was reduced by events at Simpson's shop opposite our house. Mrs. Simpson died and left her daughter Annie as the sole occupant. She was a spinster, quite a few years older than Barbara, but as she found herself lonely and saddened at living alone, she offered to have Barbara sleep at her house every night. We became used to the routine of we boys going upstairs to bed, and Barbara crossing the road to spend the night with Annie Simpson. Annie was so grateful, and Barbara appreciated the extra space and privacy, so it all worked well.

Eventually, Barbara and Cousin Bill Hood spent more time together as Bill, like Carrie Jnr, loved to visit us. They married after a few years and went together to live in Lock Cottage by the canal at Rode Heath. Bill, from leaving school, had always worked for the Canal Company (by then incorporated into the British Rail and Waterways Organisation).

Bill was a qualified and skilled joiner with an education in building practices, and it wasn't long before he was promoted to be the "length foreman". He was responsible for the length of the Mersey Weaver Canal from Kidsgrove, where it started, up to Sandbach. His team was responsible for building and repairing bridges, canal maintenance and repairs, together with the caring for the many locks in that length. So, he was given the tenancy of company house, Lock Cottage. Bill and Barbara had two children, Simon and Jane. Simon had no children, Jane had two, a boy, then a girl.

Back to Grannie Gaskell. She had a small bed in the front room. This overcame her difficulty in climbing stairs. She wasn't any trouble; her wants were few. She ate little and her clothing looked like that of a stereotypical Mediterranean widow. She wore black. Every item of clothing was black. Her only problem, in my father's eyes, was her drinking. I never saw her drunk, nor did she show any signs of being inebriated. She never went out, just sat quietly by the kitchen range.

She did send me out, however, every single evening, armed with two large screw-top bottles, to the small off licence shop on the opposite side of the street, about ten houses down. Granny gave me the cash to pay for "three halves of bitter" in one bottle and "three halves of mixed" (mild and bitter) in the second bottle. That amounted to three pints every single night.

The lady who kept the off licence shop seemed always to be worried at serving a young lad with such a quantity of alcoholic beer. She went to a great deal of trouble, after filling the two bottles, to seal the stoppers with an adhesive paper seal. I guess this would have appeased anybody in authority questioning me carrying such an intoxicating load. Three pints might have been a tolerable quantity for a young adult, but for a woman in her eighties it could be considered to be a bit too much.

Her food intake by then consisted almost always of a mug of Oxo with a slice of bread broken into it. She complained of stomach-ache and gave that as the reason for wanting no other food. I can't think now of amore unsuitable diet. The Oxo drink was basically, salted hot water. After a few years, perhaps unsurprisingly given her diet, she passed away at age 82.

My sister Barbara still, at the time of this writing, lives in Lock Cottage. She told me recently that Grannie was an alcoholic and that was the cause of her demise. I would like to say that Grannie entertained me with stories of life in the Victorian Age, or her early life and employment, but she didn't talk much. She just made sure I knew what beer to order each night.

The neighbourhood

The neighbourhood was populated generally by decent working-class families. There was no crime I ever saw or heard about. As I explained, earlier, we closed the latch on the front door when going to bed but never used the key to lock it. People would help if needed but there was no "neighbouring" that I knew of. I heard, when I grew older, of districts where people would literally walk into a neighbour's house to borrow a cup of sugar. Perhaps it was the influence of the Primitive Methodist chapel at the head of the street that prevented such over familiarity.

I remember several of the neighbours being quite keen gardeners, growing beautiful flowers in their back gardens. We didn't. A lot of the garden was taken up by the Anderson air raid shelter that father had constructed during the war. He was too busy working, or looking for work, to do any gardening.

I remember when one of the many horse-drawn carts passed our house. Mr. Barlow, who lived three doors down, must have kept a look out from his front room window, because if the horse left its droppings on the road, Mr Barlow would dash out with a bucket and a little shovel. He would gather up the dung and rush back up the entry to his back-gate to add the contents of his bucket to the earth around his beautiful roses.

Our next-door neighbour at No. 10 was a strange little man, never speaking to his neighbours. He was called up into the army at the beginning of the war. If, when he was home on leave at the time of the regular air raids, he would parade up and down the length of his back garden with his rifle and fixed bayonet. We were never actually bombed. As I mentioned earlier, apart from the occasional stray bomb, the

193

Luftwaffe always carried on flying over us in a north-westerly direction towards Manchester and Liverpool.

Next door below at No 14 were Mr. and Mrs. Pedley. Mr. Pedley was also named Arthur, and he and Father became good friends. Mrs. Pedley, unfortunately, was a bit of a "shrew", suspicious by nature and not very much of a neighbour. They had a daughter, Nora, about five years older than me and a son, Tom, the same age as me.

Tom and I, with other neighbours' boys, would play together in the street. No danger from road traffic in those days. The occasional carthorse gave plenty of warning of its approach. We played football with an old tennis ball. Cricket with the same ball and a couple of staves from a barrel fashioned into a bat.

Some games followed the seasons. When the weather was warm and dry it became, suddenly, the craze for marbles, which we played in the gutter. The kerb was useful in preventing the "shotties" from rolling away when we played a game called "follows on" along the gutter.

Then it would be the season for "top and whip". The many sweet shops sold them. The tops and whips were well made, but for some reason the whip had a leather boot lace which was useless for the job. We soon replaced them with a length of stout string.

After that, there was "bowling hoops", sold in the same shops, a slim iron ring and a short iron rod to propel and guide it. If any of us couldn't afford one, we would search around the shawd ruck or the fields bordering the canal for an old tyre.

Very often, instead of these manufactured games, we would play "tick". The first person nominated to be "it" chased after the crowd. When he then touched one of the crowd, that person now was "it" and carried on chasing until he caught the next to be "it".

A big favourite, however, was "hide and seek". The rows of terraced houses had entry ways leading on to the back gates of the two houses, one on each side. A few of these "entries" gave way to a long entry stretching past the back of a number of gardens. This all created a maze of hiding places.

After school we would either play in this fashion or a small gang would set off to the fields across the canal. There we could explore the "shawd ruck" where broken pottery had been dumped, along with other hardware type of rubbish, over goodness knows how many years.

The main ruck behind and beyond Middleport Pottery stretched for over half a mile, reaching almost to the London Midland Railway. Then, if we had played and strolled that far, we could dare one another on who could stand on the path under the railway bridge when a train, especially an express train, was passing.

The railway line served as an unwritten border to us. Our parents warned us not to carry onwards, under the bridge, to Orford Street and the start of the very steep path up to Wolstanton. This massive, steep slope was largely rough grassland but was broken by a very large quarry, cut into the hillside, from which red clay for tile making, was extracted. The hole cut into the hillside left a high cliff face. Children from Wolstanton, playing on the grass above the quarry had sometimes, fallen into the huge hole and been killed. So, our parents told us, we must never venture that far. The fact that it was too far for little legs to walk and to get back, helped keep us away.

Special Days

We children were brought up on Santa Claus, or Father Christmas as he is called by older children, still believing in the fantasy. He has other names. My grandchildren in Hungary expected St. Nicholas to call but not on the night of Christmas Eve. I have to confess; I don't remember exactly when. It is either before or after our Christmas Day.

As a child, I remember the uncontrollable excitement. On a year when my father was in work, I was treated to a visit to Lewis's department store in Hanley. It was a very large store, modern and brightly lit. At Christmas time, the store created a wonderful display of almost life-size marionettes of fairy story characters with reindeer and Cinderella, Jack the Beanstalk and other characters. They were manufactured to a very high standard and all moving to the sound of Christmas Carols.

If parents paid extra the visit included a meeting with Santa Claus who gave each child a wrapped gift. I was always disappointed with mine. In contrast to the expensive displays, it turned out to be a little tin car or similar toy.

At home we were helped by Mother and Father to hang up our stockings. Next morning, parents would be forced to let the children get up at a ridiculously early hour. We rushed to our stockings first. Always, the toe held an orange and the heel an apple. Nuts, sweets and chocolates filled the remaining space and often a little toy. Then the parcels.

I don't know how they did it, but the presents were always wonderful. I wonder how they afforded them. Mother, when she wasn't ill, pregnant or suffering a migraine, was an excellent cook and Christmas dinner was always so good. However, I regret that as a child I never appreciated the effort Mother made in preparing and cooking our meals.

One Christmas, 1939, was a bit disappointing. Father had only just started at H&R Johnson on the gas producer, and he and Mother couldn't afford the usual generous load of presents. There were a few new toys but supplemented by toys and books which were clearly second hand. I learned in later years that the senior manager, responsible for all the kilns and other power issues, had learned from Father about the "tight" Christmas that year. He very kindly dug out stuff his now grown-up children had left in the house. I was six years old at the time. I had kept secret my realisation that Santa Claus was a ruse to justify unwarranted generosity by parents. Seeing these second-hand books and toys sealed my conviction.

Birthdays also were another excitement. My best birthday present was on my fourth birthday, when I was awoken by Mother and Father, who dropped onto the bed, on my lap, a small wriggling puppy. He was a foxhound, all white apart from his brown ears and a large brown patch on his right shoulder. He was tiny and had a pink ribbon tied round his neck. I fell in love with him straightaway and quickly gave him a name, "Spot" because of the large brown spot on his shoulder. He was a good and faithful childhood companion. Unfortunately, I didn't see him in his last years. He died when I was away in the army and just about to leave Egypt. Dad, in his weekly letter, told me how he went to sleep of old age.

My siblings and their sizes

I was the smallest of the children in our family. The younger we were, the taller we grew. Bill, two years younger, was much bigger and heavier than me. Eric, again after another two years, was bigger and taller still. Barbara was one of the first war babies, born on the 2nd of October 1939. She wasn't as tall as we boys but bigger boned and heavier. When she was sixteen, she weighed sixteen stone and was not what I would term "fat". There was a then a gap then of five years before the youngest, Mavis. She was slimmer than Barbara but just over six feet tall. When Sheila had our first child, Gary, my father exclaimed when he say him, "He is going to be a giant". I don't know how he could tell, but Gary grew up to be quite a big man.

Chapter 11. Starting School

Prelude

Schooling has changed so much since I was a child. Then there was no recognition of special needs, no parents' evenings, no school holidays abroad, and no exchange visits. Most working-class children studied for many fewer years than they do today. I hope over the next few pages I can give you a flavour of what it was like then.

Middleport Infant School

When I reached the age of five, I started at Middleport Infant's School. I remember my first teacher, Mrs Booth. Unlike the other teachers, who all were young women, Mrs. Booth was an older lady, very large, with grey hair. She didn't wear pretty clothes like her colleagues, but always a green wrap-round overall which concealed whatever dress, skirt etc. she was wearing. She wasn't unkind. She wasn't overly kind either. She just seemed to be efficient in what she did. Looking back, I wonder if she had lost her husband or something.

She settled me down at a tiny desk in the middle of the classroom. There was no induction course. I was left to discover for myself how to ask to go to the toilet, where the toilet was and the route to avoid getting lost.

Mrs Booth brought me a sheet of foolscap paper (the forerunner to today's metric equivalent, the A4), a sharpened pencil and a strip of pink card bearing in neat handprint, (not in double-writing) as we later called it, my name Arthur Johnson. This strip had horizontal lines drawn on it to guide the student as to the height of the letters. There was a base line upon which the letters would be written, and a middle line which marked the top of the main form of letters and a slightly taller line denoting the height of the taller letters like b, d, f, h, j, k, l, and t. Then there was a final line at the top where capital letters reached. Using this card as a guide she showed me the foolscap sheet which was ruled in the same way and told me to copy my name until the sheet was filled.

I don't remember much of those early days. It was winter when I started at school. In later months when the warmer weather came, my mother sent me to school dressed in the homemade pastel cotton clothes she had hand sewn.

I have to admit her ideas were strange and the clothes quite impractical. I had a primrose, short sleeve top with buttons spaced around the hem. Then a pair of blue cotton shorts with buttonholes around the top. These were fastened onto the buttons on the shirt. No pockets in either garment. On my feet I had white ankle socks and black patent leather shoes with a strap over the instep which buttoned onto the other side.

You can imagine what it was like, in a rough working-class area, surrounded in the school yard by the other boys dressed in warm shop-bought short trousers and shirts or jerseys, their feet clad in stout boots to withstand the rigours of boys' play activities. My hair was long too. I remember the boys laughing and pointing to my shoes saying, "Are you a girl?" and "Why are you wearing girl's shoes?"

I complained to my father when I got home, and he put his foot down. He said something to the effect that he could understand my mother making clothes, because we couldn't afford to buy them. However, he must have persuaded her to get an "Alcocks' check" so she could buy some proper boy's clothes for me.

Alcocks was a local moneylender. The "club man" would call every week to collect money from the housewives. If a loan was required, he would write out a "check" (it wasn't called a "cheque") for, say, £10. This would be honoured by a retailer. If the full amount on the check was not spent, the retailer would write on the back leaving the balance to be spent at a shoe shop or other retailer.

When I was taken by Mother to get a pair of trousers or whatever, I always felt embarrassed when she produced a check instead of cash. I don't know why, nobody ever explained things to me, but I felt, instinctively, that it was infra dig to borrow in this way. Even as a child, it seemed to indicate to me an inability to manage money.

Bill, my younger brother, had a similar experience with my mother decking him out effeminately. This culminated in my mother becoming extremely distressed when she found father had cut off Bill's golden curls and made him look like a proper boy. In later years, my father confirmed my suspicion that mother wanted a daughter and was dressing us in what I thought was an effeminate style. A strange person in some ways.

I enjoyed school apart from maths. I am convinced to this day that all the maths teachers at all the schools I attended had some sort of communication problem. I enjoyed English, geography, history and other subjects. The teachers seemed to explain things clearly and were prepared in most cases to answer a student's queries. Not so with maths teachers. They all just scribbled at high speed on the blackboard, talking at the same time to the board instead of facing the class.

"What you do on one side of an equation, you must do on the opposite side, like this," pointing to the blackboard. It wasn't until many years later, working at H&R Johnson with Bill, that he explained some of the basics to me, and, helped by the newly available electronic calculators, I taught myself a bit more.

St Paul's Junior School

I spent three years at Middleport Infants School before transferring to St Paul's junior school opposite St. Paul's Church. This, like Middleport, being in a built-up city, was in easy walking distance, so we never had transport problems. I remember the last year's teacher at Middleport Junior School. Mrs. Howell, she was called. As you might guess from the name, she was Welsh. Always kind and considerate, a young middle-aged lady, she made lessons interesting. She also took us for music, which involved a lot of singing. She taught us some songs in Welsh. (Remember that Stoke-on-Trent is less than fifty miles from the border with Wales.) *Land of my Fathers, Men of Harlech*, though I can't remember a word now. A few days before the Christmas Holidays, school broke up. I then discovered that lovely Mrs Howell suffered with epilepsy.

Just before the bell rang for school closing, she started with a major "grand mal" fit. She fell to the floor, writhing and jerking spasmodically and foaming at the mouth. Every single child, apart from me, started screaming and ran out frantically through the door. I stopped and knelt by her. I could see her dentures had slipped and were almost falling out of her mouth. I felt worried she might choke on them, so I took hold of them, pulled them out and placed them by her head. The headmistress appeared only a minute or so later and thanked me, before she and another teacher began to care for Mrs. Howell.

Chapter 12. A Child in Wartime

Prelude

Today, our social memory of the war comes from movies – and even TV shows like *Dad's Army*. From these, you get the impression that everyone was at war – all the time. But they weren't. For most people, life went on. It was different, but it went on.

Outbreak of war

I was three months shy of my seventh birthday when World War II was declared. Prime Minister Neville Chamberlain announced it on BBC Radio. It was a Sunday, but I didn't learn of it until the following day. I was returning from school dinners at about 1.30 pm. School meals were not cooked and served in the actual schools in those days. There was a central kitchen near the centre of Burslem which served several schools around that area. We had a walk of over a mile to a methodist chapel hall, which had been adapted for the purpose well before the war. I had reached the bottom of the hill and had just crossed a stretch of waste land which had a curious name with the locals, "Corny Eyes".

I never knew how it got its name, but it had the appearance of the site of a demolished factory area. There was no grass or other vegetation, just a flat stretch of black cinder-covered ground. We boys used it as a play area for football and, in summer, cricket. Old barrel staves were used as bats and an old tennis ball served as a cricket ball. Stumps were drawn on the factory wall which bordered the area using a lump of broken pottery mould from the shawdruck for chalk.

To get back from that digression, there was no-one around because of the lunch break, but suddenly a boy, a few years older than me, ran past me. He had an air of panic about him, and he was shouting for anybody around to hear: "There's a war. We are at war with Germany." He seemed almost hysterical, but there was only me to hear him. So, I continued on my return walk home. I think it was school mid-afternoon lessons but decided to call at home to hear about it from my mother.

She was alone as Father was out walking the streets of the Potteries, as usual, looking for work. I asked my mother if it was true and if she had any more information. She just shrugged and said, "Ask your dad when he comes home. He'll tell you."

The school meal centre

I shudder at the memories of the meal centre. Quite ungrateful of me, but I hated it. The building, for a start, was a large dark hall with a high roof. There was no internal ceiling, just the beams and rafters. Tables were rows of long trestles with forms each side to sit on. All like a drab version of a Harry Potter dining hall. Before getting in, we queued in the street. Unsupervised, a lot of the city children were rough and ill-behaved with bullying and fighting rampant. Once inside we queued again by a long servery.

Ladies with large aprons piled on to your plates as you passed, meat – often a substitute like a rissole or Spam, then a dollop of mashed potato, followed by veg and gravy. Lastly there was a pudding, usually a steamed pud with custard or an ersatz rice pudding. Imports like rice were scarce, but the Ministry of Food under Lord Woolton worked hard to come up with ideas. They introduced "Farina", which was a form of starch made into flakes and boiled with milk was not unlike a rice pudding. Actually, although I didn't know what it was made from, I quite liked it.

After the meal we queued again to return our trays to racks at the end of the servery. We needed to pass rows of dustbins where uneaten food was tipped. They were often overflowing with the contents which would be boiled up for pig food.

Although I was only a child, in my mind, the whole experience was unwholesome and distasteful.

I couldn't help feeling part of the poor community. Added to this was the routine each week at school when meal tickets were issued. These tickets were printed in rows on a thin card, separated by perforations. Pupils were called up, one at a time, to the teacher's desk at the front of the class. After their name has been ticked ticking off, they were each handed a card covering the week.

First of all, the paying pupils were handed their tickets on pink card. After them the pupils who qualified for free dinners were issued with their tickets printed on white card. I'm sure, in retrospect, that I was oversensitive about such matters, but couldn't help feeling I had been regarded as lower class.

Our air raid shelter

My memories of that time are mostly vague with a few vivid ones. I remember, even at that age, thinking how clever the world of officialdom was. So many things were organised. For example, nearly all iron railings around schools, churches and public buildings were cut down to help avoid metal shortages. Public air-raid shelters were built of brick and concrete, at least one in every street.

Nearly all the houses were given an Anderson shelter, which the house occupant installed in the back garden. These shelters were constructed of sheets of galvanised steel, some of them bent, so that when fitted together with the loads of bolts and nuts provided, they made a hut-like structure with a rounded roof. The base and corners were joined with lengths of angle iron. The house occupant needed to dig a hole about twelve feet long, eight feet wide in which the shelter would be erected.

Dad, never one to do things by halves, dug a pit conforming to the measurements but instead of four feet deep he dug it a foot deeper. He laboured mightily at the task. Then the spoil from the pit was piled onto the corrugated shelter to a depth of about a foot, and then firmly tamped down. The front and rear walls were supplied ready cut to size, and the front panels had an opening where a rough door could be fitted.

Dad also built a set of steps out of scrap wood leading down to the floor. The floor was the local earth, which was heavily clay based, tamped down with the back of a spade. Again, using his stock of scrap wood, he built five bunk beds. (Mavis, my youngest sibling, had not yet been born). Finally, with dry bricks he constructed the base for a type of stove using candles under clay plant pots. That sounds absolutely unbelievable to many people today. It is true! It has been borne out by YouTube videos published recently showing people's variations on that theme. I remember Father boiling a lightweight kettle on his contraption and making a pot of hot tea. Then, to finish off the furnishings, a hurricane lamp for the dark nights.

Unfortunately, he and most of the neighbours didn't take into account the British weather. As the autumn wore on it proved a wet one with long periods of rain which, because of the impervious clay floors of our shelters, became flooded. It would have needed a mechanical pump to keep each shelter dry.

The wetness didn't appear to be a problem during the first air raids. However, having to wake the children when the air raid siren went off, carry them down to the shelter bundled with blanket became a real ordeal, what with Father also trying to bail out the flood water. So, we, and most of neighbours abandoned using the shelters.

Fortunately, every house in those terraced houses – two down, two up – had a generous sized cellar, which had been constructed to stay dry. After that, we used the cellar during the air raid warnings. I have an idea, can't where I got it from, that in the event of a bomb blast – apart from a direct hit – the cellar was a safer place than the Anderson shelter.

Gas masks

Another of the precautions that the clever civil servants had organised was the production and issue of gas masks. It must have been quite an undertaking. Every single person in the country was issued with one. Small children had a brightly coloured one. In an attempt to encourage them, they were designed to look like Mickey or Minnie Mouse There was even a specially designed one for babies. In my memory, it looked like a cot in which the baby lay complete with blankets and pillow. The whole thing was encased in a transparent plastic hood. It was completely airtight, and so as to enable the baby to continue breathing, it had a bellows pump incorporated. During an air-raid, the parent would sit by the cot pumping steadily to supply filtered air to the baby.

Once a week, the school carried out a gas mask drill and test. We each had to don our mask, and teacher would inspect us to see that the straps were straight and properly placed. Then, each pupil had a fresh piece of foolscap paper to hold against the filter where the incoming air was drawn. When we breathed in the paper was sucked against the base of the mask. If the paper didn't stick to the filter, the teacher would examine the pupil's mask. It was always a twisted strap. I never witnessed a faulty gas mask.

We had to carry our masks with us everywhere. When first issued, each mask came in a square cardboard box with a string attached so we could hang it over the shoulder. As the months went by, these boxes became worse for wear, so shopkeepers began to sell more serviceable types. These were not cheap, and my father found a cheaper version in Woolworth's. It was a black tubular metal tin with two holes in the lid where the string could be threaded.

At the weekly inspection, I was brought out to the front of the class where the teacher responsible for gas mask drill explained to the class how unsatisfactory the tin was. The mask had to be squeezed into a tubular shape to fit the tin. This he said, weakened the material and could lead to it splitting. I, and everybody else, was unaware of this. We had not been briefed about the acceptable types of containers.

The teacher, Mr. Miller, was not our class teacher, but his gas mask remit covered the whole school. We pupils went in dread of him. Tall, cadaverous, unsmiling, he was, looking back, a sadist. He decided to make an example of me, "pour encourager les autres" and produced his cane.

I was ordered to hold out my hand whereupon he slashed down the cane very forcibly. The pain was incredible. My whole hand and arm were on fire for hours afternoon, with a vivid blue bruise across the palm. Tears filled my eyes, but I wouldn't give him the satisfaction of crying in front of the class. I wonder what the authorities today would think about such treatment of an innocent eight-year-old. I didn't complain to my parents. I felt they were too occupied with their own problems. I told my parents that the teachers said my mask tin was not approved, so Dad got me a better cardboard box.

Air raids start

Continuing my recollections of the war, the air raids didn't start until months later. We had been briefed by newspapers and the radio on what to do.

The sirens sounded, a loud wailing noise that rose and fell in waves of rising and falling notes. At first, we were all scared and huddled in the shelter awaiting events. Then the sound of the approaching bombers. It got steadily louder as they neared, until they were right overhead. I learned after that they were heading in a north-westerly direction heading for Manchester and Liverpool.

Many people have since commented on the sound they made. It was different from British planes. Instead of a steady roar, the sound was a rhythmic loud humming noise like a woo-woo woo-woo sound. It was quite loud and menacing. I asked father why they made that unique sound, and he said it was because the Germans always used diesel engines. Because I was quite well read for my age, I knew that was nonsense – diesel engines would be much heavier than petrol ones, quite unsuitable for an aeroplane. I never heard an explanation for it, but as an adult I've heard different opinions. One was that the planes set at differing revs. That doesn't make sense to me. Another opinion was that it was deliberately set that way as a terror weapon, like the siren on the Stuka dive-bombers that had no other function other than to terrorise the recipients of their attacks. It certainly had that effect on me.

At first there were no bomb explosions. It seemed to prove the speculation that the raids were directed at ports or industrial complexes. It was some months before we heard the occasional explosion. Again, the speculations were that they were returning bombers jettisoning the occasional bomb which had failed to release with the rest of the load during its attack. There were some ideas floated that they were searching for the large royal ordnance factories at Swynnerton to our south and Radway Green near Crewe. Eventually, well after the bombers had passed, we would hear the siren sounding the "all clear". This was a loud, continuous note, causing great sighs of relief from the family.

Put that light out!

Making our way back to the house could be a bit tricky because of the darkness. Very strict rules had been enforced forbidding naked lights, which, apparently, could easily be spotted by enemy planes and could aid their navigation. We were taught that even the simple act of lighting a cigarette in the open could be seen even at altitude. All streetlights were switched off during the war. All buildings had to have light-proof blinds or heavy curtains, including commercial buildings, schools, hospitals and private houses.

The government had set up throughout the country an organised force of "air raid wardens". These were mainly volunteers who gave sterling service to the country, patrolling all the streets and public areas for possible spies, aiding the public in the event of a raid, helping the police, ambulance crews and the fire-brigades. They also helped escort occupants into public air raid shelters. They constantly patrolled the streets, knocking on the doors of delinquent households whose blinds were inadequate and calling out wherever a chink could be seen, "Put that light out!" This became a comic phrase after the war in the TV series *Dad's Army*.

Father made a set of blinds out of a light timber frame covered with roofing felt. It made a snug fit inside the front and back windows. Also, Dad reasoned it would help in some way to prevent flying glass in the event of a bomb blast outside the house. The risk of flying glass was a big concern to the authorities and the public. All windows in schools and public buildings had strips of white adhesive tape in the form of a cross over each individual pane.

Not only were streetlights extinguished, but motor vehicle headlamps had to be fitted with a metal hood which concealed the lens and permitted only a small amount of light through two narrow horizontal slits.

Inevitably, these precautions led to an increased rate of accidents and crime because of more opportunities to crooks in their criminal activities.

Call up

Father was only 25 years old when war was declared, so he was eligible for call-up into the armed forces. He underwent the usual medical examination, and he was graded C, the unfit category. He never discussed it with me, but I knew that he had suffered rheumatic fever as a child which left scarring of the heart, also his eyesight was poor.

So, we were fortunate in some ways, because I know Mother wouldn't have coped with her poorly constitution and her intellectual capabilities. I suspect she couldn't read or write properly, as evidenced during my national service when she never wrote to me.

Father wrote, unfailingly, every week, a long letter full of the latest news and events at home. I know that I am wrong in disrespecting Mother's memory. I feel so guilty about it, but this is not the time and place for a confessional or a psychological analysis of our family dynamics. Suffice it to say for the moment that many families of my generation from poor, working class backgrounds have suffered emotional trauma, many of them beyond ours. For the time being, I will continue my recollections of living and coping with wartime.

People unfit for military service but fit enough for other occupations could be directed by the Ministry of Labour. So, Father was sent to work at Radway Green royal ordnance factory just outside Alsager in Cheshire.

In the early part of the war, before he was redeployed by the Ministry of Labour, Father was working at H&R Johnson tile factory in Tunstall. It was a dirty job but reasonably paid. His job was a gas production operative. H&R Johnson had a couple of large modern tunnel kilns, fired by gas and the fuel costs were always their biggest costs in production.

So, they invested in the construction of a "gas producer" which brought down this cost considerably. It wasn't a large building but quite high. An underground basement held tons of anthracite. This was supplied in small pieces about the size of a Brazil nut. An empty space above the basement provided access for lorries. Then a corrugated iron work chamber housed the cooker where the anthracite was burned in a closed atmosphere so as to give off gas, which was then piped to the main factory. Above this work chamber stood a large hopper containing several tons of anthracite. Alongside the whole structure was a tall, narrow tower about a hundred feet tall. Inside this was a vertical conveyor with small pans which descended into the anthracite in the basement. It was in effect a vertical conveyor belt. On its upward journey it went right to the top where it emptied continuously into the hopper.

Dad's job was to check that everything continued to operate properly. This involved inspecting the various taps, valves and recording instruments. Then more physical jobs, like opening the base of the retort to discharge burnt cinders into a lorry below. He worked shifts, two weeks on "day shift", then two weeks "noons", followed by two weeks on "nights".

There were a few incidents he told me about. Once, on night shift, he was working at the top of the conveyor tower. Dawn was just breaking, when suddenly a lone German bomber roared above him in a southerly direction, trailing flames and smoke. It was flying at high speed, and a few seconds later a Spitfire appeared, chasing after it. They both disappeared into the distance without any danger to the local populace. The air raid sirens hadn't sounded, so he assumed the bomber had passed our area over to the west and then got separated from the rest of the fleet.

The second incident was when Father was gassed. The gas producer could be dangerous at times, if the retort was over filled for example, and it appears on this occasion a leak of gas into the work area had overcome Father. He always worked alone, but fortunately a workmate called at intervals to collect Father's readings and the thermocouple's printouts. He had to check and record the instruments regular measurements of temperatures, pressures, loadings etc. He ran to the factory and phoned for an ambulance, and Father was rushed to Haywood Hospital in Tunstall. After a few hours there, he recovered and started to worry about the family with only his somewhat inadequate wife to cope. So, he found his clothes in the bed-side locker, climbed through a window, and walked home.

The third incident involved him being arrested as a spy, signalling to overhead enemy planes. A lot of the public were, understandably, paranoid about security. The government was constantly broadcasting announcements with slogans like, "Walls have ears" etc. At the cinemas, each film was preceded by a newsreel telling the public how our wonderful, heroic armed forces were performing. Also, they repeated warnings and advice about keeping quiet about our work activities, and how to watch out for saboteurs, fifth columnists and spies.

On this particular night, the electric motor which powered the conveyor, or "elevator" as it was sometimes called, developed a short and was giving out quite bright blue sparks at regular intervals. The motor was situated right at the top of the elevator and workpeople on night shift had spotted it and phoned the police. Very quickly a couple of burly police constables climbed the ladder to Father's workplace above the retort. They didn't question him, but quickly bundled him down the ladder, into a police car and on to Tunstall police station. It was only there that he was questioned, and a senior police office 'phoned Father's manager and, after waking him, heard a warm description of Father's bona fides. He was released to walk home.

Although we were very fortunate in not being bombed, there were a few bombs dropped around us. Speculation had it that they were lone bombers jettisoning their load, possibly because they were singled out for attack by Allied fighter planes.

There was great excitement when a bomb exploded nearby in Wolstanton, about two miles away. We were woken in the night by this frightful bang. The bed I was sleeping in, with Bill and Eric, seemed to jump off the floor, and the whole house shook. This was a bomb exploding two miles away. I couldn't begin to imagine what it was like for the people nearby. It must have been a weekend, because on the following day I joined a lot of people, adults and children who walked down Albion Street and across the fields to the hill-top of Wolstanton.

The bomb had dropped at the end of a street of smart semi-detached houses. Wolstanton was a posh area, and the houses weren't the old-fashioned terrace cottages in Middleport. The explosion had completely obliterated the end house, but there was no evidence of damage to its adjoining neighbour. The bedroom inside wall of the remaining house was intact with its brightly coloured wallpaper, and it was as though a giant hand had sliced off the end house, scattered rubble far and wide and left a clear space where the house had stood. I've heard many tales about the peculiarities of bomb blasts. The newsreels often mentioned such incidents.

We listened to the radio – no TV. Then, also watching newsreels at the cinema, we thought about the poor soldiers, airmen and also the navy and the merchant navy sailors. It was only in recent years I learned that when a merchant ship was torpedoed, the sailors' pay was stopped immediately. No sick pay, no compensation.

I think of the 3,000 British merchant ships sunk with 15,000 merchant navy seamen killed! It's heartbreaking. Winston Churchill is quoted as saying that the only thing that kept him awake at times was the battle of the Atlantic. Over 383,000 Servicemen killed in the war too!

So, as I was saying, the "reserved occupation" regulations were a blessing to our family. Radway was the making of Father. After years of insecure work in the Potteries, with its regular layoffs and long periods on the "dole", suffering the indignities of being questioned and scrutinised about how we spent the dole money, Dad was in a relatively secure job with the luxury of being, like civil servants, in a superannuated scheme with a pension at the end of it.

He started as a near labourer in the furnace block, smelting brass for cartridges and other munitions. After a while he became a charge hand. Soon he was transferred in a responsible position in safely disposing of questionable explosive ammunition. He finished up being an inspector in the bullet manufacturing.

He retired in the early eighties and really enjoyed his retirement. The only thing that marred his life was the situation with my brother, Eric, who suffered with schizophrenia from his late teens. Poor father had to put up with several unhappy incidents which I won't relate here. I just leave the memories of the happy times in his retirement.

Recollections of my mother ("Ma") and wartime food

I have never researched our family tree and know little of the history of Granny Gaskell, my mother's mother. From the house at the bottom of "Knob Hill", Porthill, I gathered the family had been much better off than the residents in the crowded terrace houses surrounding the factories (pottery works) where our house was situated in Albion Street. I was very young when Granny Gaskell told me some stories about the past. These were confirmed in conversations with Auntie Carrie, mother's older sister. They told a family tale which our generation has always dismissed as "moonshine". I will repeat it here. Perhaps it may happen that someone with an acute memory or resources will, if they wish to, research it.

The story was that Grannie's great, great, great grandfather was French. An officer in the French army who rose to become an aid-de-camp to Napoleon Bonaparte. Ma even told me his name, Arundel Pender Polgrain. After Waterloo, he came to Britain and fell in love with a girl, who was in service at a grand household. Arundel's father was a very rich man who objected strongly to his son's wish to marry a girl below his social station. When Arundel persisted, his father cut him out of his will, which now stipulated that the inheritance should be "put into chancery". Whatever that means. I don't know. All I've ever discovered from my meagre readings is that it is one of the divisions of the English Court of Law.

Apparently, the arrangement was that Arundel wouldn't inherit it directly, instead it would be inherited by the third generation of his descendants. This, presumably, should have been Granny and her siblings. I asked Auntie Carrie about it, as she always appeared to be more aware of what had gone on. She said that their generation had been cheated by some dubious legal action, and that a distant relative had successfully claimed the money and decamped to America with it. She said that one of the distant relatives was related to the popular singer Jo Stafford. Carrie had no evidence for any of this. It sounded incongruous to me, so I forgot about it.

I referred to this story to illustrate that Granny was believed to have had connections with a wealthy set. It is allegedly because of this that she found employment for Mother as an under-maid at a large estate in Shropshire. During her stay at this place, she worked for a time as a kitchen maid. The cook was kind to her and taught her the basic techniques for choosing and cooking food. After several months, the owner said she was bringing Bertha (my mother) back to Porthill. The story is that they had persisted in training Bertha, but in the end, they said she was too weak and also too "slow" to make anything of. So, regretfully they brought her back, all the way in a coach, to Granny.

This could explain why Mother was a really good cook. I've tried, unsuccessfully, to reproduce the way she cooked onions: for example, liver and onions, and French onion soup. She had a large iron frying pan and, with lard, would gently fry the onions for a long time until they were a deep brown. They were delicious, and I never discovered how she browned them without any trace of burning. When she was not unwell, we always had a hot cooked dinner.

Every week, Bill and I were sent to do the food shopping. After we had returned from the Co-op with a large cardboard box, which we carried together, we went out again to Price's butcher's shop in Dale Hall. There we bought a large joint. First it was a shoulder of lamb, then the following week a "nose end of brisket". Most of this meat was imported, and I remember the "New Zealand" mark, stamped on the lamb joint. The merchant marine had managed to fulfil the country's ration quota.

This choice of joint never varied throughout the war. Mr Price was a big jolly man, and he rather took to me, making sure I had a generous supply of sausages or offal, which were "off ration". Rationing, of course, lasted throughout the war, and after – it didn't end for some items until 1956. The joint was enough to last the family for several days. On Monday and Tuesday, we had cold cuts of meat with hot vegetables and gravy. Wednesday and Thursday a lovely stew with the broth made from the remnants of the joint. Fridays, we had thick slices of toast slathered with lovely beef dripping from the nose end of brisket, which Mother chose because of its fat content. This incorporated the dark brown jelly from the roast. On Saturdays we had bacon and cheese with North Staffordshire oatcakes. These were bought from a neighbour who had a "backstone" – a sheet of cast iron which was placed over all four burners of her gas stove. On this, she cooked delicious oatcakes. We ran home to with them to enjoy them cooked with the bacon and cheese, grilled on a tin plate. Mother baked delicious cakes, and her "upside down pudding" served with real egg custard was to die for.

Barbara, the fourth child in our family, was born on the 2nd of October 1939, so she was one of the first "war babies". The Government really tried to pull out all the stops for children at that time. Because of the war, the import of fresh fruit was stopped. I never again saw a banana or an orange, which I enjoyed before 1939, until after the war. However, to offset this, expectant and nursing mothers and babies had a free ration of concentrated orange juice and a bottle of cod-liver oil. They also had, not on a regular basis but when supplies were available, a large tin of dried, full cream milk. This was labelled as unsuitable for bottle feeding to infants. All of us children absolutely loved this; we preferred it to fresh milk. Then came an isolated issue of dried chocolate and milk. This, when added to hot water, made an absolutely delicious drink. Each family with children was issued with a huge tin. I remember fetching ours from the co-op and carrying it home. Pity we couldn't have it on a regular basis.

Wartime family life

I know that I have disrespected the memories of my mother and the problems we endured because of her poor health, and I feel so guilty about it. However, perhaps an analysis of our family dynamics might be appropriate. I'm sure they didn't differ markedly from those of most of my generation of working-class people.

I now, in my old age, have a greater appreciation for what she went through. Housework was hard without modern aids like vacuum cleaners, modern flooring and heating. We had to break up huge chunks of coal which were cheaper than "cobble size" or "nuts".

I remember particularly Mondays, the "washing" day. Being the eldest, I often, not always, helped. First, the laborious filling of buckets with cold water from the household's single tap. Then, emptying that into the gas boiler. All the "whites" and "fast coloureds" were boiled. Then, using a pair of wooden tongs, we lifted the boiler contents, one at a time, into the "dolly tub" with other pieces of clothing. Then, the "dolly peg" was lifted into the tub. This was a stout wooden post with a wooden disc at its foot. Descending from this disk were five wooden pegs, about ten inches long with rounded ends. A horizontal bar had been threaded through the top of its post. This served as a handle – left hand under it and right hand over it. The dolly peg was then rotated back and forth to agitate the washing.

After removing the dolly peg, the tub was manoeuvred to stand beside the "mangle". This was a huge contraption made of cast iron with two great wooden rollers driven by a large wheel with a bar handle. The pieces of clothing were picked up from the washing tub with one hand and fed into the rollers, while the other hand turned the wheel. This squeezed most of the water onto a drip tray directed to return the water to the tub. Below the mangle, on the other side, was placed a tin bath to catch the squeezed clothes. Finally, the cloths were rinsed and mangled again. (The whites had a "blue bag" added for their rinse to create a vivid blue whiteness.)

Mother sometimes collared me as I was about to go out to play and asked me to turn the handle. I was glad to help; it wasn't too hard for an adult but a bit heavy for a child. However, the two of us together got through the washing more quickly. The worst part for me was the "dollying". The dolly-peg was big for me to handle, and I can understand how Mother found it so tiring.

If the weather wasn't threatening, we hung out the mangled clothes on a line that stretched the length of our long and narrow garden. The English climate, being as it is, the washing often needed to be dried indoors. To deal with that, we had a long, broad clothes rack hanging from the ceiling of our dining/living room. Effectively, this was our sole living area. The upstairs was just bedrooms. The front room, which we called the parlour, was reserved for Christmas and other special occasions. On such days Father lit a fire in the modern tiled surround. This seemed to make it quite luxurious to me.

Getting back to the washing, the clothes rack was suspended from the ceiling by a stout cord running through pulleys and operated by pulling the end of the cord, which was kept in place by wrapping through and round a sort of capstan on the wall. You can imagine the atmosphere in that small kitchen/living room with a blazing fire in the black-leaded oven/range. It was quite fuggy, and we were all glad when Tuesday came around and the clothes were unloaded from the rack and piled up for ironing.

I don't know whether ironing-boards had been invented at that time. I never saw one in any of the houses I visited. Mother used the kitchen/dining table with a folded sheet on it, and on this she used a flat iron. She had two of these. The first was placed on the edge of the fire at the side of the oven, and when she judged it to be hot enough by spitting on it (the spit fizzed and jumped off when hot enough), she would clean it by rubbing it on the hearth rug then set to work. The heat in the iron lasted for only ten minutes, when she placed it back on the iron, switching it for the second iron which by then was ready. The irons were heavy and added to the labour of the laundry task.

My paper round

Earlier, when I took you on a tour of the pot bank, I introduced the carrier down, Thomas Findlay. He was actually, the sister of Mrs. Findlay, the newsagent, and he lived with her over the shop. One day, he was hobbling home when he came by my mother. He mentioned that his sister had a vacancy for a paper boy. My mother offered my services without consulting me.

I started my newspaper round at age eleven, despite the law which forbade children under thirteen being involved in any wage-earning activity. I was cautioned, when I set out with my loaded newspaper bag in the morning, "Keep a look out for the Bobbies. If you see one, then dodge into the nearest "entry way" (a sort of tunnel between terraced houses) until he's passed. Actually, I quite enjoyed the job.

Mrs Findlay gave me a little black book listing each house, the bill for the week and a column for me to enter the amount collected. This was the start of my memory training, because I soon carried the book but made no entries until I got back to the shop. There I sat down with Mrs. Findlay to settle up. I completed the entries, from memory and counted out the cash I'd collected. It always balanced, to Mrs Findlay's amazement. If she had a query because, for example, a customer's usual magazine hadn't been delivered by the wholesaler, I could explain that against Mrs Findlay's records. I could even remember what coins or notes had been handed to me by each customer and the change I'd given. Many people today seem to think this sort of ability is unusual but, in those days, most people were too busy in their jobs for paperwork and relied on memory for all sorts of details.

Mrs Findlay

Mrs Findlay was a real contrast to Tommy. Tommy was sleight and timid, whereas Mrs Findlay was a big, almost fat, woman, with a strong personality. I got on well with her. She was quiet but business-like, and she and I worked well together when unloading the newly delivered parcels of newspapers and organising them for delivery. As I said, she was quiet with an air of almost sadness about her. I had an instinctive feeling that she was suffering from the loss of her husband. I guessed later that she had lost a son who must have been about my age.

I realised this when one day I loaded up my paper bag and set off to deliver them. This wasn't a difficult job because the terraced houses were tightly packed, and my round needed only three or four streets to complete my stint. Other boys had rounds farther afield. Halfway through my round on one day, it started to rain. A really heavy downpour. I didn't have a coat; Mother couldn't afford one for me and a shirt and jersey sufficed, with an extra jersey in cold weather.

Mrs Findlay was horrified when I returned to the shop, soaking wet. She hurried me into her living room, produced a load of towels which, when wrapped round me, absorbed a lot of the water from my clothes. She then produced what looked to me a high-quality oilcloth raincoat in my size with a 'Sou-Wester' in the same material. She said, "I am going to lend you these. Keep them here in the shop to use when the weather is wet. When the rain has paused, you can run home" (which was only four hundred yards away). It was the way she talked about the clothes that gave me the feeling that she had an emotional attachment to them.

By the way, that Sou-Wester was a godsend in foul weather. I wonder why they went out of fashion. They were more effective than modern rain hoods. I could turn my head with ease and the rainwater ran off the deep rim at the back, keeping one's neck warm and dry. There were even sewn in earflaps, lined in warm material, which was great in very cold weather.

I quite enjoyed my part-time job. It was different from school, and I enjoyed the sense of responsibility.

Father's medications

It was at that time, two years before the war ended, that Father began to be plagued by bouts of "lumbago". This is a layman's term for one of the symptoms of lumbar spinal injuries, usually a slipped (herniated) disk. These were the days before the introduction of the NHS. Contrary to popular belief, basic health care was available through private insurance schemes. A cheap version of this was taken out by our family, but Father was always reluctant to consult a doctor. He preferred home remedies or old wives' tales.

For example, a chap had sworn that his wife ironed his back with brown paper and a hot smoothing iron. He tried that, only to get burned.

Another chap said he'd heard that a spoonful of paraffin (kerosene) helped a lot. Father tried that too but, as I've said earlier, he didn't do things by half. Instead of a spoonful, he drank a glass-full of paraffin. He was ill for days and came out with a dreadful rash all over his body.

Not deterred by this, he listened to another story that guaiacum was helpful. Actually, it is well attested as a helpful herbal cure for rheumatic type disorders. So, I was sent off to Colwell's chemist in Dalehall to buy a supply of it. It came in a medium-sized bottle. A jet-black liquid which, I learned from reading the label, was a tincture of lignum vitae (supposedly the hardest wood in existence.) The instructions were to take a teaspoonful twice a day. "Important – to be taken in a full glass of water," the label instructed.

At this juncture, I think it timely to re-cap on our living arrangements. At the front of our house, we had the parlour, which was reserved for very important occasions. At the back of the house was the "back-kitchen". This contained our cold water tap over a "slopstone" (a forerunner of the kitchen sink), the gas stove, and, in the corner, a heap of coal, our sole source of heating.

In between these two rooms was the kitchen/living room. It didn't have a tiled fireplace. It still had the old-fashioned kitchen range made of cast iron, which needed to be cleaned with black lead (graphite). This range occupied nearly all the width of one wall. In the centre was the fire grate made of iron bars nesting between an oven on one side and a warming part like a smaller oven on the other side. The fire grate in the centre had these two ovens each side, and the tops formed a hob on which a kettle and saucepans would rest. These were moved to nestle on top of the burning coals when they needed to be heated. This room, effectively, was the living space for all six of us. You can imagine the scene. Pa, with his armchair in the centre, pulled up to within a yard of the blazing fire, the rest of us, on smaller chairs, sat on each side.

It was a cold night, and I came back from Colwell's with this bottle of black liquid. "Give it here," said Pa. I handed it over and went to fetch a teaspoon and a tumbler of cold water. "Don't bother with that, bring me a big spoon," said Pa.

"But," I protested, "it says here, clearly, 'a teaspoonful to be taken with a full glass of water.'"

"That's for cissies," said Pa. He always tried to portray himself as a macho male. I think it was because he was such a fan of cowboy heroes and gangsters from his frequent visits to the cinema. Reluctantly, I handed him the large spoon and the bottle. He proceeded to fill the spoon and place it in his mouth, but, before he could swallow it, his face turned a dark shade of puce, his eyes bulged from his head, and he forcefully spat a spray of the liquid straight into the red hot coals, which were only two feet from his face as he leaned forward in his agony.

If you didn't know, "tincture" means dissolved in alcohol. This spray, on contact with the coals, was the correct mixture of alcohol and air to create an explosive mixture. There wasn't a bang, it was more of a loud "whump" sound. This "explosion" blew back straight into his face. Not only that, but he was also still holding the bottle, so his involuntary jerk caused him to fling a good quarter into the fire. So, following the 'whump' there was a bright flash, and a ball of white flames hovered over him before, fortunately, it was drawn up the chimney.

Pa's skin was red, like sunburn, his eyebrows had disappeared and the front of his "short back and sides" had vanished. He always wore his glasses, so his eyes and eyelashes weren't damaged, but the glasses frame was melted, though still intact. He didn't say anything. He sat in stunned silence, which remained unbroken as Ma never remonstrated him for his stupidity. None of us children said anything, we didn't dare laugh because, although he was a good and loving dad, he had a fearsome temper.

Just a few more recollections about rationing. As well as food, many other things were rationed. Clothes for example. As with food, a booklet containing perforated coupons was issued for each household. There was a separate book for apparel (clothes, shoes and household linen.) Alongside each item's price was listed how many coupons had to be handed over along with the cash.

Petrol was rationed too, and a flourishing black market developed, with people who only needed to make short journeys selling off a few coupons to friends and colleagues who needed to travel greater distances.

Coal too, was rationed, but coke (when it became available) was "off ration". Coke is the cinder like residue after coal had been cooked to release coal gas for the town's gas supply. When the local furnace, near to Longport railway station, had released a batch of coke for sale to the public, people queued up to get some. Each customer paid a small sum and was allotted a quantity, decided quite arbitrarily. Usually they were sold a hundredweight (112 pounds or about 50 kilos in today's money). It wasn't advertised. The news spread by word of mouth, so from time-to-time, Pa collared me to accompany him to walk to Longport (just a mile away) with his ancient rusty wheelbarrow to fetch our allotted hundredweight.

Coke, when burnt knowledgeably, produced great heat. The difficulty was burning it in a domestic fire-grate. The trick was to get a good coal fire going, and when the blazing of the coals died down into really red-hot embers, keep it topped up with coke.

Harking back to food rationing, items like sausages and brawn (a jellified mixture of pork scraps, usually made from a pig's head) plus certain pieces of offal, such as liver, kidneys and lights (lungs – usually fed to pets), could be bought. Customers would deposit their meat ration book with their local butcher to ensure they were treated as a valued customer, and after buying the usual weekly joint, chops or steaks (when available), customers would ask "have you anything off ration?" The butcher would then slip his hand, almost furtively, under the counter and produce a pre-wrapped paper parcel containing either sausage or "savoury ducks", a Potteries term for what are called "faggots" in other parts of the country.

On my regular missions to Price's butchers, housewives would quietly ask, "Anything off ration this week?" This was asked usually in a lowered tone with sometimes a blatant batting of the eyelashes or a meaningful look. As I got older, I wondered about this non-verbal communication and was sure it was all innocent banter. There were quite a few rumours about the meaning behind these exchanges, and I chided myself for wondering why Jimmy Price had the air of a well fed, contented cat.

Rationing ended after the war. Not suddenly, a few goods were rationed until 1956, eleven years after.

I remember VE Day, Wednesday 8th May 1945. Banner headlines in the newspapers. Loud announcements on the radio, with repeated playing of the national anthem. Every street was decorated with coloured bunting – streamers of little triangular flags in red, white and blue strung across the street from upstairs windows to the neighbour on the opposite side.

Also, each street organised a street party for the children. I marvelled at the ingenuity of housewives, who had scrimped and saved, despite rationing, to accumulate material for the flags and the food for the parties. I couldn't believe it when I joined the other children at the Albion Street party. Trestle tables, borrowed from the chapel at the top of the street, were covered in white tablecloths and loaded with delicious sandwiches, pastries, cakes and great glass bowls of trifle, made with cake suspended in fruit jelly with pieces of canned fruit in it, and custard made with eggs and thick double cream.

Somebody had produced a record player, and jolly dance music filled the air. Even now, it brings real tears to my eyes when I remember and appreciate this lavish spread had been provided by coupons saved from rations for so long. It was clearly a deeply felt love by the housewives for us children. The air of relief also was palpable. The days of fear doubt and uncertainty seemed over. Church bells added to the music and the laughter from the children. Truly, a day to remember. Sadly, there must have been many tears shed during these celebrations by families who had lost sons, daughters, husbands and wives, to the war. Life went on, however, relief, joy and sadness mixed, after a world-changing era.

Chapter 13. Childhood Holidays

Prelude

As I said earlier, when I was a child, for working-class people, a holiday by the British seaside was the best they could hope for. Often it was that or nothing. But although my childhood holidays were not globe-trotting, they could still be fantastic.

Our first holiday: Talacre

It must have been during the war years when we had the first family holiday that I can remember. Mother was a bit of a broken reed when it came to organising things. Poor health was always a handicap to her (although she lived until she was ninety-seven). Father was extremely capable; despite his eyesight problem, he could get things done.

He decided we would go camping in North Wales, our closest coastal area. He was an excellent card player, and he had won, from one of his card-playing oppos, a second-hand bell tent. It was in excellent condition and proved to be extremely weatherproof, even in the occasional summer gale and downpours of rain.

Dad was still on good terms with Charlie Bryant, the owner of the lock-up garage next door to number 20 and a small lorry. During the Great Depression, Charlie was a great help to Father, employing him on casual jobs, including the occasional house-move (or "flitting" as it was called in our Potteries dialect). Charlie was a nice man, not at all a rough or semi-criminal type, though some of his operations to earn a crust sailed a bit close to the wind.

During the war, petrol was severely rationed, but in addition to his ration, Charlie always seemed to be able to get enough for his needs. There was, of course, the black market, though I never learned if Charlie had to resort to this. However, Father hired Charlie to take us to Talacre in Flintshire, about twenty miles short of Prestatyn on the North Wales Coast Road.

Father packed all our gear on to the lorry, the bell tent, large ground sheet and an old carpet for added comfort. He also loaded enamel tin bowls, plates and mugs, cutlery, and a wooden table he had made for cooking, and another with chairs for dining. Then came a primus stove, meths and paraffin for fuel, even some dry kindling to make a start on our initial campfire. Next, bedding, blankets and rugs with two or more "tick mattresses". These were simply a stout cotton bag which would be filled with flock filling to create a comfortable mattress. He threw away the flock and replaced it after the holiday. Mother, Bill, Eric and I, plus baby Barbara were added to the lorry load. Sitting on the lorry floor wasn't really uncomfortable, and, very fortunately, the journey to Talacre and our return were dry, no rain.

Father hadn't booked a campsite. In those days, commercial camp sites hadn't been developed. He had Charlie take the first little road off the coast road, where he'd spotted a farmhouse. The farmer, a tiny Welshman, was glad of the opportunity for a little extra cash, and he escorted the lorry down the track to the field next to the orchard. It was a lovely little field, flat and dry, also sheltered from the occasional gales that blew in that region. The shelter was provided by the trees surrounding the field on three sides.

The trees were the start of the thick woodland that stretched from Williams's farm up to the abbey (Talacre Abbey). A minor road ran along the top of this escarpment, and off this road ran a track to the abbey. There was no village or houses nearby. The escarpment is about 500 feet high, and a footpath ran from the farm up to the very top.

It was a beautiful walk; I remember it with great fondness. The woods were really dense, with some really large mature trees. The path was so steep that most of it consisted of steps. No problem for young energetic folk. At the very top, at the beginning of the road that ran to the abbey, was a pub. No other buildings but this solitary Talacre Arms.

The view, once we had reached the pub, was wonderful. We could see across the sea for miles. The coast at that spot was a triangle jutting out to the Irish Sea. It was called the Point of Ayr, with a solitary lighthouse on the point. Behind the lighthouse was a broad, beautiful, sandy beach then, carrying on inland, a stretch of giant sand-dunes. After that, still heading inland, was an area of smaller dunes with small sea-meadows. This whole area has now been classed as an area of outstanding natural beauty and as a wild-life park.

Also, in recent years, a very smart holiday caravan resort has been built, with shops, open-air swimming pool, restaurants and entertainment centres. Continuing inland, there was the coastal main line railway, then some small farms, then the coast road to Prestatyn, Rhyl and Llandudno. Off the road was Williams's Farm and our camp. Nowadays the whole area is a quite smart holiday destination, but, at the time I'm talking about it, was wonderfully unspoilt and a place of absolute magic for us children.

I can remember in the summers we spent there, the wonderful weather (with the occasional storm), and walking with Mother and Father up the wide track that ran from the farm up to and across the railway crossing and onto the dunes and the beach, which seemed to be absolutely endless and with few people on it. There was the fascination of walking across the wide, flat beach to paddle in the sea.

At that point stood the Point of Ayr Lighthouse, completely alone with no other buildings anywhere close. Painted in vivid bands of white and scarlet, it was an outstanding landmark.

The dunes were fascinating, so tall and steep. I remember climbing with Bill to the top and then jumping down, a drop of at least fifteen feet. Landing was so easy and soft, because we landed on a downward slope into soft sand which cushioned our fall. It was exhilarating.

Sorry, my nostalgia and enthusiasm has caused me to leap ahead from our arrival on Charlie Bryant's lorry.

Mr Williams, as I said, was extremely welcoming. "Anything you need, just knock at the kitchen door," he said. "If you want milk, eggs, butter from the dairy, or information, just knock." He added, "There is a small newsagents and grocery shop about a quarter of a mile along the coast road. You can get bread, veg or any grocery there."

Father then asked if he could buy some straw to fill our mattresses. "Certainly, no charge for that just help yourself from the barn here." So, Father carried the tick mattresses to the barn and stuffed them with clean, sweet-smelling straw.

At the edge of the field, not far from our tent, was a cattle trough, with standpoint and tap from which we could help ourselves to water for cooking and bathing. As I mentioned earlier, Mother was a good cook, and with the set-up that Father had created, and his shopping trips, she had the wherewithal to cook good food for us all. Dining out was unthinkable for we working-class people in those days.

Cooking was a problem at first with only a primus stove, but, with Mr. Williams's permission, Father had gathered stones that were scattered around an old dry-stone wall and built a shallow fire-pit. He had also found a piece of metal fencing made of thick mesh and this made an excellent hob and barbecue. We children were sent into the woods on firewood foraging duty, which wasn't difficult, the woods were so thick that spare branches and twigs were plentiful.

Later returns to Talacre

We didn't have a holiday every year. I guess money was tight at times, and feeding and clothing a family of five children must have been a challenge. When the war ended and we children were a bit older, we had more holidays, always at Williams's farm with our bell tent. It was so idyllic; we never contemplated any other holiday after that first magical trip. In fact, in later years, Father organised taking us, setting up the camp at the beginning of the six-week school holidays, and then went back home to work until, at the end of the school holidays, he could take the final fortnight to spend with us and organise our return home.

One year, Charlie Bryant was not available to take us on our annual camping holiday. I don't know if he was ill, or perhaps one of his "flitting" jobs had taken him out of our district. However, Father to my utter surprise found a taxi which was prepared to take us. He must have negotiated well to afford the fare, as Talacre was over sixty miles away. The car was a Humber Snipe. A beautiful car, the largest in the Humber range. During my national service, I saw a few of these, painted khaki green and used for generals and other high-ranking staff officers. I remember from when I began to take an interest in cars that it was a real "class" car. It was big enough to take our family of six and, in its cavernous boot, had room for our bell tent and equipment.

As usual it was a wonderful holiday. The excitement of camping hadn't worn off, and there was the prospect of exploring farther afield, as we children were bigger and able to walk the deserted roads in the Mold hills. The weather was good for most of that holiday, except for a violent storm which lasted for two days and nights. The wind was so powerful that, even in our sheltered little, field our trusted bell tent had problems.

It was secured to the ground by more than twenty tent pegs around the perimeter. The pegs were old-fashioned ones, made of wood. Not as long or well-shaped as modern pegs that resist being pulled out of the ground. During the first night, when a particularly violent squall broke, some of the pegs were pulled out completely. It fell to me as the eldest to deal with the problem. (Father had gone home and would come back for the last two weeks, as usual.) I hammered in the loosened pegs, only to find later during the night that another squall had lifted a series of pegs in another part of the perimeter. No damage was done and no water damage, just the nuisance of having to replace the pegs at intervals.

It was on that holiday that Father took just me to visit Talacre Abbey. It was a lovely experience. A beautiful building, not over-ornate like some ecclesiastical places, with an atmosphere of a serene silence. The nuns could only be glimpsed through a wooden lattice screen. There were a few, presumably novices or lay people, manning a counter where they sold produce from their garden. I remember we bought honey, jam and pickles to take back to the tent.

I spied a little notice appealing for donations of old Christmas cards out of which the nuns created art works to sell for fund raising. After that, for many years, even after Sheila and I were married, I remember parcelling up the cards we had received and mailing them to the abbey. I shall never forget my first, but not last, visit to that abbey – a beautiful and enchanting place.

The abbey stood just below the escarpment ridge, nestled in the deep woodlands and overlooking the farmland where we were camped. It wasn't directly above our tent, perhaps about half a mile along the ridge, but close enough for us to hear the bells. The abbey had a campanile in a little tower at the end of the abbey. It rang the hours, and also, a magical experience, it played a hymn each evening. The whole area was so quiet and peaceful, and to hear those wonderful notes floating down in the quiet of the evening was a calming, dare I say, spiritual experience. I remember it vividly.

What a shame the abbey is no more. About five years ago, I Googled it to see if they had a website. They had. It announced that due to the falling number of novitiates, the abbey had been sold and was being converted into a business conference centre.

Though I am something of an agnostic and generally suspicious of the Roman Catholic Church, it is with great fondness that I remember our visits to that abbey The atmosphere was so serene and seemed to soak into me, body and soul. The gentle, smiling faces of the lay nuns and the others who were allowed to communicate with visitors, were so friendly. Last of all, in the balmy summer evenings, snug in our bell tent, I recall falling asleep while listening to the evening hymn on the campanile.

Chapter 14. Life Before National Service

Prelude

Some things never change. What makes life great, now and back then, is human relationships. Here I would like share with you times spent with some of my pals in the run up to my national service.

The gang of four

When I was about sixteen, I sort of gathered a few friends: Peter Hall, whose father was Middleport Pottery's lodge keeper, Simon Wilson, who I met when playing tennis in Burslem Park and Denis Ford, who later came to work as an apprentice packer. We were a sort of gang of four, who knocked about together after work on evenings when I wasn't attending the City School of Commerce in the Wedgwood Institute at Burslem.

One Saturday afternoon, three of us went to Denis Ford's house in Orford Street, Porthill (the very street where Grannie Gaskell used to live). Denis hadn't finished his "tea" (which is what we called the evening meal), so we were invited in to wait for him. They were a nice, agreeable family. Denis's father had not returned from work, but his grandad was there sitting by the fire in an armchair that was "his" chair and a feature of the home.

Grandad was a veteran of the Great War. He had been gassed with mustard gas. He was a pitiful sight. Although in good spirits, he was constantly struggling to breathe. Every word was an effort. Nowadays, patients with breathing difficulties can be helped, sometimes, with oxygen bottles and the necessary breathing apparatus, all provided by the NHS. It would be some years before we reached today's standards, with patients being helped at home.

Our small gang carried on with just playing tennis or exploring the local countryside (on foot until we graduated on to cycles to explore further afield). By the time we were seventeen, we knew the prospect of national service was looming. This meant we were probably going to go our separate ways, so Simon came up with the idea of going away together for a holiday.

The Isle of Man

Somehow the idea of the Isle of Man cropped up. It was "overseas" without being "abroad", and the holiday accommodation was cheaper than other U.K. resorts.

Simon got hold of a brochure about holidays in the Isle of Man. The town of Douglas seemed quite inviting; it had public parks aplenty with tennis courts. It claimed to hold several sunshine records, so we chose a little private hotel on the front at Douglas.

We were all in complete ignorance about travelling to the Isle of Man. It was stuck out in the middle of the Irish Sea, and we didn't know about its reputation for stormy crossings. We booked passage from Liverpool on the midnight sailing – because it was much cheaper than the daytime crossing. We did without a cabin, again because of the cost. We opted for a saloon chair. These were comfortable recliners, almost like a bed.

It turned out that we wouldn't need a bed. We were all sea-sick for the entire voyage. None of us had been on the sea before, and we couldn't believe how rough it was, so rough that the toilets, which were clean and smart at the beginning of the crossings were swimming with sea water after huge waves had broken over the gunwales and over the high lintels to the toilet doors.

We were warned by the crew not to be sick over the side of the ship but to use the toilets, a really unpleasant experience. Daylight had broken before we docked at Douglas. To this day, I cannot understand why it should take all night to get there. Youth was on our side, however, and, after booking into our little hotel, which by the way was smart, warm and very comfortable, and having a good breakfast to warm us up, we were excited to explore our holiday base.

The weather was glorious, all week, and we played lots of tennis on the beautiful grass courts in the parks, well-kept and ridiculously cheap, even on our budgets. We booked a coach tour of the island following the route of the Isle of Man T.T. motorcycle race. It is a beautiful island, clean and quiet, without the bustle of traffic of the mainland.

We were surprised when the coach passed up and over the mountain at the centre of the northern part. We crossed a deserted moorland landscape before descending to the northern coast. On to the Laxey Wheel (the largest surviving original working waterwheel in the world), then lunch at a lovely little café, and back to Douglas.

A couple of days later, Ben spotted a board on the promenade at Douglas advertising fishing trips. This offered a short trip out into Douglas Bay, so we were reassured that we weren't risking the rough Irish Sea again. We boarded a little motor cruiser, open except for a small wheelhouse for the pilot. Each of us was handed a simple spool of stout line with a large hook. Also, in the centre of the launch were a few buckets filled with fish-heads. These were bait for conger eel, which was to be our quarry once out on the bay.

The weather was calm, warm and sunny. The sea was like a lake, so calm. Interestingly, the water was crystal clear and deep, and although deep, we had a good view of the sea-bottom which was a lovely sky blue. I never found out why this was, whether the bottom was a slate-like rock or white sand coloured blue by the depth of water. We could also spot an occasional huge conger sliding along the bottom.

Once we had reached the outer part of the bay, we baited our hooks and simply hung them over the side. No fishing rods or floats. Conger were bottom feeders, so we were told, so we didn't need sophisticated gear. "You'll know if you hook one, just hang onto the line if he pulls away, and I'll come to help you haul him in," said the pilot. So passed a pleasant hour basking in the wonderful sunshine. Also, a gentle breeze prevented us from overheated.

My reverie was broken, however, when the weather changed unbelievably quickly. A dense black cloud appeared out of nowhere, and a fierce wind began to whip up waves. The open boat was pitching and rolling violently. Being, at that stage of my life, the world's worst sailor, I began to be seasick. Nobody else was affected. I hung over the side and, with the violent pitching, I began to slide along the bench seat towards the stern of the boat.

Suddenly, the fishing line screamed through my fingers. I couldn't hold it, It would have burned me. I thought a monster conger had taken my bait and was running away with it. After only a short while – seconds it seemed – the line stopped. At the same time the engine of the launch made peculiar sounds, then stopped. The pilot appeared grabbed my line and, giving me a murderous look, said, "Now you've done it. The line has been caught by the propeller and wrapped around it." He dashed into the wheelhouse. Fortunately for those days, he was equipped with ship to shore radio, and we heard him calling for help.

In a short time, although it felt longer in that pitching sea, the inshore lifeboat appeared and drew up alongside us. The lifeboat crew assisted the passengers from our launch over to the lifeboat. Fortunately, all the passengers were like my friends and me, young and fit. Nevertheless, it was a scary business. The sea was unbelievably choppy. When I poised myself on the bench seat, readying myself to step over onto the lifeboat, the gap between the vessels suddenly either widened, or one or the other of the two craft dropped or rose making it impossible to cross. Eventually, with the aid of the lifeboat crew, we were each man-handled across. The lifeboat made short work of the journey back to the promenade. I wasn't very much concerned; however, the seasickness made me almost oblivious to other dangers.

We were all discharged onto the prom at Douglas when, instantaneously, the wind disappeared, and the sun came out again, as we made our way back to our hotel and a nice evening meal.

We all enjoyed the rest of our holiday, and our return journey to Liverpool was calm and comfortable. We jumped onto a train to Longport Station, from where we were able to walk home.

That was our final adventure before national service. Peter wasn't called up – he didn't pass the medical exam. Neither did Simon, our ace tennis player – he didn't have the required eyesight. Ben was drafted into the Pay Corps, and I was called up into the Royal Army Ordnance Corps, rated as a "technical clerk" because of my work experience and, apparently, problem solving aptitude.

We are now back at the beginning of this narrative, just out of training and bound for Egypt.

Chapter 15: Later Career and Later Life

Prelude

Another thing that never changes is the uncertainty of business life. The Austrian economist Joseph Schumpeter famously wrote about "gales of creative destruction" – whereby waves of innovation sweep aside and destroy outmoded businesses which are replaced by new and vibrant businesses. But, then as now, there are also what we might call "gales of destructive destruction". Here I will tell you about one of those, and the aftermath.

The asset strippers arrive at H&R Johnson

I had a successful career at H&R Johnson, but that came to an end abruptly.

When Derek Johnson, the chairman, died, the ownership of the company was in limbo. He was both the chairman and the managing director and, with members of his family, the major shareholder in the company. A few months before he died suddenly from cancer, he divorced his long-standing wife, Diana, a lovely and charming lady, and he married a lady who was the widow of one of the Cullinan diamond family. He had known her for some time from his visits to South Africa.

After Derek's death, the family split into two camps: Diana and the children, and Mrs. Cullinan and her tribe. No agreement was reached as to the future of the company, so it was, in effect, put up for sale.

The story explained to me was that after negotiations with a number of large organisations, the successful bidder was the Norcross company. Norcross was a conglomerate which owned several disparate companies. There was no particular manufacturing or trading philosophy. Norcross received proposals from any of their many companies for expansion or new trading ventures and would finance ones they considered worth backing, then monitor their respective progress.

A few of the senior managers at H&R Johnson who claimed to have had experience with companies owned by Norcross said, "They're nothing but asset strippers."

The chairman of Norcross and his management team addressed the assembled Johnson's managers in the canteen one day. He started by stating that he wanted to dispel the fears that he had gathered that they were "asset strippers". The very next thing he went on to say was, "We look at a company and look for any natural lines of cleavage that would enable us to re-organise it into a more profitable base."

In the first week after taking over, Norcross sold off Thomas Peake Ltd. This was an engineering company, wholly owned by H&R Johnson, that designed the innovative plant and equipment that had contributed so much to Johnsons' success.

Next, they sold off H&R Johnson's garage, along with its staff of skilled mechanics who had maintained the fleet of lorries and company cars. "You are in the business of making tiles," Norcross said. "You can buy in any mechanics' services you need."

They sold off the builders' shop, which provided builders and joiners for factory maintenance, expansions. They sold off the specialist joiners division which designed and built the displays that were installed at builders' merchants and other customers. The specialist joiners also created special displays for exhibitions held at places like the National Conference Centre.

So much for "not asset stripping".

The staff at H&R Johnson was reduced and streamlined. The marketing design team were made redundant. They disbanded the junior Operating Board of Directors, where I was the Commercial Director. I was given a job as a clerk in the company's secretariat.

I complained about that, saying "You have, effectively, made me redundant. I would prefer to have my redundancy pay and leave."

The new Managing Director had, by then, gained a reputation for some outrageous ideas. He saw the flames through inspection ports in the walls of the tunnel kilns. "You must be burning a lot of gas. Reduce it and with it our costs."

He viewed the conveyer belt where the finished tiles passed along before the inspectors. Here the instectors picked out any seconds: those imperfect tiles that had chips or crazes, or were misshapen had a slightly different shade. The MD instructed them to feed half of the rejects back on to the "inspected and approved line" rationalising that customers wouldn't complain about a few seconds.

He met with me in his office. He had seen my file in the Personnel Department. "You have no qualifications," he said. "I, for an example, have a certificate in accountancy. That is my 'meal ticket'." To his credit, he said he was loth to cast me onto the job market without a qualification. But he was obsessed with paper qualifications and had no insight into the projects I had fathered. Projects like the model equal pay scheme I had created, and which was adopted by the British Pottery Manufacturers Federation.

"I'm sending you onto a training scheme run by the National Computer Council, for prospective systems analysts," he told me. So, I went to Manchester for a six-week residential course, and to the surprise of many at H&R Johnson, I gained the required qualification.

However, I was, effectively, made redundant by Norcross. I was approaching my fiftieth birthday in the midst of a bad recession. It wasn't a good time.

I was constantly being cheered up by my colleagues at Johnsons. "Sorry about your situation."; "Good show standing up to those bastards."; "It' won't be the same without you." And from the Jeremiahs: "Hope you get on OK, but with the country in the state it's in, you'll probably never work again."

Never finding another job was, sad-to-say, the case for many of my ex-colleagues from H&R Johnson. However, as if to give the lie to those pessimistic comments from colleagues, I only missed two days' work from then on and into my later career.

Transition to Working Life

I was sought after by Manpower Services Commission to run the Transition to Work Life (TWL) scheme for North Staffordshire. I was actually employed by the Co-op. The Pilot Committee which originally set up the scheme up got the Co-op involved and got it to employ me and provide me with an office.

The Co-op were very supportive and provided the finance for my meagre requirements. The people I used in the scheme were volunteers recruited from local employers, and whose salaries were unaffected by helping TWL.

The TWL was the brainchild of the Grubb Institute. They had been studying unemployment for years and had become concerned about the worsening situation for school leavers. The institutes liaison officer coordinated between the Glasgow and the Wolverhampton schemes. And now she added our North Staffs operation to her roster. Her name was Ms Jean Hutton.

Jean was very able lady. She was a devout Christian, and the Grubb Institute was a Christian organisation. However, their approach was completely secular and professional. There was never any proselytising. Jean spent time explaining to me and the Pilot Committee the thinking behind TWL.

In normal circumstances, a young school leaver needs support in the massive jump from childhood to adult working life. Talented and fortunate boys could find an apprenticeship where a "journey man" would be assigned to the trainee to teach him the trade and help in learning to relate to adults and to, in the words of the Grubb Institute, "take authority for oneself". In this way, he/she would graduate into the adult world.

The mass unemployment of school-leavers in 1979 and the 1980s meant that many school leavers would grow up without this adult mentoring, which could be a significant handicap to them in later years. Using the experience of running the scheme in Glasgow and Wolverhampton, we set out to create the same system.

I sought help from any local employers who were prepared to assist. The first was the Co-op, not unexpectedly considering their whole philosophy was to help the community. Then Marks and Spencer. The Grubb Institute had longstanding relations with Lord Marks and his successors. One of these, Mr Marks, was keen to help, and he persuaded the manager of the Hanley store to help us. I was invited to Hanley to meet the manager and a few of his senior staff.

Hanley, I was surprised to learn, was one of the biggest M&S branches in the provinces. The manager had considerable autonomy. He was, I recognised straight away, a power-conscious individual. He wasn't difficult to deal with, but he had a slightly cynical view of the thinking behind my scheme, and it was clear that it was because of Mr. Marks suggestions that he was co-operating.

Behind the scenes in the store, his office was quite grand. He invited me to lunch with him and his senior staff. The dining room was like something from a four-star hotel, and the food, being Marks and Spencer, was absolutely excellent. From the demeanour of the manager and his staff, it was clear that he ran the store as his personal fiefdom. His word was law, and the product range and displays etc. were all designed to his personal approval, with almost no regard to the dictates of head office. He didn't tolerate any interference in his running the store because, I learned, it was so successful and profitable for the Marks organisation.

To get the TWL project going, I needed firstly organisations which were prepared to provide a mature workwomen or workmen to act as a leader. I would also need a room where he or she could meet with a group of school leavers. There, the experienced adults would help the youngsters in confronting the difficulties that they were having because of the recession. And they could provide the adult mentoring, which these stranded school leavers were missing, the lack of which would make it difficult to transition into a functioning adult.

The North Staffs Co-operative Society, with its ethos of public involvement, helped by providing me an office that I could use as a base. It was on the third floor of their flagship emporium in Newcastle-under-Lyme. This was handy for the local road network, so it made it practicable for me to get out to visit employers to seek their co-operation.

You can imagine the difficulty I faced. The recession created a general air of depression and insecurity, which were a big obstacle in finding firms willing to co-operate. I experienced the frustration and the pain of rejection which people in sales operations face. The employers were willing to see me, and all said how they sympathised with the plight of youngsters at that time. Few, however, could spare the people or facilities to help. Despite this, I managed to get a small group together, Marks and Spencer, British Rail and the Co-op of course.

The next problem was to recruit the youngsters. Surprisingly, this turned out to be the biggest difficulty. The first thing to learn was how to deal with civil servants. The two principal civil service groups were, first, Manpower Services a branch of the Ministry of Employment. They dealt with employment issues for adults; the Unemployment Office was their base. The second group was the Youth Employment Service, who acted as the unemployment office for school leavers.

The Manpower Services didn't figure much in my operations. They were, generally, a professional sort of people, hampered by so much bureaucracy. There were so many rules which seemed to militate against making decisions. They were good people and as co-operative as they were allowed to be.

The second group, Youth Employment, were employed by the local education authority. They had the biggest influence on school leavers, and I found them difficult to deal with. They tended to be quite amateurish in their approach, with little experience of the real world. At the end of the academic year, they would "assist" school leavers in finding suitable employment.

In the shocking absence of jobs, they looked for training establishments to take on the youngsters. Being quite academic in their approach, their practice was to sort out the sheep from the goats among the school leavers. The bright ones were snapped up first of all by the Michelin Company, who were famed for their excellent training and the apprentice schemes, which they still operated despite the recession.

The next group in the academic league were allocated by the Youth Training Service to the training scheme run by the pottery industry on behalf of employers like Wedgwood, Doulton and others.

Next came the school leavers who were adjudged by YTS to be suitable for engineering training. They were sent off to the Staffs Technical College.

This left a remainder who were considered to be virtually unemployable. They had no academic abilities or record. This was the rump that YTS was prepared to make available to me. The whole project was a "mature learning experience" for me personally.

Assistance came to me from the Co-op. A high-class small pottery company in Longton had become bankrupt in the recession. The Co-op took it over as a workers' co-operative. They retained three of the managers and brought in a managing director, named Kevin Dickin, who was an industrial accountant. I found later that he was a distant relative to my family. My father's eldest sister, Betsie, was married to a Dickin, and he was a relative to her husband.

He was a difficult man to work with. He'd had a chequered career, and I guessed his fierce volatile temper had influenced it. My role changed to be the training officer for that firm. I was given a large group of the sheep and goats to put to work in the factory at the standard training rate of £25 per week, which would be financed by Manpower Services.

We employed experienced pottery workers and started manufacturing in a limited way compared with the firm's original operation. It did, though, provided opportunities for the youngsters to learn from the adult they were paired with and, as I rotated them to give them as varied experience as could be managed, it was quite successful as a training operation but less so as a viable pottery manufacturer.

From time to time, I took the place of the adult for one of the groups. At the first meeting, there was a long silence. I had deliberately refrained from saying anything. I wanted them to learn from experience how to organise themselves and deal with an adult instead of being students in class.

Eventually, one girl spoke up and asked, "What is happening; what are we here for?" I explained my ideas and gradually they came to understand and were quite enthusiastic about it. Instead of asking, who was in charge or what was the agenda, they began to loosen up and talk amongst themselves, occasionally involving me in their discussions. I had explained that I could arrange visits for them to see adult working places.

"Where are we going to visit?" they asked.

"You are involved in this as much as I am," I replied. "Give me some ideas of things you think you would like to see."

After a pause and some muttering, the girl who had been the first to speak up said, "I would like to visit an undertaker. Is that possible?"

241

I guessed straightaway that the general idea was working. As children it wasn't appropriate to visit such places. Their curiosity about the adult world began to take shape and other suggestions flowed thick and fast. "I would like to visit a slaughterhouse," one lad suggested. A cinema and projectionists came next. I collected a list then set them the task of playing a part in organising things. I would help them compose, type and mail letters. (This was in the days before e-mail and mobile phones.) So, they, together, searched through Yellow Pages for an abattoir and composed a letter explaining that they were trainees seeking experience of the adult world which, up to now, had been denied them.

We got a prompt response, and a week later, the group of a dozen lads and girls boarded the back of a transit van the firm owned, and off we went to the abattoir. It was a deeply shocking experience for me personally. It took me years to really get over it. Four of the boys fainted but none of the girls. They seemed to be made of sterner stuff.

At the following week's meeting, there was an animated discussion of the experience, and it was fascinating to see them grow up in attitude in such a short space of time. I rotated them among the mature workers, so that they could get a taste of the different skills. It also helped to combat the biggest general problem with the youngsters – boredom. If you weren't careful, they easily became distracted. I noticed that after a quite exciting start of our meetings they would suddenly become bored until something cropped up that grabbed their attention.

We were having a discussion one day about entertainment. "What's your favourite TV programme?" I asked.

They answered, almost in one voice, *Brookside*. They all seemed to enjoy this soap opera. I'd never seen it. Soap operas were not my scene, but I was intrigued by the unanimous enthusiasm for the programme, so I found it on early evening TV and watched it. The storylines were simple, almost banal, so that as soon as one topic had opened and the characters' interactions developed, it would switch to another scene, then on to a further one. I found it quite irritating, there was no opportunity to get your teeth into a story line before it had jumped to another one.

I then realised that the makers of the programme had a brilliant idea which catered for their particular audience's characteristic, a short attention span. These youngsters had been written off by some of the educational establishment as "thick" (my words) and incapable of receiving an orthodox education. I found them in fact, with only a few exceptions, to be bright and interesting, when you got engaged with them. Their problem was their short attention span. They seemed incapable, or unwilling, to maintain their concentration. I've often wondered since, if the world of education has got on to this problem and addressed it.

However, as Harold MacMillan famously replied to a TV interviewer's question about the biggest problem of his premiership, "Events, dear boy, events."

The co-op had taken over the pottery and tried to run it with less than a fifth of its original workforce. I was not privy to their inner workings and the financial arrangements, but it became clear that the operation was starved of funds.

I was still organising systems and procedures for the training operation with no staff. I found a stationery storeroom full of stuff, but most of it the wrong sort. I found a supply of file folders which I used for various purposes. One for an attendance register. Another for personnel histories. Then training programmes, progress reports etc. etc.

I found a pack of A4 white paper, but it was not regular typing paper. All the stock of paper was the type used in the old-fashioned Roneo machine. The paper was absorbent to take the ink. This machine held a wax paper sheet on which one typed a document and wrapped it onto the drum, which was filled with black ink. When paper was fed, sheet by sheet, under the drum, it printed copies of the wax image. As there was no other paper, I used the paper for letter writing. Soon the pack was empty and there was no further supply.

I asked Kevin Dickin if he could order in some more stationery. His reply was, "We're broke, I can't afford to buy stationery. There's a storeroom full of it. Use that."

"But," I said, "there's loads of paper in all the colours of the rainbow, but no white paper."

"You'll just have to manage with colours then." He shrugged and walked away.

I selected the palest yellow paper as a substitute for white, then had a thought. I could turn a problem into an opportunity. I could use the various colours for the many different records I was keeping. Pink for the register, blue for personnel and so on.

I could see, however, that the writing was on the wall. The whole operation was going to wind down for lack of finance, so I began to search for a new job. I wrote to the Co-op and the Grubb Institute, thanking them for their support, but pointing out that the project was no longer financially viable, and I was looking for alternative employment.

It so happened that Manpower Services at that time 'phoned me to announce they were coming to audit the scheme, which they were partly financing. I fixed a date for later that week, and their team of three people came. They interviewed a few of the trainees, examined the workplace, then turned their attention to the way I had organised things. This was a further insight for me into the civil service mind.

To my surprise, they were thrilled at the whole set-up. They implied it had advantages over the "professional" schemes I mentioned earlier when talking about the Youth Employment people.

"This idea," enthused the lady who was the team leader, "of a colour scheme to classify the whole operation, is admirable. I am so impressed that I would like your permission to use it as a model for organisations who are about to set up new training schemes." A bit late in the day!

Further events followed. The co-op had twigged that Dickin, despite his alleged qualifications, was a bit of a fly-boy, so he was encouraged to depart. They then recruited an experienced pottery factory manager, who had just returned to the UK after running a factory in Brazil. This new chap was a different kettle of fish altogether. He had no patience with a training scheme. His idea was to get the factory back to full production and concentrate on a smaller product range.

Dairy Crest

In the meantime, I had received a reply to my response to an advert in the Sentinel newspaper. This was for a sales administrator wanted by the Dairy Crest Northern Division, based at the newish depot in Crewe vacated by the Emberton's Cheese distributors. So, again without losing any days in unemployment, I was the successful applicant and started at Dairy Crest in 1984 at the age of fifty-two.

Dairy Crest was only a few years old. Its creation came about when, at the start of the recession, a large international organisation, which owned the biggest chain of dairy/creamery businesses in the UK, told the Milk Marketing Board that they would be losing the biggest outlet for their members' milk production. Their creameries had been neglected of funding for so long and were making such losses that they were prepared to cut their losses and leave the market.

I never saw any record of the transactions, but it was explained to me that Unilever had effectively held a pistol to the head of the MMB. "Buy from us our chain of cheese and butter creameries up and down England and Wales, or we shall abandon it completely. "Where will your farmers then find outlets for their milk production then?"

Out of this hurried situation MMB created a separate organisation, a commercial company called Dairy Crest. This was because the MMB itself had no real commercial experience. It acted just as an organising board for the nation's farmers.

The headquarters of the MMB was in Thames Ditton, about ten miles west of Kingston-on-Thames in Surrey. They acquired a building a mile away along the river at Surbiton, which they christened Dairy Crest House. They then, apparently, spent a fortune on consultants to create a functioning company. The consultants recruited a highly paid chief executive, then a management team of research and development, production, sales and marketing, personnel, finance, etc...

Then they recruited a team of managers to fill the slots on their theoretically based organisation chart, then working downwards a succession of staff to fill the then required vacancies.

All this was done before they reached the stage when Dairy Crest took over Emberton's operation in Crewe. This northern depot had a huge, refrigerated warehouse and a fleet of lorries to service grocery wholesalers and supermarkets in the north of England, Wales and Scotland. Another Depot was created from scratch at Hemel Hempstead, north of London, to supply the South and West of England.

I don't know when they actually took over the creameries from Unilever, but Dairy Crest's sales and distribution had become established by the time I was engaged.

The Crewe operation was split into two: warehouse and distribution one part; sales was the other part. It consisted of a team of telesales ladies, who had minimal contact with the other office, Terry Foden, the sales manager for the North and Scotland, me as his Sales Administrator, and a couple of clerks/typists.

It was, in some ways, a relatively cushy number for me with my previous experiences at Johnsons, but it had, inevitably, its confusions while I learned the ropes. Basically, the two excellent clerks had the job of digesting the sales statistics from the main frame computer printouts each month. This enabled the Regional Sales Manager, Terry and the General Sales Manager, based at Dairy Crest House, Surbiton, to track the performance of the salesmen - twenty or so in each region.

An incentive prize scheme was run, worth a bit to the winners, so the results were eagerly awaited by the managers.

I was continually amazed at the unscientific ways of thinking by the sales and the marketing people. We had a General Sales Manager who, without fail, 'phoned me at 5 o-clock on Friday to ask what the sales figures were. I tried, unsuccessfully, to explain to him that the computer was still printing out the sales figures, which had to be collated by product and sales area in order to be made readable sense.

"Yes, I understand," he said, although the obviously didn't or wouldn't. "But the week has ended now, so surely you have the figures?" Frankly, although he was an intelligent man with lots of sales experience, it was like talking to the village idiot. In the end I just let him ramble while we got on the job of digesting the printouts.

These prints were available to the sales team so that they could examine their relative performance, but the system had been designed by computer people, not by any sales or non-computer person. Nobody knew which print out contained which sector of sales information. The only people who could make sense of the system were the computer manager in Hemel Hempstead and the two women in our office, plus our counterparts in the Hemel regional office.

The women at Crewe were, at first, a bit suspicious at my digging into the set up in order to make it intelligible. I think that, in their way, they were a little bit jealous that their arcane knowledge of the system was being taken away from them. After a while, their fears were allayed, and I printed out an analysis, which I created from my PC, tabulating the various reports which were identified in the cumbersome computer system simply by numbers.

I shrank this document to fit inside the cover of my diary and, armed that, I could talk to the computer people when it came, inevitably, to designing a new system. It proved a godsend in meetings with the sales management and the computer staff, so I was co-opted onto the committee involved in designing the new system.

The training course in Manchester, before I left Johnsons, had been quite a help. There, I had sat the examination set by the National Computer Centre and gained a certificate as a qualified systems analyst. Passing an exam was not enough in itself to enable me to work as a systems analyst. It needed quite a lot of experience with computers. However, as the NCC inspectors told me, there were very many systems analysts skilled in computing, but in practice they lacked the business experience and outlook. A person with both was described as a "business analyst", and they felt with my experience I should prove useful in that role.

Back to Crewe

At any rate, returning to Weston Road, Crewe, the Northern Depot and Sales HQ.

I was responsible for a number of tasks which included dealing with sales statistics and running the incentive scheme, which awarded prizes to the best performing salesmen.

The incentive scheme took the form of modest cash awards and other perks, such as tickets to an entertainment event. I produced a league table each month based on sales figures, for use by the sales manager when adjudging performance.

However, to my continued amazement at the thinking of salespeople, the prizes seemed to have only a passing relationship with the stats. Other factors, not so measurable, were on the mind of the manager. I guessed there was no favouritism, but a salesman's performance at the monthly sales meetings had an influence. A good solid presentation, from which his colleagues could learn, and ideas for the coming sales promotions were taken into consideration.

The salesmen, from both the North and South Divisions, were generally a good crowd of people, and even though I was far older than them, I was happy to learn from them. They saw me, not as a father figure, but as a sort of helpful uncle, who would help them in connection with general knowledge and my knowledge of cheese and butter, which I had boned up on before joining the company. Dealing with these great chaps was a real pleasure. They grew to trust me in that I didn't manipulate figures as my predecessor had allegedly done, and I tried to be consistently straightforward with them.

I mentioned earlier, the organisation split at the depot between the sales department and the distribution side of the operation. The distribution side worked on strict lines, something like the civil service. There was no willing co-operation. They seemed to resent the sales team and, on the other hand, our sales manager and a few of his colleagues referred to them as the "sales prevention department".

This was a factor in another of my jobs, that of supplying samples to a prospective customer or a sample of a product different from those usually taken by an established customer. The system was that I had to place an order with the telesales office for a complete case of cheese, for example.

Most cheeses were produced in huge blocks weighing 20 Kg. These were wrapped in saran (tough cling film) and then put into a stout cardboard "case". These would be sold to large wholesalers, who would sometimes cut the cheese into pieces and wrap them individually wrapped for sale in their outlets. Sales to, for example, cash and carry wholesalers consisted of cases each containing the standard 20 Kg block but cut and saran-wrapped into four 5 Kg blocks, suitable for a retailer to buy from the cash and carry. A block could also be cut and wrapped into eight 2.5 Kg blocks, for smaller retailers.

If a salesman was trying to get a customer interested in the 2.5 Kg blocks, for example, he would ask me to send one to the customer. The distribution side of the depot would not sell me a "part case". Consequently, I had to buy eight blocks, send one to the customer and place the remaining seven blocks in my samples cage.

The samples cage was constructed out of mesh and stood in the corner of our refrigerated warehouse. (Dairy products could not be stored in "ambient" conditions.) I had to hope that there would be other requests from salesmen for the leftover 2.5 Kg or 5Kg samples.

Dairy products have a shelf life stretching up to six months, and I needed to send them to a customer before their sell by date expired. If I couldn't, I had the problem of disposing of the extra samples.

Management didn't want to know about this problem. The only solution was to take a block out of a case and then return the remaining blocks to the distribution side of the business.

This was easier said than done, however. I had to go through the same procedure as a customer returning a part case. I was asked to fill out lengthy forms giving the reasons for the return, for example, quality, damage, wrong product and so on. This would give rise to correspondence from head office trying to solve customers' dissatisfactions. However, the system paid no regard to the need for samples for the sales operation. It was a Kafkaesque nightmare.

My opposite number at Hemel Hempstead had the same problem and dealt with it as I did, by taking a block or two home. Fortunately, this happened very occasionally, so we could cope with consuming extra cheese. (Perhaps I should have omitted such an admission for fear of CID involvement!)

So, I spent four happy years at Crewe. I wasn't stuck in the office while there. Every month, the sales meeting was held at either Hemel Hempstead or combined with a visit to one of Dairy Crest's creameries, where I learned something about cheese and butter production. We would stay for a night at a good hotel.

The meetings were quite painless; the company of the sales chaps was enjoyable, and we had the interesting experiences of seeing the creameries in action. I remember visiting: Haslington, famed for its Stilton; Wensleydale again famous for the eponymous cheese; Nantwich, to see Cheshire Cheese produced; unpronounceable creameries in Wales where they produced (geographically misplaced)

249

Lancashire cheese, double Gloucester and others; also, the giant flagship creamery at Crudgington in Shropshire, where huge volumes of Cheddar were produced in massive "cheddaring towers". (Cheese was continuously loaded into the top of these towers and then, later, drawn from the bottom, having spent weeks being compressed by its own weight into their excellent cheddar cheese.)

I look back with grateful memories of how good Dairy Crest was to me at that late stage in my career, exposing me to such nice people and interesting experiences. I recall being sent on courses about sales techniques, statistical analysis etc, in lovely venues. One was held in the former home of WS Gilbert of Gilbert and Sullivan fame. It was preserved in its original state with his study, library and examples of his work for us to see.

Finally, I was invited, with a few of our notable salesmen, to a residential course on cheese and butter making held at Reese Heath Agricultural College, just outside Nantwich. I really enjoyed that. It wasn't very technical, more to give delegates a general knowledge about the products. It was led by a recent recruit to Dairy Crest's management team. This lady, with an encyclopaedic knowledge of cheeses from the whole world over, had been the head buyer at Marks and Spencer for such products.

On the last day, she showed us a long trestle table on which were amassed so many different products, each still in their colourful packaging. There were hard cheeses from the Netherlands and Switzerland, soft mold-ripened cheeses from France, Germany and Spain and others I can't remember.

The move to Cobham

Then came the day the world changed again for me. The day before the monthly sales meeting, the head office sales manager came to Crewe. Terry Foden was away, so we used his office for a private chat.

"We are progressively transferring more of our operations to the Hemel Hempstead depot," he explained. "They will be taking over a lot of the work you have been doing at Crewe. As it happens, we have created a vacancy in Dairy Crest House for some-one with your experience to aid in sales administration. You will be working for the National Sales Administrator and have special responsibilities to liaise with the national management team, who are designing a completely new computer system."

In effect, he was telling me I could be made redundant from my job at Crewe and leave the company or be transferred to this new position at head office.

I expected that Sheila would be apprehensive about moving to Surrey. We were both well aware of the huge difference in house prices since we kept in touch with Martin, Sheila's eldest brother, who, after leaving the RAF after 20 years' service, had lived in Epsom. We, with our children, had visited him a few times and met his wife, a divorcee with a teenage son. Surrey seemed a pleasant, civilised area, so it was the house prices which were the only major concern.

Nevertheless, I took the job. When I started to work at the Surbiton office, I stayed in a small hotel in Kingston on Thames, only ten miles away, while I settled in and started house hunting. My first port of call was an estate agency in Esher, the town next door to Surbiton. Their office was located by the entrance to Sandown Racecourse. I explained that I was looking for a small house for my wife and me. (Our children had, by then, left home and were married.) Our little bungalow in Rode Heath no longer had a mortgage, but we were prepared to take on another loan at the age of 55, and this didn't appear to be an obstacle.

The agent was an upper middle-class type of chap who sounded like a pre-war BBC announcer. He asked what sort of price bracket I was considering. Our bungalow had been valued at £60,000, so I guessed we would need to pay something like 25 percent more for a similar property in Surrey. The agent, with a supremely condescending air, said, "Oh you won't find a house round here, sir, for that sort of price. You would be lucky to get a run-down old terrace house for £100,000 at least."

Colleagues at Surbiton sympathised and explained that staff joining from the North found it necessary to find rented accommodation. However, I found an advert in the local paper for a semi-detached cottage with two main bedrooms and another small bedroom too, on the main Portsmouth Road. It was sound with a long garden, typical in

Surrey. It didn't have a garage, but the owner said that a neighbour owned a small courtyard round the corner with lock-up garages available to rent.

The owner and his wife had a somewhat unusual outlook on life. They had spent some time decorating and arranging the house into its original Victorian condition. They had installed a modern gas central heating system, but any fitted furniture had been removed. Each room, including the bedrooms, had its own Victorian cast iron fireplace. Actually, it had a certain charm, but Sheila and I couldn't live without a more modern kitchen with decent sink unit, cooker and washing machine.

The asking price was £110,000. Negotiation was difficult, because at that time, property was scarce. It was very much a seller's market. However, I managed to get him to agree to £100,000 because he and his wife were keen to move near to her parents.

Getting a mortgage wasn't difficult, so we prepared for the big move. Then, to my surprise, the Dairy Crest personnel manager asked me to call in at his office to discuss any problems I might have concerning the move. He was already aware that I would be facing the house price differential and explained that Dairy Crest had a policy of assisting staff with house moves. Apparently, with the major re-organisation they were undergoing, they had difficulty in filling vacancies with staff from areas outside London. The scheme paid all the interest on my new mortgage during the first year, then 10 percent of it on the second year and so on for a period of 5 years, by which time, with the payments I had made from savings, the mortgage was paid off.

We set about modernising the house. Fortunately, with the different courses I had taken at evening classes, I had a number of skills and Sheila proved to be really adapt, particularly with plumbing. The kitchen was big enough but, like all the surrounding houses, was longer than it was wide. However, we made it into a fitted kitchen using individual cupboards, shelving and fitments. To the surprise of the neighbours, who were really helpful and friendly, it was quite smart.

We bought compact wardrobes and beds etc. to complete the project. We retained the cast iron fireplaces. When situated in a more modern décor they added charm to the house's appearance. In fact, it became a big selling feature when our estate agent, years later, put it on the market.

We really enjoyed Cobham. Contrary to the common assumption in our native Staffordshire/Cheshire, the southerners were no different from our friends and neighbours back home. We had a good social life with a social activities club for seniors in Cobham. It was not a drinking club, but there were pubs dotted around.

Our favourite pub was the Black Bear at the end of the High Street, where it faced the River Mole. In summer, it was delightful. It sat at a bend in the river and for children there was a broad paved area shelving gradually into the water, so they could paddle safely or feed the many ducks and swans.

A bonus was the weather. Winters were milder; in fact, in the ten years we lived there, we had only one light snowfall. Summers were much warmer; in fact, for a lot of those months, it was almost like a heatwave.

Lovely place, shame about the job

The only drawback for me was the work. A few visitors from head office to our Crewe depot had mentioned that Dairy Crest House was marred by politics. I found, in the different places I had worked in or visited after leaving Johnsons, that some of them had an unsettling atmosphere. Poor, weak or absent management meant that staff had time for gossiping, forming cliques and jockeying for position. That was the negative side of Dairy Crest head office.

The Director of Sales and Marketing was a highly educated Australian chap. In complete contrast to the down-to-earth image of an Aussie, he was an urbane, academic, hands-off type. He seemed proud of his presentation skills and made appearances at our sales meetings to announce new innovations.

He didn't delegate he abdicated. As sales manager, he concentrated solely on the salesforce itself. This left all the power in organising things to the Chief Sales Administrator. This guy was the epitome of a micro-manager. He had worked all his life in a supermarket, starting as a shelf-filler. Supermarkets are extremely detail orientated, and this guy had not known any other working environment.

He was bright and well-meaning, but my heart sank when he spoke to me for the first time. He had telephoned me to advise me on how to get to Dairy Crest House from Crewe. He launched into a verbal version of an RAC route guide. "First you have to take the A51 from Emberton's which will take you to Junction 16 of the M.6. There you will need to take the first exit from the roundabout onto the motorway. When you get to Junction X take the M.25 to Junction Y."

This was years before sat-nav, and I had years driving experience finding my way around the country. "It's O.K. Steve," I said. "I am well used to driving and I have an excellent road atlas in the case of difficulty."

"Yes," he ploughed on, "but you need to be aware of x.y.z..."

It was more than this manager's micro-management that caused my disillusionment with Dairy Crest. I had a slight suspicion from the sales manager's explanation of the new position, that I might be something of a supernumerary.

Apart from my contribution to the design committee for the new computer system, my role was inserted between the sales administration team and the "micro manager". The staff had a slight resentment at an extra, unnecessary, layer of management, and this was compounded by the manager's obsession with detail.

It came to a head when I had something of a row with him, and after that he consulted human resources, the new title for the personnel department. They were still working, all those years later, on re-organising the Crewe depot. They decided they would make the two girls who had previously worked for me redundant, and, as our jobs were related, they took the opportunity at the same time to offer me early retirement.

I had reached the age of 60 and I welcomed it. In many ways, Dairy Crest had been a generous employer with the subsidised mortgage scheme and generous travel expenses for my monthly trips to sales meeting venues. It was unfortunate that a lack of real leadership at a senior level caused so much politicking.

Moving back to Cheshire

Sheila and I enjoyed a further four years in Cobham. In some ways I still miss being there: the real difference in climate, the local amenities and high standard of living.

But then, events intervened again. Martin, Sheila's eldest brother, had divorced his wife and left Epsom. He was renting a room in the house of his ex-wife's old lady friend. He wasn't being properly looked after, and couldn't cook, so most of the time he was eating at a local "greasy spoon".

My guess is that his unsatisfactory diet gave rise to him developing colo-rectal cancer. Sheila and I spent some time visiting him in hospital at Guildford. In the process, Sheila was dismayed at the living conditions in his rented room. So, I suggested that Martin should come over to Cobham and live with us.

He was a gentle, amiable chap and I'd always liked him, almost like a brother. He used to chat with Sheila and me about their early life in Scholar Green. I sensed that Sheila, after enjoying ten great years in Cobham, had become home sick, and we all came to the idea of returning to Cheshire to enjoy the rest of our retirement.

By the time we left there though, it wasn't simply the nostalgia for Cheshire that influenced our decision. There had been a steady increase in road traffic, not only on the Portsmouth Road where we lived, but in that corner of Surrey. It was so convenient as a living centre. Cobham was just one mile from Junction 10 on the M.25 and the Portsmouth Road gave onto the A3, making it only an hour away from the centre of London. The traffic became so heavy that rush hours expanded in the morning and evening with not much of a gap in between.

Our house was well situated. On the other side of the road was Cobham Common, a great place to walk our dog. However, the lack of breaks in the traffic meant a walk for half a mile to where a footbridge took pedestrians across to the common.

The recession which began in 1980 had by then run its course, but the housing market remained depressed. It so happened that Martin had a time-share apartment in Tenerife. We spent a lovely fortnight's holiday there, and when we returned and the taxi dropped us off outside our house, I was amazed to see all up the Portsmouth Road, "For Sale" signs outside so many of the houses.

Another co-incidence was that Leonard, Sheila's youngest brother, had just put his house at Rode Heath on the market. It was in a beautiful location on the canal side; it was a detached with four bedrooms and a large double garage. We snapped it up. Our house in Cobham had appreciated in value and this, with the North/South differential, made it possible for us to buy Leonard's house and a new car for cash and still have money in the bank.

Rode Heath was a lovely, peaceful village to live in. However, we came to realise that, for shopping and for our social life, we were driving the couple of miles to and from Alsager, which had grown to the size of a small town. It had shops, restaurants and take-aways, some nice pubs, an active library and a thriving civic centre.

So, we decided to move again to Alsager. Martin, unfortunately, had died, and by then we were beginning to feel our age, so we looked for a bungalow. They were extremely scarce and pricey, because the aging population was driving up demand. We found one, from where I am typing this autobiography, in Grosvenor Avenue. A lovely quiet cul-de-sac, backing on to open countryside stretching up to Lawton Heath.

The U3A

Sheila and I were looking for leisure activities or hobbies when I saw a notice in the window of the library announcing a new venture being started by a couple of the more active residents. One of them was Frank Guy. I had known Frank for many years. He was the representative for Thomas Meadows, the forwarding agent and air freight specialist in Stoke-on-Trent. He used to call on me regularly when I was in the Export Department at H&R Johnson. He was a very pleasant, straightforward chap, and I was delighted at the opportunity of meeting him again.

He and Norman Williams had started to create an Alsager branch of the U3A. The "University of the Third Age" (which is what the initials stood for) had been in existence for a few years in France, and now was spreading in the UK. The idea was the brainchild of a group of academics at the university in Lyons, I believe.

They viewed our lives as being in three stages, or ages. The first age was infancy and school life; the second age was work or profession; and the third age was retirement.

This group of French academics were reflecting on what a waste of experience, skills and wisdom it was when, after an active life, people were left, in many cases, without any further use for their experience. Life is a continuous learning experience, they considered, and a wider collection of people could benefit by the sharing of this experience and various skill sets. On top of that, there would be the social advantage of belonging to a community with shared interests.

Frank and Norman found that Alsager was particularly suitable for such an enterprise. For many years, Alsager had a large teacher training college, which had now been subsumed into the Manchester Metropolitan University. The college had recently moved to a new large campus in Crewe. Many of the retired lecturers and staff from the college lived in Alsager. Also, Alsager is a residential area for many professional and managerial people without many outlets for retirees' energies.

Sheila and I turned up at enrolment day at the civic centre in Alsager. There was a queue of people stretching round the centre and spilling out onto the town car park. Fortunately, the help desk inside had a large staff, so the line was processed quite quickly.

The U3A was open to anybody over the age of 50 who was not engaged in full-time employment. After paying our modest fees, we passed into the large venue hall, where more desks had been set up for the various groups/interests. Sheila and I both enrolled at the travel and excursions desk. There were others, for example, photography, short medium and long walking group, local history, French and other languages, arts and crafts, etc.

I wasn't quite as fit as I had been, and Sheila had persuaded me to retire my set of tools and to employ tradesmen instead of doing so much DIY. After some thought, I recalled my school days when I found the art classes enjoyable, so I joined the Art Group No.1. Art was so popular they had four different groups meeting at different venues around Alsager.

Sheila was looking for something different as a hobby, so she joined the Mah Jong group. With her Arrowsmith mind, she took to this very quickly and, until she became ill, never missed a meeting.

Finally, we both joined "Talk Time" where, every Monday at 11am, they had a visiting speaker on all sorts of subjects. After there was tea/coffee and lots of interesting, lovely people to talk with.

Each group had a leader, a volunteer member of U3A. My group was led by Ewart Edge. Sheila and I had known Ewart and his family for years. They lived in Scholar Green. Their children were the same age as ours and went to the same schools. Ewart was much older than me. He had been a fighter pilot in WWII, and after he was the export manager for Wedgwoods. He and his wife were a cultured couple, who met as students at Oxford. Ewart was fluent in German and other languages, hence his job as export manager at the famous pottery firm. He was a brilliantly talented watercolourist, and his paintings were much in demand.

I found water colour painting interesting but complex and difficult for a starter. With Ewart's kind expert advice, I built up a kit of the proper types of paper, paints and brushes. Sable brushes were extremely expensive, but I had a selection of the best size and types. After three years under Ewart, I gained some skills and even sold a few paintings at the annual exhibition we held in Alsager.

Ewart was well into his eighties when I started at the group, and one day we had the sad news that he'd died. The U3A searched for someone to take over with no success. The only prospect was to close the group and find places for the members in one of the other groups. Our group was so convenient, meeting in the main hall at the civic centre, and we were all loth to travel farther to join a strange group.

So, I undertook to take Ewart's place. The idea, in U3A, was to have a leader, not a teacher. I didn't need to teach so much as to organise and to encourage less able members. I did want to impart some of the valuable knowledge and techniques that Ewart had coached me in, so I began to plan a series of sessions for that purpose. Looking back, I remember for some reason the song from *The King and I* film when

Anna's lines included words, "When as a teacher you start, from your pupils you learn your art." Perhaps not the literal words, but the meaning was relevant.

I found the internet a massive resource for creating a lesson on a topic. For example, I found a way of explaining perspective. The textbooks and even parts of the internet made it so technical, but I found ways of being able to demonstrate it to the grateful members of our group. Other topics like aerial perspective, colour mixing, sketching ideas, and so on. These thinking exercises were a help to me. They enabled me to understand better and to put them into practice.

I am quite proud of some of my watercolours, but, as for most of the group, they didn't sell well. The amateur painting hobby is an overcrowded area for anyone interested in it as a commercial venture. It wasn't my aim to learn painting for commercial purposes. I found it interesting to study different techniques so I could create more of an atmosphere in painting – mainly landscapes and buildings.

Sheila's health declines

I was starting to explore portraiture when MacMillan's predictions happened once more. "Events, dear boy, events."

Sheila had not been as lively and challenging for some time. The progress of this development in our lives was so gradual, unnoticed, insidious I believe is the word, that it was months before I realised that it was becoming a problem. It was the onset of vascular dementia, a dreadful and ultimately terminal illness. It is difficult even to describe it and how its effects worsened.

I need to take you back to our time in Cobham to explain a possible cause of Sheila's health problems.

While we were at Cobham, Sheila had experienced the onset of the menopause. We both read up on it and decided that hormone replacement therapy (HRT) appeared to be a useful treatment, which we could explore with our GP. Dr Sarah MacKay was a great family doctor. She was kind, thorough and always keen to help. She prescribed HRT. This was wonderfully effective; it restored Sheila to her usual vivacious self.

She had been receiving this treatment for some years before Dr MacKay said she was concerned about Sheila being on this regime for so long. She was concerned about the risks of blood clots, breast cancer and other complications. We respectfully declined the offer of an alternative, a drug from a group called bisphosphonates. This medicine was used to re-mineralise bone cells lost through potential osteoporosis. The doctor reminded Sheila several times of the risks that she, as a doctor, felt needed to be addressed. So, eventually, Sheila accepted the offer of the new drug, "Didronel".

Dr Mackay wanted to monitor its effectiveness, so she sent off a sample of Sheila's blood at the start of the treatment and followed this by another sample one month later. The result of the second test showed a reduction in Sheila's red blood cell count. In effect it was making her anaemic. So, the Didronel was stopped, and Sheila was referred to a consultant haematologist.

All this happened as we were arranging our move back to Cheshire. Eventually, we had an appointment with Dr Tarkovacs, the consultant haematologist at Leighton Hospital, near Crewe. He strongly advised against reverting to HRT. Careful monitoring of her aplastic anaemia, as it was termed, was the best way forward.

The anaemia didn't improve. A course of iron tablets didn't work; it caused her to accumulate too much iron in her blood, but not in the red corpuscles. Something had caused Sheila's bone barrow to reduce its ability to produce new red corpuscles. So, a course of a hormone called erythropoietin was tried. A one-month course. A blood test at the end of the course showed that she had produced an excess of red corpuscles, which the doctors described as making her blood too sticky. This had caused a series of what they called "ischaemic events", in effect, mini strokes.

These had affected Sheila's balance. I escorted her everywhere after that. She had an appointment with the optician, and, despite me holding on to her arm, she tripped over the step at the entrance and fell, breaking her left hip. An ambulance took her to Leighton Hospital, and the following day she had a hip replacement operation.

This was successful, but three months later we were talking in the lounge when she suddenly fell backwards breaking her right hip. Again, no time was lost in having an operation, but this time the operation had complications. Something had severed tendons in her right hip, so she could no longer move her right leg. Her general condition had also deteriorated, so she was bed-fast at home. On top of this, it was becoming clear that her memory and thinking were gradually deteriorating.

After nursing Sheila at home with the assistance of carers, who visited twice a day, she suddenly deteriorated further. Just before Christmas 2019, she fell into a sleep. I couldn't wake her. Our G., Dr Bennett, came and decided she should be admitted to Leighton Hospital. I knew Sheila hated hospitals. She had been admitted for a couple of weeks the previous year with a chest infection, and both of us were dissatisfied with the care she had received. It wasn't an actual lack of clinical care, but the nursing staff were not the same as in years gone by. In my view, the standards in the NHS had declined after many financial cuts by the government.

So, instead of Leighton Hospital, Dr Bennett found a room at Lawton Manor Care Home, which was reserved for NHS patients, and I agreed Sheila should go there. Our GP urged me on in this saying, "You are 86 not 36 and you are damaging your own health by dealing with her toilet and other needs." We couldn't find a care agency that could provide all day care, never mind the cost that this would involve.

Just as Sheila was admitted to Lawton Manor, the Covid crisis was brewing. I visited Sheila the day after she was admitted, finding her terribly upset. Her thinking had declined somewhat, so she was confused. She was so used to me being with her 24/7 and couldn't understand what was going on. I should try to explain that vascular dementia is different from Alzheimer's disease, where the memory is affected. Sheila's memory had been affected but differently. She could remember but with confusion about the time scale.

I had a word with the manager of Lawton Manor, and she offered me a room for £950 per week. It was a large room and could hold two beds. All this happened as the first lockdown was imposed by the Government during the Covid Crisis. So, after moving in we were confined for months in the care home.

It was quite a high-class home; the furnishing and the food were excellent. The carers were mainly young, single mothers on minimum wage. They were as good as they could reasonably be expected to be.

As I mentioned, Sheila's vascular dementia wasn't quite like Alzheimer's. She could be lucid and fully engaged with us at times. I have a video on my mobile phone, taken just before she had the relapse which caused her to be admitted to Lawton Manor. She was sitting up in bed and reciting *Albert and the Lion*, one of Stanley Holloway's monologues. The family always loved to hear her perform this poem at Christmas and other gatherings. She used to recite it at the Rode Player's nights. In my video, she recited the whole piece without mistakes or hesitations.

Occasionally, when she was feeling well, she would recite it for the carers at Lawton Manor after her daily bed-bath. They loved it and other carers would come into the room when the word got out that she was reciting. On those occasions, she was quick-witted and full of jokes and fun with the carers.

However, it was not the care I wanted for Sheila, and I found myself, at times, in conflict with the nurses, the carers and the manager. The big problem was that the carers, and the nurses to an extent, worked in a robotic manner as I called it. When she needed the toilet, Sheila needed to be helped by a crane-hoist device with which two carers lifted her up from the bed and lowered her onto a wheeled commode. The carers' response to the call button was lacking in a sense of urgency. They went round the individual rooms in the home on "toilet duty" whether the patient had requested a visit or not.

I insisted they respond to Sheila's needs as they arose, instead of waiting her turn. The manager, when I complained, agreed with me but used shortage of staff as an excuse. In emergency situations, I rang the manager, and she came personally with a nurse to "toilet" Sheila. Not a proper solution to the problem, which only improved when Lawton Manor was taken over by Barchester, a large chain of homes. Then they obviously could afford to employ more carers.

One of the joys of our married life was to go to bed together, where I could cuddle her and get her off to sleep. In our room we had two single hospital beds at opposite sides of the room. On the floor beside

Sheila's bed, a "crash mat" was placed in case she fell out of bed. I lowered her bed to the floor, transferred my bedding to the mat making it resemble a double bed, and in this way, we spent the nights together. I feel it was a great comfort to her for the twenty months we spent at Lawton Manor.

On 19th July 2021, we celebrated Sheila's 88th Birthday. Nick, the brilliant chef, baked a beautiful birthday cake for her, and the nurses and carers brought her a huge bouquet of flowers. A week later, on the 25th, she died suddenly. I can't and won't try to describe what that was like.

All the time we were in Lawton Manor, I had kept the bungalow in Alsager. Edwina did a super job in checking it every week. I planned to leave Lawton Manor and find a small home for myself. I found that difficult, so decided, in the end, to return to our bungalow. It is a large bungalow, too large for a single person.

However, I only use the smallest of the three bedrooms and that leaves plenty of room for family visits.

On the 19th of June, three weeks ago as I write this, Bill my younger brother died aged 87. Eric, the next in descending order of age, died 25 years ago. Mavis, my youngest sibling, died 3 years ago. Barbara still lives in Rode Heath in the foreman's cottage that she and her husband Bill had. So that leaves Barbara and me, the survivors of Arthur and Bertha's five children.

Chapter 16: Conclusion

Prelude

Thank you for letting me share some memories of my life with you. I hope you found something of interest. My grandchildren sometimes ask me what the most lessons I have learned in my more than nine decades. I think they are hoping for some insights and lessons — "life hacks" they call them – to help them navigate their way through life. For what is worth, and in no particular order, here they are.

Thoughts on what I have written here

This book is the first stab I've taken at writing other than business and management reports. It was prompted by my children and grandchildren as I reached my 90th birthday. They were keen to know more about the "old days", how different life was then and the problems their Mum and I had surmounted.

Looking back after reading it, I feel I've not succeeded in describing a lot of things I ought to have expanded on. Things like my parent's marriage, my early years, the war years, and how these impacted all our lives. My children heard, second hand from me, Harold MacMillan's famous quote, "You've never had it so good." They weren't born when he said it. However, this speech marked the economic and social revolution in the early sixties when they were so young.

These recollections have prompted me into thinking of a possible epilogue which would give me an opportunity to fill in some of the gaps and the emotional impact those changes had on my family and me. I hope that time is on my side and that I can provide some of the necessary rounding out in the form of that epilogue.

In the meantime, these are my concluding notes.

Memories of my wife, Sheila

Learning together as we went along

Sheila's death hit me very hard. It made me realise that my parents, like so many parents of my generation, made a bad job of educating their children in social and life skills. Sheila and I had no sex education. We just picked up snippets from older colleagues at work. Consequently, in those days of pre-marital chastity, once we decided to get married, we discussed our mutual ignorance, and I followed up by buying the now famous book by Dr Marie Stopes entitled *Married Life*. It dispelled all the old wives' tales and common misconceptions.

It was a great help, and I like to think it started us off on the right foot for our sixty-five-year marriage. Nobody had told us about what it was like to fall in love, for example, and to cope with the whirlwind of emotions it brought. Fortunately, we had planned to get married in St. Andrews church in Porthill where the vicar was a modernistic and thoughtful character. He held a short course involving an hour's talk over many evenings during the weeks before our wedding day.

One thing that surprised us was when he said, "The most common difficulties in married life revolve around money." He explained that many couples don't understand how to budget and plan to care for the household. This advice was taken up ardently by Sheila and, as I described earlier, in those days before bank accounts were commonplace, she placed the budgeted weekly amounts in separate envelopes for each of the tradesmen. I, meanwhile, drew up a plan for the year so we could anticipate when quarterly or annual payments were expected so we could save for those months of heavy bills.

Our children now

Popular culture, both then and now, prepares you for the overwhelming emotions when you fall in love. However, there isn't the same priming for becoming a parent. For me, the feelings I felt for our children were utterly overwhelming. And, over time, my love and pride in our children grew.

When I think back to my childhood, having to leave school at fourteen, the paucity of books, and never having even dreamed of going abroad, I can hardly believe how educated and cosmopolitan Shiela and my little family has become.

Our children are all adults now – our grandchildren too.

Gary and his wife Karen (who was born in Kenya), have four children. Three boys, Ben, Sam and Harry and a girl, Rebecca. Kevin and Andrea have a girl, Emese, and a boy, Jimmy.

Edwina pursued her career in banking. After taking early retirement, she gained a degree in engineering and joined her husband Kelvin in his business at a work efficiency consultant. Both are now retired and, for the moment, live locally but will eventually move abroad. They visit regularly. Every Sunday, they pick me up and take me to their house for lunch with involves much laughter – and lasts well into the evening until it is time for them to drive me home.

Gary, after studying medicine, went into work in the pharmaceutical industry. Later he and his wife, Karen, set up their own consulting company developing sophisticated computer-based models and market simulators for forecasting and pricing pharmaceuticals. They started their business from home and, as it grew, moved into a succession of larger premises. They now own an office block in the Chiltern Hills and their clients include every major pharmaceutical company in the world.

As you know, after qualifying in sociology at Nottingham University, Kevin took part in a post-graduation exchange visit to the University of Debrecen in Hungary. There he met Andrea who was studying linguistics but already fluent in several European languages. They married in a marvellous Hungarian civil ceremony and Kevin, who couldn't speak a word of Hungarian, decided to move to Hungary and take whatever work he could while Andrea finished her degree.

They started married life in rented a flat with Kevin coaching students in English. He eventually found an excellent and rewarding job as the Hungarian representative for a Scottish surgical instrument firm. Meanwhile, Andrea forged a successful business as a translator and later as a qualified interpreter at internation conferences.

Both are now partly retired. They have sold their house in Budapest and bought a lovely traditional house in the countryside. It has a large plot of land including an orchard and an acre of forest. In May of 2024

I travelled, alone, on the disabled assistance scheme and spent time with them in their new home.

Emese, Kevin and Andrea's daughter, studied to become a midwife while her British husband, Gareth, studied to become a doctor in Hungary. They moved from Hungary to Nottingham where Gareth now works in obstetrics and Emese is a midwife. Their daughter, Lara, who started swimming at five-months-old in the local pools near their home in Budapest, has ambitions to be an Olympic swimmer.

Kevin and Andrea's son, Jimmy, has settled in England and lives near Oxford. He has a PhD in materials science and is working on the latest nuclear fusion research. He travels all over the world.

After his second master's degree, Gary and Karen's eldest son, Ben worked as a senior health economist in the National Institute of Clinical and Health Excellence before becoming a Senior Director of Health Economics and Outcomes at a major Japanese pharmaceutical company. He regularly travels to America, Japan and Europe.

Sam, Gary and Karen's next eldest, is board director and head of R&D for their company. Gary and Karen love Malta and have had home there for decades so I suppose it was inevitable that one of their three sons would fall in love with a beautiful Maltese girl. Sam and Ella have a beautiful house in the Chilterns and will get married in Malta next year. Ella works at the John Radcliffe Hospital on a cancer study for Oxford University.

Rebecca (Becky) is now a Senior Product Owner (whatever that is!) in the software industry and lives in a converted farm labourer's cottage in the beautiful Berkshire countryside with her partner, Nick, who is half American and half Welsh and an expert software designer.

Harry, Gary and Karen's youngest, graduated with a master's in health economics and now works for consultancy in Manchester. He has little flat which he loves and, because he lives relatively close, he often drives down to Alsager to spend the day with me. He is so interesting to talk with and seems to enjoy listening to my stories.

Altogether, not a bad epitaph for a fourteen-year-old office boy from Stoke!

Lessons learned in my lifetime

My grandchildren ask me about lessons I have learned in my life. I wish I could claim that life has provided me with unique lessons; I think most oldies have probably learned the same things! But there are many lessons I wished I could have learned earlier than I did. I think a few might be worth reproducing here.

Education

I had little formal education and left school at fourteen. I studied at night school and learned a great deal about commercial matters including commercial geography. I still find this subject fascinating. However, I lacked opportunity, and perhaps aptitude, for serious study. I never obtained a degree or professional qualification. However, throughout my life, I have maintained a strong curiosity about the world, a love of books and reading. Through this I have picked up a number of skills which make me somewhat of an autodidact.

So, my lesson: Follow your curiosity. Ask questions; seek knowledge. And if you need help, there is a treasure trove: it is called books.

Decision making

A tough one. Some people say, "Follow your head." Others say, "Follow your heart." I believe you need to do both. Get the facts, examine and weigh them. Then sleep on the problem. While you slumber, your subconscious will do its work. Then as you wake, invariably, your heart will have popped the right answer into your head. In matters relating to work, you should then *check* the result!

Personal relationships

Emotion is a powerful driver. You should not abandon thinking rationally about something, but, at the end of the day when you have done your thinking, your heart will provide a good guide.

Judging people

Again, I have found a dual approach is best. Listen to your instincts, but also consult your past experience. For example, I am usually suspicious of the laughing boy, the office clown, and the gossip. They often turn out to be real back stabbers. This is, of course, a generalisation: a good sense of humour is essential in most walks of life and some incorrigible jokers can prove to be loyal friends.

Finally

Be brave! After conversations with many different people on various subjects, I have found that people seldom regret the things they've done. They regret the things they never did.

That's it, kids!

Acknowledgements

I would like to thank my children, Gary, Kevin and Edwina and their spouses for urging me to record my life experiences.

Thanks especially to Gary and his wife, Karen, for their hard work editing and publishing my memories.

And thanks too to my parents Arthur and Bertha for doing their best according to their lights in sometimes very difficult circumstances.

Index

271